Letter
FROM THE *Heart*

The Real Story Behind the Iconic Photograph

A Memoir by Sue Massey

LITTLE CREEK PRESS®
A DIVISION OF KRISTIN MITCHELL DESIGN, LLC

Mineral Point, Wisconsin USA

Copyright © 2014 Sue Massey
Little Creek Press®
A Division of Kristin Mitchell Design, LLC
5341 Sunny Ridge Road
Mineral Point, Wisconsin 53565

Editor: Jill Muehrcke

Book Design and Project Coordination:
Little Creek Press

Limited First Edition
May 2014

Printed in Wisconsin, United States of America

For more information or to order books:
www.letterfromtheheart.com or www.littlecreekpress.com

Library of Congress Control Number: 2014938592

ISBN-10: 0989978044
ISBN-13: 978-0-9899780-4-0

This is a memoir and subject to the imperfections of memory and
perception. In the interest of narrative and people's privacy, I have slightly
altered some events and dialogue and changed some names.

The wind lifts us, a tiny brown seed attached to a plume,
like a hot-air balloon's woven basket, into an endless sea of blue.
A seed of hope, of what is to come.

With me, in flight, my family sails in the basket of life we call home.
The wind guides us, her voice, our faith, sometimes a strong gust,
and sometimes a gentle breeze, always with us.

My love, like the span of the sky, has no boundaries.

Letter from the Heart, dedicated to
Kenny, Kelli, Danelle, Corey, Maron, and Naomi.

Table of Contents

PART IV **HEALING THROUGH THE EARTH** . 247

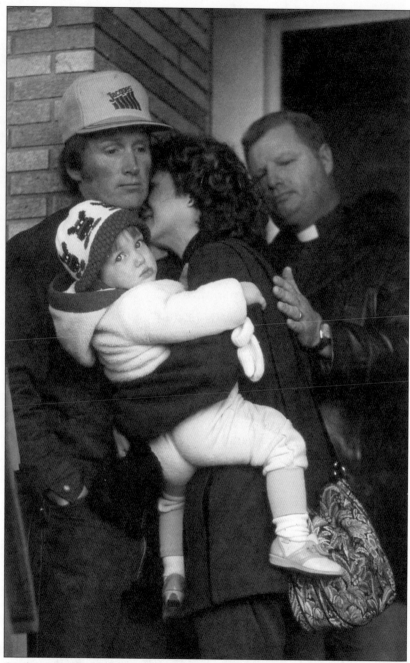

On the cover: Sue Massey grieves with her husband and youngest daughter, as a local clergyman comforts her. The clergy had rallied to offer support to Sue and her family. "I sometimes see it as if God placed a hand upon my back at this moment of despair," Sue says. Photo credit: L. Roger Turner, *Wisconsin State Journal.*

Introduction

Decades ago, I wrote a simple letter never dreaming it would place my family and me on national TV and change our lives forever. My father-in-law told me anybody who could write like that needed to pursue it. With his urging, I signed up for a writing class taught by Ben Logan, author of *The Land Remembers*. During the class, Ben learned of my story. He told me I had a book and paired me with an accomplished writer in the class to help me create it.

I had very little experience with writing and little perspective on my family's situation. The co-author was a nice man, willing to take on the gigantic task of writing a manuscript with a young woman who had more stories and feelings than she knew what to do with. Above all, it was a woman's story, a narrative of day-to-day struggles, of babies, home and hearth, the constant juggling of household responsibilities, the search for a creative outlet, desperate feminist yearnings while brushed with fame under the most trying circumstances.

The writing drafts went back and forth, back and forth, and sometime during the process, my voice was lost, or perhaps my voice was just beginning to develop. I sent it off to several publishers and agents and eventually placed it on a shelf in the basement, too busy meeting family obligations to take on one more task.

In my heart, I never truly gave it up; I just placed it on hold. I was stretched thin raising five kids, working at a demanding job, and managing a household. Looking back, I'm glad the manuscript wasn't published, for there was so much of my life yet to unfold as a result of the adversities that were yet to come. And in learning to embrace life's challenges and acquiring coping skills, I would discover my voice.

Years later, I was thrust into a job that I never would have predicted. I was working as a part-time receptionist when my manager encouraged me to consider the position of communications editor. Given my love for writing and people, she was confident in my ability

Sue Massey

to grow into the position. To my amazement, it was one of the best decisions in my lifetime. It opened my eyes to the inner workings of a large corporation, one that would eventually guide me into becoming a managing partner-owner with my husband in our own small business.

One of the many perks of that wonderful job was a paid membership in a professional organization, so I joined Women in Communications. There I met and became friends with a writer and editor named Jill Muehrcke. She and the other members of the organization taught me a great deal and spurred my interest in writing.

When I told Jill that I'd decided to take a new stab at writing my memoir, she offered to edit it for me. Thus began a friendship, adventure, and collaboration that continue to this day.

Immediately I could sense that Jill understood my story on a deep level. She saw that it was, at its core, a love story. Underneath the train of tragedies, catastrophes, and misadventures we endured was, always, the love my husband and I had for each other, which spilled over into our devotion to our family. Our struggles did not define us; they were only the stage upon which our deep love unfolded. What was important was how we handled the adversities that came our way. The plot of our life together may be unique, but all of us have the ability to become better people, not allowing our circumstances to define our futures.

Jill also understood the themes that ran through my story — the motifs of nature, the elements, home, family, metamorphosis — and helped tease out the parts that were hard for me to write about — the discovery of mental illnesses, disabilities, and imperfections I had tried to hide from everyone, including myself, the monsters that lived deep inside me.

Jill and I became a close working team. She was not only my editor; she was my saving grace. She was like a skilled therapist who listened to the things I could not rationalize about myself and still loved and accepted me. As she and I together coaxed my demons out of hiding, the epiphanies that occurred were life-changing. Finally, the end of the story became clear, and it was far more triumphant than either of us had ever expected. I am still in utter awe today of what flowed out my fingertips and left me free to open my hand and release it. It has caught the wind and disappeared into the wide open blue sky where it belongs.

Because the four elements of nature — air, fire, water, and earth — have always been a source of strength and guidance for me, I've broken my story into four parts to match the four elements. Growing up on the land as I did, I found that these four essentials of life are woven into my very being.

My story begins with air. The element of air is the power of the mind, the force of intellect, inspiration, and imagination. It is ideas, knowledge, dreams, and wishes. Air is the element of new life and possibilities. It's the vital spirit passing through all things, giving life to all things, moving and filling all things: the medium that binds everything together. The wind, the sky, the birds, and the clouds are some of my most important touchstones.

But air is elusive, intangible, wispy. I begin the book with "Up in the Air" because that's how I was in my early life. I've always been "in the clouds," especially in my late teens and early twenties when Kenny and I were first married. The events that blindsided us in those years left me floating helplessly in the stratosphere, wondering what would become of us, whether I would ever find my place in the world.

The second element, fire, is dangerous and impulsive. It can smolder and suddenly burst. It is the destroyer. I've titled the second part of the book "Into the Fire," partly because of the way that circumstances consumed and demolished the life Kenny and I were building, leaving us with five young children in the middle of total wreckage.

And yet, paradoxically, fire is also the creator. It cooks our food, warms our homes, and fuels our passion. It can give wings of courage, compassion, and devotion. Part II, in addition to narrating the catastrophic events that toppled my world, also describes the warmth of family and hearth that were so essential in my slow recovery and rebuilding.

Water, the third of the four elements, is cleansing, soothing, psychic, and loving. It's the element that aligns with Scorpio, my zodiac sign, signifying a personality that's emotional and intuitive. I call Part III of the book "Caught in the Wave" because of the way conditions beyond our control once again flung our family into misalignment. Yet as wild and tumultuous as water can be, it also has regenerative powers. The period of my life discussed in Part III was one of rebirth and realignment after swimming my way out of the turbulence.

Earth is the final one of the four essential elements. Its association with the seasons, crops, and fertility resonates with someone like me who earns her living from the land. "Mother Nature" has been my constant companion as far back as I can remember.

People describe me as "earthy." I think they mean that I'm in touch with my natural surroundings and all five of my senses. Or perhaps they mean that I'm "grounded," oriented toward what's real, able to create tangible results.

On a more literal level, I'm earthy because I'm never happier than when I'm digging in the soil, planting flowers and vegetables, moving dirt around to create gardens and landscapes that will nourish our souls and beautify our homes and corporate offices. The final section of the book, "Healing through the Earth," highlights the ways in which the earth has helped me find my way home.

I can't choose a favorite element, for I love them all equally. It isn't always easy to keep those four elements in proper alignment. My life has been, and continues to be, a balancing act. I have often lost my balance, but it's always the four elements of my world that have helped me regain it, and that is the essence of my story.

To paraphrase Nelson Mandela, if you talk to people in your language, it goes to their heads. If you talk to them in their own language, it goes to their hearts. I hope my story reaches into your heart and fosters an understanding for circumstances beyond our control — how each of us faces the journey of life with all its unexpected twists and turns.

Perhaps some of my words will land and sprout like the tiny seed of the milkweed plant, perhaps spark a memory hidden within your heart, waiting to be released. Perhaps some will float on the wind until the right time and place arrive for them to land, burst open, and grow.

Sue Massey

PART I
UP IN THE AIR

The wind blows hard among the pines
Toward the beginning
Of an endless past.
Listen: you've heard everything.

~ Shinkichi Takahashi

CHAPTER 1

Blowin' in the Wind

I opened my eyes, as if it were any other morning. Glancing at my husband Kenny's scrunched pillow, then at our alarm clock, I saw that it was six thirty. In just one hour, we would learn the fate of our small business — the family-owned business we had poured our heart and soul into for over two decades.

The sun dappled the ceiling, and a faint chirping filtered through a crack in the patio doors. A family of finches hung, some upside down like little bats, from the mesh feeder outside our bedroom window. A dog barked in the distance. I heard a faint snoring and knew it was our little dog, Sophie, at the foot of our bed. Beside me, a warm fur pillow cuddled near — Jack, our cat. He had come to bed in the middle of the night when he felt cold, and we warmed each other.

Kenny was in the kitchen getting ready for our meeting at the bank, scheduled for seven thirty. Soon we would learn if we would receive a loan to keep our small, family-owned landscaping business afloat.

Could this really be happening? Could one family lose everything twice in one lifetime? It had happened to us two decades ago, and we had just begun recovering from that devastating loss. After struggling so hard to get back on our feet, would we be a fatality once again? We were first caught in the nationwide devastation of so many family farms, and now as a struggling small business digging out from the recent recession. It was one thing to start over in our early thirties, but now I was in my fifties and Kenny in his sixties. Did we have the stamina to do it all again? Our kids were grown and involved in the business, and our home and all we owned were held as collateral for the bank business loans. If the business failed, we stood to lose everything. Again.

Shutting my eyes, I let twenty years loop through my mind: twenty springs, twenty summers, twenty falls, and twenty winters. From farming to our landscaping business, our lives had revolved around Mother Nature. We drew strength from her, but we also knew how unpredictable she was. A ton of sweat and tears had grown our business into something we could be proud of. This morning our future would be dealt us.

I heard a soft shuffle approach, and then a whiff of freshly brewed coffee drew near. Kenny leaned over to give me a kiss and set a steaming mug on my bed stand. Then he reached for Sophie and placed her beside my face in our bed.

"There, your mom needs you, Sophie," he said.

The bed squeaked as Kenny crawled back in and lay quietly staring at the ceiling.

"I'm scared," I said as I stroked the long, silky hair on Sophie's ear. Jack snuggled closer so that I could pet him too. They lay quietly, like sponges absorbing the sad energy in the room.

"I know. Me too," Kenny said, not moving. There was little else to say. We had lived in day-to-day uncertainty for so long that we'd almost grown to accept it as our lot.

This man, I thought — the hardest working man I know — feels like such a failure. It didn't seem possible.

I wondered what a fly looking down might see. A husband and wife lying in bed with a cat and a dog nestled between them as they held each other's outstretched fingertips. I tried to imagine how life would be when we came home from the bank meeting. Would this be the defining moment when our business would be forced to close its doors? The down-turned economy had taken a toll. Once current on all payments, we had slipped behind on taxes and bills. The IRS and state were brutal, demanding to take our seller's permit and tax ID if we didn't pay in full. They had already garnished our wages.

I glanced at the glowing crimson numbers on the alarm clock. They matched the red numbers in our business checkbook. I could barely remember the last time our bottom line was black. I wanted so badly to turn back the hands of time. Instead, our future lay in the hands of our banker. Would he see us as too high-risk, or a risk worth taking? We were about to find out.

As Kenny and I sat in the bank waiting for the banker to come talk to us, I let my mind scroll back over our life together. What had brought us to this point? I thought of all we'd been through, how much we had changed and grown.

It all began, I recalled, with a letter.

I've always been a letter writer. When my soul wishes to speak, I send a letter. It seems like a small thing, a tiny twinkle in my personality, but that stirring to express on paper what lives within me has shaped my life.

I wrote two letters, twelve years apart, that completely changed the course of my life. I often wonder where I would be now, what my life would look like, if I hadn't written those two letters.

While the second was the one that gained world attention, it would never have happened without the first. It was that first letter that steered my world in a direction I couldn't have imagined. There were times I would have given anything to have an ordinary rather than an "interesting," somewhat drama-filled life. But, if I had it to do over today, I wouldn't hesitate. I still would write that letter. My mother told me, when I was very young, to stand up for myself. If I didn't, nobody else would. So, whether voicing a concern, a heartfelt compliment, or an idea, I always reached for a pen.

Sue Massey

My parents had a rule: "No dating until you're sixteen." It had been true for my older brother and sister, and it wasn't any different for me. Just shy of my sixteenth birthday, though, I was really into dancing and boys, interests that I shared with my best friend, Shay.

One hot July Saturday night, Shay and I hitched a ride with some local boys to a neighboring town for an outdoor teen dance. We had tossed our favorite blue jeans into the dryer so they shrank, and we had to lie back on Shelley's bed to zip ourselves into them. The fact we could barely breathe didn't matter; the tighter, the better.

Shay was the tallest girl in our class, and her full figure made her look older than she was. When we walked side by side, heads would turn, and I knew it was for Shay. When boys came up to ask for a dance, it would be for Shay, and that was OK with me. I'd grown used to it. I would just turn toward the band and dance among the others. I never minded solo.

The live band drew hundreds of kids to the park shelter house in Mineral Point, Wisconsin. It was *the* place to hang out and meet kids our age. Aside from a handful of cops, we pretty much were on our own, and it was the ultimate feeling of freedom, like being an adult without the responsibility.

The lights streamed like ribbons of red, green, and yellow, then flashed while the floor vibrated with an intense beat from the guitars and drums. It was the early seventies, and heavy rock was in. I felt as wild and free as the horse I'd been breaking in to ride, back home on the family farm. It was as though I was standing on the edge of the world and anything was possible.

As I glanced around the shelter, my eyes fell upon a guy standing alone at the edge of the dance floor. His jeans and denim jacket were a natural faded, worn blue, his hands tucked casually into his front pockets, his hair long, blond, and wild. He looked rugged and outdoorsy, not overly concerned with his appearance.

My heart began to swell and beat like the drumming of a ruffed grouse. I wanted to open my wings and fly to him, yet at the same time I wanted to blend into my surroundings, simply feel the throbbing intensify.

I peered between the thickets of teenagers, my eyes never veering from him. I was powerless against the surging of my heart. I'd never felt anything like this before. How could I be so drawn to someone I'd never even met?

The song "Just My Imagination (Running Away With Me)" by the Temptations began to play, and I wondered if it were speaking to me. My heart seemed to fall into beat with the music's pounding rhythm.

Shay grabbed my hand and pulled me onto the dance floor. We laughed and danced our hearts out, not a care in the world. During intermission, the kids mingled: Some made out in cars in the parking lot, some sipped beer hidden on the floors of their cars, and some smoked pot. The moon was full and glowing as we stood under a blanket of twinkling stars. The heat of the day had dissipated, and the cool air felt glorious against my bare arms. Someone handed me a wine cooler, and I took a sip.

I looked around for the boy and saw him, still standing by himself. He reminded me of a lost puppy. Who was he? There was something different about him. He wasn't loud and cocky like so many of the guys trying to impress the pretty girls who were flitting around the park.

Shay came up beside me and whispered in my ear, "He's too old for you."

My cheeks felt warm: embarrassed to think she had noticed me staring at the boy.

She laughed. "I think his name is Kenny Massey, and he's outta school. He works on his parents' farm near Hollandale."

Hmm, I thought. No wonder his hair is sun-bleached; he must be out in the fields working all day. Maybe that was the intangible thing that drew me to him, because I too lived on my parents' farm and loved nothing more than being outside on the land.

Sue Massey

The lights began to dim, the dance floor cleared, and cars sped off into the night. Shay and I headed out, looking for someone to give us a ride.

Once home, I locked the heavy oak door behind me as I had so many times before. The last one in had to lock the door. Now that my older brother and sister were out of the house, the last one in was usually me.

I crawled beneath the cool sheets of my bed and stared at the ceiling with an image of that boy still twisting in my head. I shut my eyes and tried to make it disappear. It wouldn't.

If only I could meet him. But how? I wracked my brain, searching for a way. If he were in high school, I could arrange to run into him. But since he had already graduated, I had no idea how I could make a chance meeting happen.

Anyway, for all I knew, he had a girlfriend.

But he sure looked lonely at the dance.

A letter, I thought. I could write him a letter. I scrambled out of bed, flipped on the amber desk lamp, grabbed a white piece of paper and began to write. I remembered Shay saying he farmed near Hollandale. I would send my letter to Kenny Massey, Hollandale, Wisconsin.

Dear Kenny,

We have never met, but I noticed you at the Mineral Point Dance tonight. I was too shy to ask you to dance. If you plan to go next week, I hope to see you there. I will be a junior at Pecatonica High School this fall. My friend and I love to go to dances. I hope you are having a good summer.

Take care,
Sue Johnson
RR 1 Box 116, Blanchardville, WI
608-523-4769

I slid open the desk drawer, felt for an envelope between my fingertips, tucked the letter inside, licked it shut, and set it on the desk to mail in the morning. Down the hall, I could hear my dad snoring.

As I climbed back into bed, my mind seemed to settle. I imagined my letter being placed in Kenny Massey's mailbox. I wondered what his reaction would be. I hoped he wouldn't think I was stupid for writing to him.

I didn't understand why or how someone I'd never met could have such an impact on me. I had no idea what would happen — whether Kenny would answer my letter or ignore it, whether I would ever meet him or if this would be one of my crazy ideas that went nowhere.

But I had done what I could, and now I could rest.

CHAPTER 2

Horizon

I lay on my back in a soft mound of meadow grass and let my thoughts shoot through the sky on the wings of the plane overhead. I wondered: Where were all the people on the plane going? What did our farm look like from the sky? Would I fly in a plane someday?

I plucked a velvet seed pod from a milkweed plant, and its sticky white sap spilled everywhere. I held the pod between my fingertips and gently pressed the thin seam open. Inside there was a work of art, a signature piece by Mother Nature. Each seed was attached to a white plume that would carry it far and wide. I lay back and watched the seeds take flight.

Our farm was sprawled on a hilltop where the wind blew constantly. The backdrop to my life was the gentle whistling of the windmill paddles from the grassy knoll above the barn. Even on sticky hot summer days, there was always a hint of a breeze. My friend, the wind, was always there.

The sky was a world of endless wonder. The clouds reminded me of different people in the sky. Today they were light and fluffy, like people who seemed to skip through life. On other days, the clouds were deep and dark and heavy with rain, like people who were difficult to understand.

Like Kenny. Why did I feel so drawn to him? If he was meant to be in my life, as part of me believed, why hadn't he answered my letter? Weeks had passed since I'd mailed it.

Another part of me was sure he wouldn't respond. I didn't see myself as one of the pretty girls, and when I sent a letter, I never had expectations of getting one back. That way I wouldn't be disappointed.

As I waited, I tried to put him out of my head. I was usually good at taking hurtful, unattainable goals, pushing them to the back of my mind, and moving on. My brain was a constant flow of ideas, which I released out into the world to see what would happen. Sometimes I was amazed at the results, but most of the time, it was like throwing a penny into a well so deep that I never even heard it land.

I thought back over my childhood, way back to the days before I learned to suppress my feelings, back when the world was a wonderland created just for me. I had an amazing childhood, one that I wouldn't exchange for all the money in the world. I couldn't imagine anything more ideal than growing up on a 125-acre farm in the beautiful, rolling hills of southwestern Wisconsin. It shaped who I am today.

I closed my eyes and remembered. Remembered a time when life was simple and my dreams seemed possible.

It was the first day of school, and I was in the first grade. The minute I sat down at my desk, I opened Dad's empty Red Dot Cigar box, which I had filled with my school supplies: scissors, glue, pencil, new box of eight crayons, and a ruler.

I looked across at my classmate. She took out her new box of sixty-four crayons.

"Wow, neat box of colors! Can I see them?" I whispered, ducking my head down low.

She smiled and handed me her box of crayons. I looked inside at all the little heads poking out. All the colors of the land, I thought. There was periwinkle, the wash across the sky at sunset. Orange like the poppies in our neighbor's yard — the ones that looked like ladies dressed in enormous lace ball gowns flowing side-to-side with the music — and emerald green, the color of the hay field where I picked alfalfa for my pet rabbit.

"Class..." The teacher's voice broke my daydream.

I closed the lid, handed the box of crayons back to my neighbor, and looked inside my Red Dot box. It smelled like my dad, like last night after supper when I sat on his lap, his tobacco pouch a pillow for my ear. I looked into my box, and his scent carried me away.

I imagined blending my eight crayons to make more shades. I wondered if I could come up with sixty-four colors on my own.

I tore a blank piece of paper from my tablet, reached for the red, then the yellow, and drew lines, one on top of the other, and a beautiful orange was born: the orange of my favorite poppy.

I felt a song in my heart. There was something about hatching an idea, an idea that came to me out of nowhere. Plucking it out, and then using my hands and whatever materials I could find to make it grow, thrilled me.

Around the poppy-like orange, I drew a frilly circle with black eyes inside. I smiled with delight. *This,* I thought, *will be a picture for my mom, for she loves flowers as much as I do.*

"Mom, I colored this for you!" I said as I handed her the picture later that day.

"That's beautiful, Sue. Thank you! I'll hang it on the refrigerator for everyone to see." She turned, dried her hands on a towel, and taped my picture on the refrigerator.

I twirled around on the heels of my bare feet and ran outside to play.

I placed the old bushel basket over the top of the hen.

"There. Now sit on your eggs," I insisted as I peeked through the tiny cracks in the woven basket to see if she was listening. She fluffed and puffed out her feathers. She squatted, shuffled the eggs with her underside, and began to cluck like a mom speaking to her children. As she settled down, so did I. Whew. Relief spread over me like a warm blanket on a chilly spring morning.

I stood up, brushed the wood chips off my shorts and bare knees, and peeped out between the cobwebs of the brooder house window. Mom was picking berries in the strawberry patch at the lower end of her garden. I opened the door latch, jumped out onto the ground, and grabbed my pail. At the nearby water hydrant, I set the pail on the ground beneath the spigot, pulled the handle up, tipped my face to the side, and ice-cold water filled both me and my bucket. I wiped my dripping face with the shirttail of my cotton top.

Mom always had chickens. Her flock provided us with eggs and meat. Every other spring, a box of fifty chicks would arrive at the post office. This year, I was determined to hatch some chicks out of our own eggs. I had watched the hens closely, and when one went into a clucking stage, I knew she was the one. I would gather fertile eggs from the coop and make her sit on them.

Every day, I fed and watered that hen. Eventually, she adopted the clutch of eggs and I no longer needed to cage her with a bushel basket. One by one, I "X'd" the days off the calendar. Around day twenty, I examined each egg, hoping for a sign of life from inside. There was a dense feeling to each egg, different from the ones we cracked for breakfast or used for baking.

"Mom, today's the day!" I sat on the sunporch floor and pulled on my everyday sneakers.

"For what?" She looked over her shoulder as she stood at the sink washing the breakfast dishes. The silverware clicked as she dropped it into the rinse water.

"The hen. She's been on the eggs for twenty-one days. This could be the day the eggs are ready to hatch." I headed for the door.

"Sue, what about breakfast?"

I looked at the empty plate sitting on the kitchen table in front of my chair.

"There's toast, eggs, cereal, bacon, fresh strawberry jam — whatever you want," Mom said.

I reached for a piece of toast. "Mom, I gotta run." I nudged the screen door open with my elbow and ran as fast as my seven-year-old legs could take me to the brooder house.

The hen was sitting there as usual. I sprinkled her morning grain into a dish, and she stood up and fluttered her night feathers, like a dog who wakes up and shakes out its coat. I dropped to my knees and lifted each egg out of the straw nest, turning them one by one.

I knew these eggs, each tiny imperfection, the dips, the pores, like mini craters on the moon's surface. As I turned the third egg over, I discovered a miniscule beak. Was it possible? Had I done it? Then I heard the faintest peep, and an eggshell chip fell into my palm. I could see a tiny yellow beak. At the top of the beak, there was a minuscule peak that the chick seemed to be using to break out of its shell. I could barely believe my eyes. I had thought I could do this, but I thought I could do a lot of things, most of which didn't exactly pan out. Somehow, though, I had done this. I had managed to hatch a baby chick on my own. Inside I felt a bubble of excitement build.

There was a wet chick in my hand: a perfectly formed chick. I saw the way it had grown inside the egg, its head tucked beside its wing, its legs tight against the underside of its tummy.

"Wow, that's amazing," I whispered. I turned it over in the palm of my hand. It had two wings, two legs, and a chubby tummy. It was perfect.

I set the chick in the straw nest, and the hen went crazy with joy. Her clucking changed to a delicate, love-like chatter, one I'd never heard before. With the curve of her beak, she gently tucked the wet frail chick beneath her to keep it warm and safe while it dried.

In my hand was an open eggshell. Inside, there were tiny veins and a thin, sheer membrane in which the baby chick had grown. I looked at the empty shell, then at the hen with her new chick, and thought what a miracle this was. I sat cross-legged, the scent of wood chip bedding all around me. I had done it. I had really done it.

～⌣⌣⌢

The car jolted to a stop. My fingertips clutched the fuzzy rim between window and door panel. It felt like the bristles of a wooly-bear caterpillar, like the ones I collected and kept in a shoebox beneath my bed.

I pushed open the gray door of our family's mint-green '57 Chevy. It was Friday night, and Main Street in the sleepy, rural village of Blanchardville had come alive with the locals, farmers dressed in clean denim and bibbed overalls, wives in lightweight cotton and gingham dresses. They mingled and gathered at street corners to visit and catch up on the gossip.

It was a warm summer night, and the scent of freshly popped corn from the stand up the street drifted in the air along with muffled chatter and the laughter of children playing curbside. Our family had come to town to pick up groceries.

My first stop was the library, a red brick building nestled beside the Pecatonica River. Main Street stretched up and over a concrete bridge, its railings so thick and so wide that I had to heave myself up to see the bellowing waters of the dam below. I always needed to peek at the dam and view the rushing waters before slipping into the library. The waters were both a wonder and comfort to me.

Inside, Mrs. Gallagher, the town librarian, greeted me from behind her honey-stained desk. The books stacked on each side of her looked like bookends framing her head. Her warm brown eyes matched the color of her hair, and her soothing voice eased me.

I hung my hooded sweatshirt on the metal hook by the door. At dusk, the cool river air would push the summer heat aside, and I'd be glad I brought my hoodie.

I went directly to the children's section and scanned the rows. There it was — a worn brown book that looked like a deer in the woods peeking out at me. I pulled it down, scurried to the antique oak table, crawled onto the cool wooden chair, and lost myself in the pages of *Brown Cow Farm*.

The large, brown eyes of the Jersey cow in the book touched me in a way I couldn't explain. We had thirty black-and-white Holsteins on our farm, and they were almost like an extension of our family. Our lives revolved around the milking chores. Seven days a week, night and morning, Dad rarely missed a milking.

When I saw the face of the Jersey in the book, I dreamed of one day owning one. Everything about the Jerseys was petite except for their huge brown eyes. Because they were so small, they consumed less feed, gave less milk, and gave birth to smaller calves. Their warm eyes and gentle nature are what captivated me.

When I turned nine, I could join the local 4-H Club in town, and I hoped to take "dairy" as my project for a fair entry. I had picked up booklets on how to select the best dairy cows based on genetics and composition. I was thrilled to learn from the pictures.

I was constantly caught up in the wonder of what I would be when I grew up. I fantasized about all the animals I would buy when I had my own farm. While some girls played with dolls, I dressed up the barn cats and rode my olive green bike with my pet rabbit in the basket.

The thing I loved about the animals was the way we were able to communicate without words. The relationship I shared with animals was seamless and easy. The barn was like a second home to me. It was always warm, clean, and filled with animals, just like in *Brown Cow Farm*. The book had pictures of every farm animal I had ever imagined.

After I'd read the book from start to finish, I didn't want to put it back on the shelf. I sat, chin in the palm of my hand, envisioning what it would be like to live on Brown Cow Farm. I didn't care that my favorite book was a numbers book for children just learning to count. It was *my* book. I hoped and dreamed that one day it would be my story.

The jingle of the bell attached to the library door rattled me out of my daydream. I knew instinctively that it was time to go. I took one last look inside the book, closed it, held it against my heart, and then placed it back on the shelf. "Until next time," I whispered. I pulled out five books and slipped *Brown Cow Farm* behind them, my own secret hiding place.

I had checked out *Brown Cow Farm* so many times that I decided to leave it at the library. That way I would have something to look forward to the next Friday night when our family came to town. As I hurried outside, I carried the story of Brown Cow Farm with me. With every step, I imagined a life on my own farm with my own animals.

I could see Dad in the window of the café across the street and knew he would buy me a strawberry malt. Most times Dad would have to help me finish it. When he was done, he would lean back and pull a tobacco pouch from the pocket of his bibbed overalls. He'd unfold the foil packet and slip his black pipe inside. He'd tap the pipe on the metal edge of the counter, cup his hand around the barrel while holding a lit match to the dried tobacco leaves, and inhale, deep and long, then exhale fragrant white puffs of smoke out the side of his mouth toward me, and smile.

I loved the sweet scent of fresh tobacco in his pipe. It sparked feelings of security, because when I sat on Dad's lap after supper, with my cheek against his flannel shirt, smelling the tobacco pouch in his pocket, I knew I had him all to myself. He was finally resting, not working. In the arms of my dad, I felt like a puddle after a hard summer rain when the earth opens and quenches its thirst; his love was mine.

I listened as Dad and the other farmers talked about the weather, the crops, their yield, and the cows. Everyone knew my dad. He had spent his entire childhood in Blanchardville. He had left to serve in the Air Force, then drove a semi for a bit before returning to the farm where he was born.

I reached to hold his hand, letting the conversation stream around me. His hand seemed ginormous to me, the skin like leather with fingers permanently bent like a wrench. I ran my fingertip across the warm blue veins and touched each freckle painted by the summer sun.

A light tap on the café window broke my thoughts and sent all eyes toward the street.

"Well, Suzie, looks like Ma is ready to go home." He smiled and pushed back his chair.

Night was creeping in. The crickets had begun their evening song beside the river banks. The street lights began to hum and awaken like the owls at night; it was their time to shine. The moon was beginning to show, and I wondered if all the animals were bedding down for the night in the pastures and barn on Brown Cow Farm.

As we pulled into our driveway, I could hear the gravel ping beneath the car. I rolled down my window and smelled the night air. In the distance, a cow bellowed. It was time to go in, time for bed. I ran upstairs, grabbed my pajamas off the hook behind my closet door, dove across my bed and looked out my open window, listening to the crickets chirp and frogs croak in the wetland between our farm hill and the horizon where the twinkling town lights began.

The rain arrived in sheets. Dad stood in the open barn door, eyes fixed on the oat field, the perfect stand of sturdy, yellow oats, just days till harvest. He watched, helpless, as the wind and rain snapped and flattened his field.

I looked up into his face. Were there even words for what we both felt? I'd watched him plow that field with his tractor, the sharp silver blades of his four-bottom plow slicing the earth, black furrows of exposed soil trailing him like railroad tracks, seemingly with no end in sight.

I had ridden on the bumpy fender of his tractor and watched the flitting cloud of red-winged blackbirds, starlings, ravens, and sparrows following in mid-air behind us. They dove, their beaks like darts, toward their target, the worms and bugs suddenly uncovered as the rich underside of the earth was turned up. The birds were keen at the game and hit the bulls-eye almost every time.

The tractor would chug along, Dad raising and lowering the plow blades as he turned each corner to start a new row. It was like a full-body workout: As he turned the wheel to steer the tractor, his legs would press the clutch and brakes, twist to see, pull levers, push buttons, and change gears from the bouncing seat of his tractor. To me, he looked like a buoy bouncing at sea.

Then, Dad would harrow and drag that oat field until it was as smooth as my mom's garden. Row by row, he'd seed it with his grain drill. Dad rarely bought new farm equipment. He'd say, "Why waste your money on new when there is a ton of life left in what we have?"

Almost like magic, within days, his field would turn a brilliant yellow-green with oat seedlings, the rows as straight and narrow as if he'd used a ruler. Almost every day, I would wander into that field, just below our barn, and check to see how much the grain had grown. I would slip deep inside the soft rows and measure the growth by seeing how far the stems would reach up on my leg. As the sheaths of grain grew, the rows disappeared and the oat heads grew tall and mature. I would scissor a stalk between two fingers and pull off the heads in my hand. Then I would open the grain heads to see what was inside.

In the heat of the summer sun, the shallow green would fade to a gorgeous golden hue. I would stand at the edge and watch the wind play in her sea of gold as she sent waves rippling from side to side. As they ripened, the shafts would dry, and the wind would whistle through the field, a song I never grew tired of hearing.

Dad would store the harvested oats in a granary, where my brother, sister, and I loved to play, dumping buckets of oats over each other's heads and using our hands like scoops to bury each other as if in sand on a beach with only our faces exposed.

"It couldn't wait, could it, Suzie?" Dad leaned against the handle of his pitchfork as the rain sprayed in through the open barn door. "Just a couple more days, and the oats would have been in the oat bin. I know we need the rain…" His voice trailed off like the cool droplets that skimmed my cheeks.

I looked toward the southwest. The ominous, gray clouds kept rolling in with no break in sight. The temperature had fallen with the sheets of rain, so heavy that I couldn't see past the gate that opened to the field, the field where I played my continuous game of adventure and discovery.

The oaks and maples bent under the billowing force of the wind. Thunder cracked, and streaks of lightning shot from the clouds to earth. Loose leaves, twigs, and debris blew in through the open barn door. There was an excitement in the fury of a storm but a sadness too.

The cows were dripping wet, happy to be in the milking barn, their udders swollen, some so full that the milk leaked down the inside of their back legs. Some of the younger cows were spooked by the thunder, while the older ones barely turned from their grain.

The sturdy shafts of grain, heavy with heads of ripened oats, were now bowed toward the ground. When the field dried out from the rain, Dad's combine would slice through the field and pick up as much of the downed oats as it could. It could only do so much. After the oats were combined, Dad would rake the cut oat shafts into windrows and bale them up as straw to use as bedding for the animals in the winter months.

Dad lifted his weathered barn hat, wiped his brow, and set it back down, covering his sweat-dampened auburn hair. I knew what he was thinking. This wind and rain would cut his oat yield in half. A small oat crop meant less money. Selling crops and animals was how we earned a living.

Farming seemed like such a gamble, I thought. A person could do everything right, and still there was no guarantee of success. Seemed as though anything could happen.

One by one, Dad clicked the stanchions shut. Each cow stood in her milking stall munching a small pile of grain.

"The ol' bossies will be happy when we finish baling that straw." Dad shot me a grin over the top of a cow as she swished his face with the end of her tail. "We'll turn the cows in and let 'em clean up the oats on the ground."

As he walked up the center of the barn, the white barn lime crunched beneath his two-buckle rubbers. He paused to turn the "on" dial of his barn radio to a lively polka channel.

"In between cows, I'll teach you how to hop polka." He flipped the switch as my brother carried in the milkers and wash pail. "Are you washing tonight, Suzie?" Dad handed me a small bucket filled with warm soapy water.

"Yes!" I reached for the bucket and stepped between the first two cows. Their massive bodies heaved as they reached for every morsel of grain they could get. They looked as happy as a kid with a sucker.

Dad called the cows "One" and "Two"; I called them "Blue Bell" and "Tracy." Dad never named any of the animals, but I did.

I squeezed the sponge semi-dry, reached under the udder, and washed each teat, one-by-one, like cleaning fingers at the sink. With the other hand, I patted Tracy. "Easy, Trace, easy."

"Remember, Sue, slow down, take your time. If you wash too fast, they'll let down their milk too soon," Dad reminded me. I nodded. He had told me this before. When I jumped into something, it was hard to contain my excitement. I loved hanging out in the barn, helping Dad with the chores.

"How'd you get outta helping your ma with dishes tonight, anyways?" Dad asked with a teasing sparkle in his blue eyes.

"Sandy's turn. I helped last night," I said as I watched Tracy's udder deflate like a balloon. I wondered what that felt like. I imagined the cows felt less pressure in their udders after milking. White gold, Dad called it. The more milk the cows gave, the bigger his check would be from the cheese factory in town that bought his milk.

Sue Massey

"Feed the cats with Number Two's milk," Dad instructed my brother. "She has one more day on antibiotics. Make sure her back right quarter is completely empty before you take off the milker." He elbowed Number Three, a.k.a. Mabel, to move over so that he could set the milker on the floor beside her.

Dad ran two milking machines, and my brother Bruce ran the other two. Between them, they carried the pails of milk to the milk house. Other farms were installing pipe-line milkers to streamline the milking process. Not my parents. They lived by a rule that if you couldn't pay cash for something, then you had to save up until you could. We didn't have an automatic washer or dryer, microwave, dishwasher, automatic barn cleaner, or pipeline milker until well into the eighties.

There was a science to milking cows, and I found every aspect fascinating. There was so much to learn and understand about the animals and farming that intrigued me.

I was drawn to all types of animals. Talking to them and touching them settled the constant swirling inside me. When I looked into their eyes, everything else melted away, and nothing else mattered.

After school, I would run home along the worn dirt path that went past my grandparents' house, cut through the woods, and then make a quick hike across the board step-over that Dad built for us kids to cross the barbed-wire fence surrounding the calf pasture. That step-over saved a bushel basket of mending for my mom.

A handful of black-and-white Holstein calves would take a break from grazing to look up in wide-eyed wonder, see it was me, and go back to munching grass. I'd climb to the top of the hill, where our farm home was perched with a big white porch wrapped halfway around it. Then it was through the metal gate, past Mom's laundry flapping and snapping in the wind on the clothesline, through the sunporch with a quick "Hi, Mom, I'm home, gotta run," followed by her trailing words, "Hi, Sue, how was school," and I was already on the second flight of steps toward the hook in my bedroom closet. I always skipped the third step from the top, as it had an awful creak to it, sounding like an old soul begging for forgiveness after living a life of toil. Down the hall, I'd pull open my closet door and reach for my everyday clothes on my hook.

It felt as if my day began when I pulled my play clothes from the hook. I'd wiggle out of my school clothes and step into my worn, patched jeans and gray sweatshirt. I'd drop my school clothes down the laundry shoot and head back down the stairs and out the door with a "Bye, Ma, see ya at supper," and off I'd go as fast as my little legs would take me to my windmill hill, where I would sit and dream.

I've always loved a hook. Some hooks changed with the calendar, while others remained constant. Dad hung his hat on his hook on the wall by the back door before each meal and at the end of a long work day. Mom's hook, next to Dad's on the wall, always held her scarf — usually one of Dad's big red cloth handkerchiefs she'd claim as hers and tie in a knot in back of her neck.

The hook evokes a welcome home to me. A place to hang your hat, a favorite sweater or vest, and just be — be at home with yourself.

Sue Massey

CHAPTER 3

The Swallows

We bounced along, my sister Sandy and I, giggling in the back of Grandpa and Grandma's car as he followed the dirt road into the pasture at the bottom of the hill on our farm. He parked beside a ten-foot maple.

Each of our four doors flew open, and Sandy and I dove out into the clumps of cool meadow grass. I swung an arm around Sandy's neck, and we tumbled to the ground laughing, our faces buried in the rough, sandpaper blades of the crabgrass. We wrestled and rolled: first Sandy on top, then me straddling her. She may have been a year older, but I was wiry and fast and could wiggle my way out of almost anything — literally and metaphorically.

I spotted the open trunk of Grandpa's car, made a dash for it, and heaved myself up and inside. The spare tire tucked deep inside was as black as the hole in which it lay. A few metal wrenches felt hard and cold against the backs of my bare legs. Sandy bounded in on top of me. She tried to tickle my ribs, but I held my elbows tight against my sides like little barricades preventing her fingertips from tunneling through. We must have looked like two sardines lying shoulder to shoulder in an open can.

We laughed so hard that the songbirds flew to nearby trees, uncertain what had invaded their quiet meadow. The June sun poured in and over us as Grandpa spaded a circle around the base of the ten-foot sugar maple. I could hear the earth slice as the blade laid open the land. Dad was cutting hay in a nearby field, and the fragrant smell of fresh-cut clover filled the air. I grabbed Sandy's braids and pretended they were the reins of a pony. She pulled off my sneaker in retaliation.

The trunk slammed shut, and with it darkness, not a splinter of light anywhere.

Startled, I clutched Sandy, and she me. The only sound was the beating of our hearts. We waited for the trunk to open. It didn't.

Thoughts deluged my mind. Did the hood accidentally close when we were horsing around? I pushed hard with both hands. It was locked, and we were trapped.

"Help! Grandma, help! Let us out! Please! I promise, we'll be good!" We kicked and pounded with our feet and fists as hard as we could, screaming, pleading.

A hint of a chuckle filtered in. Then Grandpa's muffled voice: "Gunhild, that's long enough," followed by some Norwegian dialect between them. A key turned, the trunk snapped open, sunlight streamed in, and tears burst.

We heaved ourselves out.

Dazed, we fell onto the grass. My knuckles were red and skinned from banging on the hood.

"That wasn't funny, Grandma!" I tried to look into her eyes, but she turned away as if she hadn't heard me.

Shocked and confused, Sandy and I watched as Grandpa and Grandma lifted the root ball of the maple into the trunk. That was our cue to crawl into the back seat. Silence and the shovel lay on the seat between us.

Licking the salty dots of blood off my skinned knuckles with the tip of my tongue, I tried to sort out what had happened. We must have been too silly and too loud, and it made Grandma mad. She could have told us to cut it out, and we would have. Or maybe this was just Grandma's quirky sense of humor. I puzzled over it as we jostled and bounced back toward our big white farmhouse.

Grandpa stopped the car in front of the brick-red gate. "I'll get it," I called as I popped out. I ran to open the gate and waved as they drove through.

"Bye, Grandpa. Bye, Grandma." I looked in at Sandy, "I'm going to the barn. See ya in a bit."

She nodded an OK. I looked over my shoulder and watched Grandpa stop the car in front of the house. Sandy sprang out and ran inside as the green Chevy made its way down the driveway, the maple tree, tied in the trunk, bobbing behind.

The barn was empty. It was between milkings, and the cows were in the pasture. I crawled onto a hay bale and called out, "Kitty-Kitty."

I heard a teeny meow and there she was, sleepy-eyed and stretching her back legs. She was so new, so little, I had yet to name her so I called her Kitty-Kitty, and she always came when she heard my voice.

She curled on my lap like a doughnut, and I could feel her purr vibrate against my bare legs. She was the only long-haired black-and-white kitten ever born on our farm. She looked up at me with a mew so tiny and sweet that it felt like a love arrow shot straight through my heart. She spoke to me, and I listened, bathed in her loving comfort.

A shimmery barn swallow swooped down, chattering her dismay. Above on the ceiling beams, she was building a nest of clumps of mud she'd collected from the edges of puddles after last night's rain shower. I was surprised how assertive the birds were when it came to protecting their young.

The dark, scary feeling of being trapped in the trunk seeped into my head, and I wondered: Where was my voice? I had yelled and screamed, but when one is little, it's hard to be heard. I wanted to tell Grandma how scared and hurt I felt, but something inside told me to swallow my voice and let it go, for I knew Grandma loved me. She just had her own way of thinking.

My grandparents had recently retired off the farm and bought a home in town. The maple tree from the farm was to grace their front yard. Our walking path to and from school crossed the upper edge of their lawn. In the coming years, I watched that maple grow and flourish. Beneath its canopy of shade, there were two metal lawn chairs. On my walk home from school, Grandpa was always there, sitting in his chair, his farmer-tanned skin dappled with shadows cast from the leaves. Grandma's chair was usually empty. She didn't sit much, and I knew she was probably rolling out her paper-thin molasses cookies, flipping the Norwegian lefse (a thin potato-based delicacy) on a grill, or plucking dead blooms off the petunias in her flower bed.

Whenever I looked at that tree, I felt the blackness of the trunk surrounding me. I convinced myself that it was a fluke and over time my fear would float away like the tiny seeds of the milkweed plant. I was wrong. Every now and then, the panicky feeling of being trapped would surface, and I kept swallowing the terror, hoping one day it would go away.

I wanted to look at that tree and see it as the beginning of my grandparents' retirement off the farm, the next chapter after a long, hard life of working on the land. I wanted the tree to remind me of the love and silliness my sister and I shared when we were kids romping in the playground of our farm.

It was a gorgeous, sunny fall day, and I ran home from school barely touching the path beneath my feet. Inside the house, I climbed the steps by two, grabbed my everyday clothes off the hook, pulled them on, and was out the door. I headed toward the barn, my second home. I was seven, released from school like an animal from its cage.

The swallows squawked at me, warning me not to come any closer to their mud nests that hung from the rafters: nests of babies with tiny skin heads, mini marble eyes, and wide-open mouths chirping, begging to be fed.

Sue Massey

"Kitty-Kitty," I called as I looked toward the wooden ladder that reached to the barn loft. On the concrete pad below the open chute was a mound of straw bales that Dad had tossed down to bed the calf pens.

Instantly, a gripping fear consumed me. *Please God, don't let my kitten be beneath one of those bales*, I prayed to myself as I grabbed the bobble twines that held the four-foot loaves of straw together. The bales were almost bigger than I was, but it didn't matter. I pulled and tugged and tossed them aside one by one, all the while praying and hoping, calling out to my kitten.

With each bale I overturned, I felt hope creep in, thinking she might be curled safely asleep in one of the mangers.

Then I saw her. She was on the floor between the bottom bale and the cold concrete floor, flattened like a pancake, her body still slightly warm. As I picked her up, my heart burst and tears drenched her crushed body. Holding her tiny corpse, no bigger than a doughnut, I thought of her sweet meow and gentle purr, hoping this was all just a bad dream — that I would wake up and she would come running when I called. She would lap the warm milk and I would clean the white droplets off her white, pin-like whiskers, and she would look up at me with her large trusting eyes as if I were her mother. I had invented games for us to play by tying a twig to the end of a piece of twine and dragging it across the straw bale so she would jump and try to grab it with her paws.

On the farm, I saw life and death on a weekly basis. But this was different. Kitty was special. She seemed to know when I was happy, sad, confused, or worried. If I had a tough day at school, I could come home and she would curl on my lap, and the outside world would fall away. Her purring soothed the mass of feelings whirling inside me — feelings I had not yet connected with words, and with Kitty I didn't have to.

Rocking her in my arms, I began kicking myself inside. Why hadn't I told my dad about Kitty and made sure he checked for her before throwing down the bales? Why hadn't I kept her in a special box for safekeeping? Why had I fallen so deeply in love with her? If loving someone caused this much pain, did I ever want to love again?

Alone in the barn with my lifeless kitten, I thought about life, about death, about love. Then I pushed the "whys" out of my mind. They seemed useless. What happened, happened. I couldn't change it.

It was there on those golden bales of straw that I decided I wouldn't let life's circumstances define me. I would refuse to let sorrow and despair flatten me. Nothing I could say or do would alter the fact that my Kitty was dead. I would push away my anguish and go on with my life.

I wouldn't tell Dad. Kittens came and went all the time on our farm. Why make Dad feel bad by pointing out what had happened? It was no one's fault. Telling him — telling anyone — wouldn't change anything.

With the cuff of my shirt sleeve, I dabbed my tears off Kitty's velvety fur. From the row of hooks on the barn wall, I lifted down a shovel.

Cradling Kitty's limp body in one arm and the shovel in the other, I walked behind the silo and, in a shadowed corner, dug a hole and buried her. I tied a cross with twigs, the same twig and twine that only yesterday my kitten and I had played with. As I patted the earth, I said a prayer.

I heard Dad's voice calling the cows for their evening milking. I could see them coming, their udders full and bulky. They waddled like a herd of very pregnant ladies, ready to have the expanding pressure within them relieved. I wondered how long it would take for this swollen, sagging sadness I felt inside to go away.

A week later, while playing in the hay mow, I came upon a mother cat with four kittens. I watched but didn't touch them as they nursed from her pink tummy. They were all short-haired and calico in color. None of them looked anything like the long-haired, black-and-white kitten I'd loved for such a short time.

Sue Massey

A pang tugged inside my heart, but I willed it away. I remembered the resolution I'd come to in the barn. The past was past, and I wouldn't dwell on useless emotions. Instead of sharing my feelings, or even acknowledging them or sorting them out, I would put them away into a part of myself that grew wider and deeper through the years. I had no idea the events that my decision would put into play, the harvest I would reap years later, or how catastrophic those results would be.

Still lying in the grass watching the clouds, I realized that no childhood is perfect, even though we'd like to think it was. I knew my parents and grandparents loved me and did what they thought was best for me. One thing I don't think they were familiar with was talking about innermost feelings. Mom's mom had died when she was six, and Dad's parents, who came from Norway, kept a tight lip.

Sandy and I didn't talk about the trunk incident until many years later, after whatever wounds our psyches may have suffered had long since become embedded scars. Sandy told me recently that she can't stand to be in elevators and will go to great lengths to walk up even the longest, steepest stairs because of her severe claustrophobia. I told her that I plan to be cremated because I have a bottomless fear of being buried alive.

Even worse than the fear and trauma of what happened was the silence surrounding it. I often recalled the question I'd asked myself after being locked in the trunk and then choking back my feelings rather than speaking up: Where was my voice? I seemed to turn everything into my fault, wondering what I'd done to deserve such treatment.

There were so many feelings I couldn't connect and form into words. And I still wondered: How could anyone understand, if I left those emotions locked inside?

The same was true of the day I saw my kitten crushed under the bales of hay. The traumatic incident might have become just another story if I'd discussed it with someone, but I didn't. It became a turning point, solidifying my belief that it was best to bury painful episodes that were beyond my control.

I created little boxes inside myself, where I could keep the emotions and longings that overwhelmed me. I tried to do the same with Kenny — to push aside feelings about him and the letter I'd written. But each time I tucked those thoughts into a compartment and closed the lid, it sprang open as if a giant grasshopper lived inside and wanted out. For some reason, I simply couldn't forget him.

I had spent hours watching the clouds and thinking, and the horizon had turned dark and heavy with rain. The colors in the landscape seemed to intensify. It was as if the fairy of the land waved her magic wand and one by one the colors came out to play. The rolling hills turned seven shades of green. My favorite patch of wild buttercups became a slick, brilliant, buttery yellow, almost tempting enough to lick. Between the paddles of the prickly pear cactus poked violets, as deeply purple as the iris that stood like little flagpoles in my mom's flower garden.

The wind picked up and tickled the tops of the trees. The rustling leaves were a chorus to the songbirds' melody. My world was a series of pictures that I snapped inside my head. When I was forced to go inside, I would take my pictures with me.

Sue Massey

CHAPTER 4

Butterfly

Summer break ended, and so did the Point dances where I'd first laid eyes on Kenny. He hadn't been at any of the dances since. I wasn't sure if I was disappointed or glad that I didn't have to run into him and feel embarrassed about the letter I'd sent him.

Still, the thought of him seemed stuck inside my head. I'd daydream during biology class, pretend in my mind that he would call and ask me out. It didn't happen: My thoughts ping-ponged between Kenny Massey and my interest in biology.

Learning about the physical body intrigued me as much as what went on inside people's minds. Like the time I watched our farm veterinarian inject a syringe-filled needle into a huge dairy cow, slice open her thick hide, and lift out a one-hundred-pound, wet, newborn calf. When I thought about what I would be when I grew up, that was the image that came into my mind. Whatever career I chose, I was sure it would have something to do with animals. I knew the magic I'd felt that day would never wear off.

One evening that fall, after our Pecatonica High basketball team won a big game, some friends and I got together at the Eagle's Nest, the local teen hangout. We were milling about, talking and laughing, when whispers of "a party off Dowd Road" flashed through the high school crowd like a grass fire. The place was abandoned within minutes. Friends clustered, jumped in cars, and all sped off toward Dowd Road, deep in the country darkness.

It was a chilly October night. The cold had never stopped our gang from having an outdoor party. This one was being held on an out-of-the-way gravel side road in the rural hills.

Seven of us were packed into the car when we arrived at the party site. Cars pulled up, and dust hung in the night air. Guys were lifting cases of beer from their car trunks, and hints of cigarettes and pot drifted in the air.

I jumped out of the car, buried my hands in my pockets, and gazed into a huge black sky filled with a gazillion sparkling stars. I heard car doors bursting open and slamming shut, bottle caps snapping off, and laughter, the essence of freedom.

Someone handed me a beer, and I took a sip. I didn't like the taste, but hoped it would relax me and help me fit in, which I desperately wanted to do.

Some kid opened his car door and blared The Doors on his eight-track cassette player. The music was great, but I really wanted to sit in the tall reeds and listen to the soft gurgling of the water that flowed nearby. I found my way down to the river bank, perched atop a large rock, and sipped at the beer.

I lost track of time and soon realized how late it was. The moon was crossing the sky. I had a curfew and needed to find a ride home.

As I came up from the river bank, I heard someone comment, "Did you see that cool Corvette?" My heart started pounding, because there was only one person in the region who drove a Corvette, and that was Kenny Massey. I had never expected him to be here. I hoped he wouldn't see me, because I felt so awkward about the letter I'd sent him. I sipped more beer, hoping it would lull my anxiety.

And then, out of nowhere, came a gentle voice. "Hi Sue, I'm Kenny. You need a ride home?"

I wasn't sure which was wider, my eyes or my dropped jaw. The

Sue Massey

beer bottle slipped from my fingers, fell to the ground, and rolled down the steep embankment. I couldn't believe the guy in my dreams was standing right beside me, calling me by name.

Although my mind was a muddle, somehow I mustered words. "Ah, yeah, um, thanks. Your timing's perfect. I have a curfew, and I can't find the friend I rode out with. Hang on a minute." I called out to my friend Cali, "Hey, I have to leave. Tell Shay I found another ride home, OK?"

I turned back to Kenny. "Where are you parked?"

"Over here." He nodded toward the cherry-red '62 Corvette. "Watch your step. There are empty bottles everywhere."

He opened the car door for me, and I stepped in. It was like lowering myself into the bullet-shaped seat of one of my favorite, scream-inducing rides at the county fair.

"Do you know where I live?" I asked as he turned the key and the engine roared.

"I have a pretty good idea: first farm outside Blanchardville, the big white farmhouse on top of the hill?" His voice was muted by the engine's thunder as we spun out onto the gravel road.

I didn't mind the loud engine, as I was at a loss for words, trying not to be shy, worried I would say something dumb, not to mention the embarrassment I felt about having written him a letter. The light of the dash illuminated his face. He looked even more handsome up close, and he smelled so good. I was certain that this would all turn out to be a wonderful dream.

The drive home was over before I knew it, and I still hadn't thought of anything to say. He too had been silent, and I wondered what he was thinking. He seemed focused on his driving, and I was impressed by the smooth, adept way he handled his car — not too fast but certainly not slow.

When he pulled up to my house, he didn't linger to talk but jumped out and came around to open my car door. I was both sorry the evening was ending and glad that I didn't have to scour my brain for conversational topics.

As we walked toward my front door, I began to worry: What if he tried to kiss me? I had never kissed a boy. Shay and I had practiced kissing our bed pillows in a fit of girlfriend silliness, but I was clueless about how a real kiss would feel. Part of me couldn't wait to find out, and part of me was scared to death.

I turned to face him, my back against the cold door, while he stood with his hands tucked tightly into his front pockets.

"Whoa, it's cold," I said. My dad had once told me that when you can't think of anything to say, discuss the weather. I blew a white breath into the sky and laughed nervously. "It'll be snowing before we know it, and I'm not ready for that."

"Me neither. I still have corn to combine." His long sun-streaked hair was outlined against the blue haze cast by the sole nightlight.

"Corn? My dad picks corn and combines oats."

"We have poultry, fifteen thousand laying hens. The combine shells the corn for chicken feed. Your dad probably picks the corn ears and has the cob and kernels ground at the feed mill for his dairy cows."

It was a real conversation, and I was beginning to feel comfortable with him. It helped that we had farming in common.

He leaned forward ever so slightly and asked, "Would you like to go out next weekend?"

"That sounds great." The words spilled out before I had a chance to collect my thoughts.

"Friday night? Pick you up at seven?"

"Perfect," I said, turning toward the door. I snuck a side glance to watch him walking down the sidewalk toward his Corvette.

Did dreams actually come true? Not only was I going on my first-ever date, but it was with the very guy I had my eye on. I could barely contain my excitement.

I was relieved that he hadn't mentioned the letter. Maybe he never even received it. But, then again, maybe it was the letter that drew him to seek me out, leading to this deliriously blissful moment. I had been wishing that I'd never written it, but now I wasn't so sure. Maybe

Sue Massey

taking that risk had been the right thing to do. Maybe it would shape my future.

Kenny arrived at 7:00 on the dot. After briefly meeting my parents, he took me to a quiet little supper club tucked amongst the rolling hills between Hollandale and Dodgeville. I was so nervous that I could hardly eat. I discovered that he was much quieter than I'd imagined, but I thought maybe we were both just shy. It turned out that this was a first date for both of us.

I asked him about his farm, and he asked about mine. Though we had grown up ten minutes from each other, he was five years older and so was out of high school before I even began. Just a few years earlier, my hometown of Blanchardville and his town of Hollandale had consolidated and formed the Pecatonica Area School District, named after the gorgeous Pecatonica River that flowed through the area.

After dinner, instead of driving me home, Kenny turned down Star Valley Road toward his farm. *Star Valley*, I thought. *What a beautiful name for a country lane.* I knew where he lived because, of course, my friend and I had driven by to check it out on our way to one of the Point dances.

All of a sudden, he pulled off the road. His Corvette jostled through weeds and grass that swept the sides of his car. Then he stopped and opened the windows. A headlight beam lit a massive oak in front of us, and he looked over at me.

"Here it is. This is my farm. Well, my dad's, but someday it'll be mine."

I squinted to see, but the cold night spilled darkness everywhere. I wondered what I was supposed to see. Or was he planning to kiss me? I wasn't sure what to think.

Kenny hopped out of the car. After opening my door for me, he took my hand in his. It felt natural, right. With his other hand, he held branches up to make it easier for me to walk as he led me through the brush. Our feet flattened and crunched the stiff, cold grass beneath our shoes. When we reached a clearing, I could see the moon reflected in a meandering river.

Something rustled and ran past the lower branches of the oak tree, lit by his car headlights. Startled, I grabbed his arm.

"Just a deer. Don't worry. There are lots of deer and lots of woods on our farm."

"Do you hunt?" I asked, secretly hoping he'd say no.

"No, that's just not me. I can't bring myself to kill something."

Standing close to Kenny felt safe. We looked up into the most beautiful star-filled sky, and I knew why the road was named Star Valley.

"You're cold. Let's head back." He was the most thoughtful guy who'd ever crossed my path.

After driving me back to my house, he walked me to the door. "Wanna get together next weekend?" he asked.

"Sounds like a plan." It was cold, but I felt a warm glow inside.

"I'll call you mid-week, and we can decide what you'd like to do. See ya, kid."

Hmm, seems I have a nickname now, I thought. Well, I *was* a kid, just turned sixteen. He was twenty-one — a mature, adult man.

I tiptoed up the steps to my bedroom, dropped my clothes, dove in under my grandmother's quilt, and stared at the ceiling. It was so late that even the highway below our house was quiet. I let the entire evening stream through my head like a home movie. Wow, was he proud of his farm, I thought. And what were the chances that it had the beautiful Pecatonica River running through it? A farm, a river, and a guy who loved the land and animals as much as I did. As I drifted off to sleep, I wondered: Was it possible that my dream could really come true?

"Morning, Mom. What did you think of Kenny?" I came bouncing down the stairway and into the kitchen, excited to hear my mother's

Sue Massey

reaction to meeting Kenny the night before.

"Well, underneath all that hair, he seems like a really nice young man," Mom said as she stacked plates into the cupboard.

"It's the seventies, Mom. Long hair is in."

I popped a wedge of Mom's homemade bread into the toaster and thought of Kenny standing in the kitchen as I introduced him to my parents. Beyond the long, unkempt, sun-bleached hair, full beard, faded denim jacket and jeans, I saw the character of the man inside.

It was like the first time I laid eyes on my colt, Bojo. He was small, covered in a matted coat of burrs. His legs were crooked, and he was wild, afraid of human touch. But when I looked at him, all I could see was what he could be. A beautiful, sleek quarter horse with a mighty chest of steel, he had a mane that would flow as I rode him in the wind. He would grow into his legs, and I would brush his coat until it was as smooth and shiny as a chestnut. It might take time, but I was up for the challenge because the end result would be worth the effort.

Kenny and I fell into a routine of getting together every Friday night. Our dates were high school games, concerts, movies, dances, and sometimes dinner out. He was so polite — took his cap off, opened doors, always treated me like a precious stone, a gem.

We often hung out with some of his friends who, like Kenny, were five years older than I was and already out of high school and on their own. They picked up his pet name for me, and I became accustomed to being called "kid."

As the dates clicked by, I began to wonder if or when he *would* kiss me. I was too young and shy to make the first move. With each date, I grew fonder and fonder of him.

I stood in front of the mirror. I looked — really looked — at the young woman gazing back at me in a new powder-blue jumpsuit, one my mom had helped me sew. Never before had I worn anything like it. It was sleeveless with a halter-styled top, cut in sharply to a standup collar. My shoulders were bare, brown from the summer sun, and the fabric was fitted at the waist, then gently fell off the curve of my hips. For the first time in my life, I looked at myself and felt both confused and curious about the new me. In so many ways, I felt like the butterfly I'd hatched from its cocoon. My wings were still damp but unfolding, fluttering with the urge to take flight.

Later that day, I stood on the squeaky wood floor of the Pecatonica High School gymnasium among a cast of fellow classmates. We were about to sing and perform to the song "Aquarius." The bleachers were packed. High schoolers had been bused in from the neighboring town of Argyle. The morning butterfly I'd viewed in the mirror was now flapping its nervous wings inside my stomach.

We sang and moved in unison, and I loved the flowing dance aspect of the performance. The audience applauded, and the gym emptied within minutes. The janitors tore down the bleachers, and everyone went back to their sixth-hour class.

For me, the next class was English. As I sat at my desk, my thoughts kept swinging between the teacher's lecturing voice and the excitement I still felt from my first performance in front of an audience.

The bell rang, the halls were jammed, lockers opened and banged shut, and a boy came up behind me, handed me a little note with my name written on the outside. "I think somebody likes you," he said and disappeared into the crowd of kids. I stuffed the note in my black backpack and ran to my next class.

On my walk home from school, along the trail that passed my grandparents' home, through the woods, and up the hill to our farm, I stopped and sat beside a white pine, the gentle wind whistling through its needled branches, and opened the note. It was from a boy from Argyle High School. It read:

Hi, Sue.

You don't know me, but I saw you today in the "Aquarius" production, and I wondered if you would like to go out with me. I don't even know if you already have a boyfriend. Here's my phone number. I hope you will call. Gary

Sue Massey

I was shocked. Boys didn't notice me. I was just there.

I was still thinking about the note on Friday when I went out with Kenny. We'd been seeing each other for a couple months now. Near the end of our date, as we sat parked beneath the large maple in front of my farm home, I told Kenny about the note.

A long silence filled the cab of his snug Corvette. I heard him fidget with the car keys that hung, swinging freely, from his dash. He took a deep breath, carefully arranged his words, and turned toward me.

"Sue, I really like you. I've never met anyone as special as you. I can see our relationship growing, but I don't want you to have any regrets. You are so young, so if you have any thoughts of wanting to go out with that guy, I understand, and you need to do that, because if we move forward, I want you to be sure of your feelings. I'm OK with you going out with him next weekend, if you want. I'll call you the week after."

This was the longest stretch of words I'd ever heard Kenny say. I was impressed with how well-reasoned his thoughts were. He was articulate and sincere.

"Thanks, Kenny. I'll have to think hard about this."

As he walked me to the door, he leaned in and kissed me for the first time. It was so natural, so effortless, like we were made for each other, and I felt a flutter, one I'd never felt before.

The other guy was every girl's dream: drop-dead good-looking, starter on the varsity football team, and Mr. Personality. I couldn't believe he wanted to take me on a date. With Kenny's blessing, I called Gary, and we made a plan to go out the following weekend.

As Gary and I spent the evening together, I kept waiting to feel the spark, the one I always felt when I sat beside Kenny. We even kissed, and he was nice, but by the end of the evening, I had my answer. Kenny was right in encouraging me to go on the date. If I hadn't, I would have always wondered "what if."

The following weekend, as I pulled on my jeans and swept a brush through my long brunette hair, I could hear the engine of Kenny's Corvette coming up our gravel driveway. I took a quick glance in the mirror and thought: I am one lucky girl. This is a special guy who totally gets me, accepts my streak of independence, and likes me for who I am. I grabbed my little handbag and dashed past Mom, who was washing supper dishes at the sink.

"See ya!" I said as I spun out the door, footloose and fancy-free, just the way I loved it.

Sue Massey

CHAPTER 5
Ginkgo

My feet fit together like a fan-shaped ginkgo leaf, I thought, looking down at them on the carpet just before I pulled on my panty hose. In history class that day we had talked about the ginkgo biloba trees that survived the atomic bomb dropped on Hiroshima in 1945. Those trees continued to live today and were considered bearers of hope and symbols of resilience and peace. I felt drawn to both the fan-shaped beauty and the meaning of the ginkgo leaf.

It was now December 1972, and Kenny had invited me to the Bett-Or Egg Farm Christmas party. It would be the first time I met Kenny's parents and his co-workers from the Massey farm.

A few years earlier, Kenny's parents had stopped raising dairy cows. Farmers like Kenny's dad, Orval, were accustomed to a condition known as "milker's knee" from the twice-daily chore of kneeling beside the cows to milk them. Over time, it had taken a toll on Orval's knees, hips, and back, and he was finding it harder to do the chores.

Instead of cows, Kenny's dad decided to switch to chickens. Kenny's mom named the farm "Bett-Or Eggs," using a segment of each of their names, Betty and Orval. They converted their dairy farm to an egg-laying operation and leased fifteen thousand laying hens.

While they transitioned from dairy to eggs, there was twice as much work for Kenny. He would run between the dairy barn and milking chores up the hill to help his dad with repairs. His parents had incorporated the farm so that one day, when they retired, the farm would become Kenny's.

I lay back, my legs in the air, tugging at the stockings, hoping I wouldn't catch a fingernail and run them before the night even began. I hated panty hose. They were so tight, so restrictive. But this was a special evening, which meant I had to wear a dress and hose.

After squeezing into the panty hose, I fanned through my closet, looking for something appropriate. Kenny had forewarned me that his parents were extremely conservative. His two older sisters weren't even allowed to wear makeup or two-piece swimsuits. Whoa, I thought, I wonder what they'll think of me.

I pulled out the most conservative dress I owned, brushed my hair, touched up my face with my rosy blusher, grabbed my coat from the hook behind my closet door, and ran down the steps and out the front door to meet Kenny, who was already walking toward the door to greet me.

"Hey, kid, you look great! You ready to meet my parents?" His hair was still wet from the shower, and he had swept it back.

"Ready as I'll ever be." I settled into the front seat of the Corvette as he closed the car door behind me.

My town of Blanchardville and Kenny's town of Hollandale were seven miles apart: seven miles of rolling southern Wisconsin hills with acres and acres of sprawling, fertile farmland and fence rows anchored by large red and white barns. Pastures of black-and-white dairy cows and handfuls of beef cows dotted the hillsides. The curving country roads were shared by tractors pulling farm machinery. Thoughts of the weather and the unfurling seasons were on everyone's mind. Farm country was like its own little island, completely apart from the rest of the world.

My town, a community of 628 people, had all the essentials: a barbershop, grocery, feed mill, hardware store, furniture store, swimming pool, fire department, park, four bars, two cafés, three churches and graveyards, a lawyer, a bank, cheese factory, and post office. What more did we need? Kenny's town was smaller with about 300 people. Fewer residents meant fewer shops and stores. Everyone leaned heavily on the larger nearby community of Dodgeville for work or supplies.

As we pulled into the restaurant parking lot, Kenny said, "My parents aren't big drinkers, but we're meeting in the bar for a cocktail, then going to our table for dinner. I think there will be around ten of us. You'll like the ladies who work at the egg farm. They're lots of fun."

It was a Saturday night, the bar thick with smoke, dimly lit, packed, loud with voices and clicking glasses. Kenny took my hand and led me through the crowd, nodding a "Hi" at everyone he knew.

I was sixteen, and the official drinking age in the seventies was eighteen. Dating a twenty-one-year old made me feel older, more mature.

Kenny walked over to a huge man, well over six feet, slightly bent, with a head of thick gray hair. "Dad, this is Sue," he said. "Sue, this is my dad, Orval." We shook hands, and Orval tipped his head, saying it was nice to meet me and he was glad I could join them. I could see instantly that Kenny resembled his dad.

After chatting briefly with Orval, Kenny led me over to a petite woman with ever-so-slightly-graying brunette hair. Although she was wearing glasses, I could see her brown bead-like eyes and defined cheekbones. He gently touched her shoulder and introduced her to me as his mom, Betty.

I felt her eyes skim me head to toe. Then she smiled warmly, held out her hand, and said it was so good to finally meet me.

I was the youngest one there and desperate to fit in, feel less nervous. I ordered a brandy old-fashioned sweet, not thinking twice about my age. I just wanted to disappear into the group.

It helped. Dinner went well. I felt my body sag with relief when we were back in Kenny's Corvette headed home through the rolling hills toward Blanchardville. It was a clear night, and thousands of twin-kling stars were reflected in the snow that covered the earth. Kenny popped in an Eagles tape.

"I don't know if you could tell, but my folks really liked you." Kenny glanced my way, brushed my knee with his hand.

"Really? How could you tell?" I was digging in my tiny clutch for my Chapstick.

"I know them pretty well. I could tell." Kenny's blue eyes seemed to sparkle in the reflected light of the dash.

I sat back into my bucket seat, set my clutch in my lap like a pillow. "Whew, I wasn't sure. They both seemed hard to read. I sup-pose that was a crazy move on my part to order a drink, but I needed something to relax me. I wanted to make a good first impression."

Kenny reached for my hand. "You did great, Sue."

Thirty minutes later, he kissed me good night at my front door. This time, he kissed me long and passionately, and I didn't want it to end.

"I'll call you this week to make plans for next weekend."

I quietly climbed the staircase, turned on my little desk lamp, and sat on the edge of my gingham checked bedspread. I could hardly wait to pull off the pantyhose. I lay back, put my legs in the air, tucked my feet together like a ginkgo leaf and thought about hope, resil-ience, and peace. I had survived the meeting of his parents. I seemed to have passed the test. I could now relax and fall peacefully asleep.

I remember the moment Kenny told me.

We'd been dating for about five months, and things were great between us. We'd become a couple, and neither of us had any desire to see anyone else.

I recall everything about this particular evening, early in March. Kenny picked me as usual. Instead of heading toward town, he pulled into a nearby wayside, a sign that he wanted to talk.

Sue Massey

The sun was just dropping below the skyline of the neighboring barns and trees. As the engine of his Vette fell silent, Kenny seemed especially quiet. There was definitely something on his mind. I'd learned to wait until he was ready to share what he was thinking.

He turned the key just enough so that Bob Dylan's voice on the radio filled the quiet space between us. The sun sank, and the sky turned a deep shade of blue. The brilliant sparkle of the North Star appeared just above the horizon, as if by magic.

Kenny's blue eyes were softly illuminated by the light of the car's dash. He was troubled about something. I waited. We listened to Dylan.

Finally he spoke. "My number's come up."

"What number?"

"For the draft. I'm number thirty-four. That means I may be drafted to serve in the Vietnam War."

He pulled a letter from his pocket and handed it to me. I read to myself:

Results for Men Facing the Draft in 1971. Lottery Numbers, by Birth Date, for Selective Service. Lottery Held July 1, 1970. This lottery will determine the order in which men born in 1951 are called to report for induction into the military.

I'd never seen such a letter. The words took with them my heart and my breath. All I could think was, *not my Kenny, oh, my God, not my Kenny.*

My mind filled with a hundred questions. "What does this mean? If you get drafted, who takes care of your farm? How long have you known this?" It was so like Kenny to hold back so as not to worry me needlessly. "What about us?"

Kenny sighed, then said, "Dad has applied for a farm deferment for me because his health isn't good enough to run the farm. So far, I haven't been notified."

I leaned over, pulled his chin toward mine, and kissed him. "I'm going to pray. I'm going to pour my heart into hoping you get the deferment. God, I hate war."

Kenny reached for my hand. We both leaned back and listened to Dylan. First, "The Times They Are a-Changin' " and then, "Blowin' in the Wind." The earthy, soul-filled lyrics of these anti-war songs always struck a chord in me, but now they seemed even more poignant.

I looked up at the North Star, now higher in the sky. Although it was the same star, it looked different to me now. The times were definitely changing.

As I opened the letter, my mom pulled out a chair across from me at the kitchen table. The Dubuque School letterhead on the cream-colored paper matched the return address on the envelope addressed to Susan Jane Johnson, RR 1 Box 116, Blanchardville, Wisconsin.

I paused to glance at my mom. She looked excited, an emotion she usually kept under a lid.

Bubbling over with anticipation, hardly able to contain myself, I said, "I feel like this letter holds the direction of my life."

"Read it. See what it says." Mom's voice was calm and reassuring. Her elbows rested on the Formica surface of the table.

I flipped open the letter. My eyes dropped to the second paragraph, just as when I opened a textbook and would always jump to the ending, scan the beginning, then skim through the pictures.

I read aloud, "I'm sorry to inform you that the operating room assistant program has been filled by in-state applicants. Best of luck in your search for higher education."

I almost didn't want to look at my mom. I knew she would be disappointed. "Shoot, Mom," I said. "Now what am I going to do?"

"Are you sure you don't want to enroll in college? Your brother Bruce is doing great in Madison at the University of Wisconsin. You know that Dad and I will pay your way through college. We've always said we'd help you kids get off to a good start, then you'd be on your own."

"Mom, Bruce has always been the brains of the family. It's only this year that I made the honor roll, and that was because I loved every class I took, and most of them were hands-on. In art, I painted a picture of our farm. In sewing class, I made Kenny a suit. In home economics, I sketched my dream house and turned out three-course meals. In technical drawing, I loved the feeling of the pencils, the rulers, and the drawing boards we worked on."

"That's true," Mom agreed. "You're always at your best when you're outside or creating something with your hands."

I nodded. "That's why I was so excited when I heard that the Dubuque School was offering a hands-on technical class where I could learn in the hospital. It sounded perfect. But now — I just don't know."

Mom pushed back her chair on the linoleum floor, gave me a hug, and reassured me that it would somehow work out. "I need to start supper. Isn't tonight your date night with Kenny?"

I nodded. "I'm going for a ride on Bojo. I'll be back by five." I wanted to gallop with the wind and wipe the disappointment from my head.

When I tightened the girth beneath Bojo's rib cage, he drew in a deep breath to puff out his chest. I waited until he exhaled and then tightened the girth one more notch.

"I know your trick, Mr. Bojangles," I told him. "You want the girth loose and comfy. But I want the saddle to stay upright rather than fall under your tummy. Let's ride out and bring the cows home for milking."

I'd learned to stay on Bojo's back while I unhinged the gate, rode him through, and then latched the gate behind us without getting out of the saddle. Once we were through the gate, I coaxed Bojo into a gallop across the pasture, letting the wind cool my face and ripple my hair so that I felt nothing but the wild joy of the moment.

I had lobbied for a horse since I was old enough to talk, and Dad had finally said OK when I was fifteen. I almost thought of Bojo as my first boyfriend. We shared a bond.

Bojo and I galloped up the dirt pasture trails, rounded up the thirty dairy cows, and herded them home, trotting along behind them. If a cow lagged, Bojo would nip her in the flank, and she'd pick up the pace.

I had long ago decided that if I had to be an animal, I would choose to be a horse. A thoroughbred, bursting through the gate and pulling forward with every ounce of energy I could muster and then running, running fast and free.

Shortly after we finished supper, Kenny's Corvette pulled in. I dashed out to meet him. I'd been relieved to hear that he'd gotten his military deferment and wouldn't be leaving. Thinking of life without him had made me realize how special he was to me.

"How was your week?" Kenny asked as we drove down our gravel driveway. Then he paused before pulling out onto Highway 78. "Right or left?"

"Right," I said. "Let's drive to the wayside and talk for a bit."

We parked beneath a grove of oaks, their leaves just beginning to bud.

"You seem a little down. Are you OK?" he asked. It was uncanny the way he sensed my moods. No one had ever done that before — no one except the animals.

"Well, not really. I just opened a letter from the Dubuque School. I passed the exam, but their technical classes have already been filled by in-state applicants. What a bummer. Shot that idea down, and I don't have a plan B."

Kenny sat deep in thought. Then a smile crept across his face.

"What?" I asked. "What are you thinking?"

"We could get married."

Sue Massey

I couldn't believe my ears. *Did he actually say marriage?* I was stunned.

"Sue, I'm serious," he said, leaning toward me. "Let's get married. Just 'cause we're married doesn't mean you can't still go to school if that's what you want." He kissed me, deep and long, and it felt as though he wanted to seal the deal.

I took a deep breath, imagining myself standing on the edge of a cliff about to dive headfirst into the unknown below. This was the last thing I'd expected to come out of his mouth.

"Yes?" It was hard to resist his gentle, no-pressure way. I felt a hint of excitement at the idea of beginning our life together, committed to one another.

I was still trying to wrap my head around all that had transpired in less than two hours. It felt like my mind had reversed itself and was charging in the opposite direction. Still, it felt like the right direction. I kissed him and breathed a "Yes. I would love to be your partner in life."

He turned the key and spun out of the wayside. A cloud of dust and gravel lifted in the air behind us. "We're going to pick out your ring right now."

I scratched my head. "I want you to pick it out. Surprise me."

With one hand on the wheel and one on my knee, he said, "Sue, I wouldn't be comfortable picking out something as important as a wedding ring. I want us to get it together."

I could see his point, but I was so young, such a romantic. All I knew about rings was what I'd seen in movies, and the guy always surprised the girl. Still, caught up in the moment, I didn't argue. "OK, let's do it."

It sparkled, brighter than the North Star rising into a clear black sky. There were a hundred different rings to choose from, but my eye went directly to the simple gold band with thinly etched swirls that fit inside a double wedding band. I couldn't take my eyes off it.

"Is that the one?" Kenny asked, peering over my shoulder.

I held my left hand out, admiring the diamond that dazzled even brighter beneath the showcase lights. It took my breath away. I couldn't believe I was helping to select a wedding ring for myself. I had turned seventeen in November, and I would graduate in May. Everything was happening so fast.

I'd always wondered what I would be when I grew up. I wanted a career, marriage, and children, and expected them to happen in that order. Now it seemed the order had been scrambled.

"Could we see a size up on the diamond?" Kenny's voice broke the train of thought streaming through my head.

I'd never even imagined getting a diamond ring. "I don't know anything about diamonds," I said. "I've only seen my mom's. A diamond ring never seemed like something that would fit in my world. Look, they have matching bands. That's pretty cool. I'd be happy with just those."

"You're getting a diamond, Kenny insisted, "and I like the matching wedding bands."

Apart from sizing adjustments, the two bands fit us as if especially designed and made for us: unique, independent, and a couple for life.

That night, I couldn't sleep. I was wound too tight, thinking about how my life had turned 360 degrees in a matter of hours.

Kenny and I had driven from the jewelry store to my farm to get my parents' blessing, which they'd given wholeheartedly. "If it were anyone other than Kenny, we might not be so happy," Mom had said. "But I think a guy like Kenny comes along once in a lifetime."

It was funny, I thought, that the letter from the Dubuque School had decided the course of my life but not at all in the way I would have imagined when I opened the envelope.

Then I thought about the letter I'd written Kenny. He still hadn't said anything about it, so neither did I. For what did it really matter? Here we were together, about to begin working on wedding plans.

Sue Massey

Many years later, I asked him what he thought when he received my letter.

"I was shocked," he said. "I couldn't believe such a pretty girl would want to go out with me."

"I never thought of myself as pretty," I said, amazed. I paused, then asked the question I'd wondered about so often: "But why didn't you answer my letter?"

"I was way too shy," he said. "But it gave me the idea that I might have a chance with you, so when I saw you alone that night, I decided I had to do something."

I came to realize that we can't possibly predict what someone else might think, say, or do. Each person comes to a situation with a totally unique perspective, and the only way to understand it is to ask. It sounds simple, but this insight came to me late in life, after I'd left way too many questions unvoiced.

I learned another important lesson, too. With my mind constantly in motion, it was a truth I needed to absorb. Sometimes the answer lies in stillness and patience.

We decided on November 16 for our wedding date. That was ten days after I turned eighteen.

From May to November, life was filled with commotion: high school graduation, wedding showers, job applications, and plans to move into a home with Kenny. In some ways I felt very grown-up, in other ways just a child, but I knew I loved Kenny, so it all seemed to fit.

The summer unfurled quickly between babysitting for the neighbors, starting a part-time job at a sheep farm, and making almost all the wedding decisions. Kenny was there if I needed to bounce ideas off him, but he was fine with almost everything I came up with.

I also started packing my things as I planned for my new life after the wedding. The idea of working on my parents' dairy farm had come up because of my love for the cows and working outdoors doing the chores. That idea was like a gull diving headfirst into the clear surface of the lake; it disappeared without a ripple and never came up again. Kenny was the only son, his destiny set in stone; he would be taking over his parents' farm, and I would be moving into the Massey farmhouse as soon as we were married. And I learned that if we had a son, his middle name would be DeWitt, another Massey family tradition. I discovered that when one is young and in love, the future seems a long way off, and in fact it really isn't.

Shortly after Kenny and I announced our wedding date, his parents picked a spot on their farm and made plans to build a house there. They would move into the new house, leaving their previous farmhouse for Kenny and me to live in. The Masseys' 365-acre farmland was sprawling with so much beauty that I wondered at first how Kenny's parents were able to decide on just one spot. But soon I realized that the location they'd chosen, tucked around a scenic bend of Star Valley Road, was perfect. It provided a gorgeous view of jutting cliff rock sculptures. Plus, it provided all of us with the convenience of living near one another as we worked on the farm while also providing some separation between the two households.

I vividly remember the day Kenny's mom told me that when she was a young bride and they lived in that same farmhouse, her mother-in-law would often pop in on her. She promised herself that if she ever had a daughter-in-law she would always call before coming over. I was thankful for that and for the natural hill of seclusion they'd created between our two homes. Although our houses were only five hundred feet apart, they weren't within view of each other, which allowed us to have our privacy and independence.

The land around Kenny's farm was very different from the farm where I'd grown up. My farm was rolling hills with wide stretches of cropland, fence rows, and groves of maple and oak. I'd always yearned for a babbling brook. When I discovered that the Pecatonica River ran through Kenny's farm, I was thrilled. The Massey farm was beyond picturesque. The river had created towering bluffs with rock outcroppings that were unbelievably majestic. It was the most beautiful farm I'd ever laid eyes on.

Kenny and his parents were all involved in the day-to-day operations of the Bett-Or Egg Farm. Betty managed the books and office end of things while also teaching full-time in the Hollandale elementary school. Orval handled most of the egg processing, candling (grading the size of the eggs and checking for imperfections under a light source), and egg delivery, while Kenny oversaw maintenance and field work.

Orval's dad had bought the farm back in the twenties and handed it down to Orval, who would soon pass it on to Kenny. If one day we had a son or daughter who was interested in farming, the Massey farmstead would move into their hands, the fourth generation.

The summer before our wedding, just before they broke ground for their new house, Kenny's parents met with their lawyer to include me in the Bett-Or Egg Farm corporation. Orval, Betty, Kenny, and I were each given board positions in the corporation — equal partners in managing the farm.

The lawyer also helped Kenny's mom and dad re-zone the land on which their new house would stand. It wouldn't be part of the farm or corporation but a separate residential area. At the time, I thought it was a smart decision, although I had no idea then how wise it would turn out to be.

Betty and Orval's new house was a Wick prefab, so it went up in a matter of days that summer. But, even though their new place was ready, they weren't quick to move from the farmhouse where Kenny and I would be living.

I understood why it was hard for them to leave. They'd lived there their entire married life. They loved their new home, but it was a huge transition for them — just as big as my transition from my bedroom to a household that I would be learning to run.

As excited as I was to start revamping the farmhouse and making it our own, I didn't want to infringe on Betty's space. I didn't want her to think that I was too eager for her to move out and let me start redecorating. So I contented myself with scribbling my ideas down on paper and making plans. Kenny and I ordered new linoleum for the kitchen floor and white paneling for the kitchen walls. Sheets of wood paneling were the "in" thing in the seventies, and I knew my dad, mom, Kenny, and I could spin things together in no time at all.

One rainy Saturday afternoon, Kenny called and asked if I'd like to go furniture shopping. I jumped at the idea. We drove to a furniture store and picked out a hutch, a dining set, a green tweed love seat, a rust multicolored tweed rocker, and a maple end table.

Imagining how I would arrange the furniture in the farmhouse made the upcoming move seem more real to me. I could hardly wait.

When we stood at the cash register after making our selections and I watched Kenny write a check for all the new furniture, I was blown away. As a single guy, he must have saved up a nice nest egg.

We then drove to an appliance store. I had a small savings account for college that instead went toward the purchase of a refrigerator, washer, and dryer. As I wrote out the check, I hoped it didn't mean the end of my dream of going on to school. I didn't know how or when I would continue my education; I just knew that I loved to learn new things.

In a blink, summer was over, rust-colored leaves were dropping from the trees, and geese were honking overhead as they winged their way south. One afternoon in early November, I was in the kitchen, checking items off my wedding planning list while Mom worked on her sewing machine nearby. For months, she'd been sewing up a storm on my wedding dress and the bridesmaids' dresses, and now she was working on her own dress for the wedding. I'd done as much of the sewing as I could, but I left the tricky parts for Mom.

Sue Massey

Her soft voice lifted slightly above the humming of her sewing machine. I was lost in my own world, trying to figure out how I was going to get everything done before the wedding.

Her voice intensified and suddenly broke my zone.

"For someone who's getting married in a week, you're as grumpy as an ol' bear. What's up with you?" Mom looked at me, two sewing pins sticking out of one side of her mouth as she pinned two pattern pieces together.

Her comment took me by surprise. I'd been so wrapped up in planning, packing up my bedroom, and moving boxes into Kenny's home that I hadn't realized how irritable I felt or how scared I was. I'd been trying to tamp down my fears, but they kept bubbling up like yeasty dough. After all, I was only seventeen, and this was the only home I'd ever known. Part of me could hardly wait to move out and be on my own, and part of me felt like I was about to plunge off the high dive at the local pool, a dare I'd yet to accomplish.

As independent as I was, I'd never lived on my own, paid rent or bills, or run a household. While I was always keen on learning by watching, I wondered about all I didn't know. As the wedding date approached and moving into the farmhouse grew near, I also wondered what it would be like sharing the Massey farm with Kenny's parents. For decades, it had been the three of them working together on the farm, and I was the wild card thrown into the mix.

"I'm sorry, Mom. I guess it must be the marriage jitters." I looked down at the RSVP list and checked off the last name. "It looks like close to two hundred people are coming to the wedding." And I suddenly realized, all eyes would be on me. Yikes, that scared me even worse.

"Sounds like almost everyone you invited is coming. That's great, honey," Mom said, cutting a piece of velvet fabric with her scissors. Her dress would blend well with those of my bridesmaids, who would be wearing simple, long velvet dresses in earthy, autumn colors of rust, gold, and forest green.

I heard Bojo whinny at the pasture gate. It was almost chore time, and he was letting me know that it was time for his evening pail of oats. Tomorrow Dad and Kenny were planning to haul Bojo to his new home, a pasture on Kenny's farm, next to the little farmhouse where we would be living. The idea of Bojo coming with me into my new life reassured me. It felt like I was taking a piece of my childhood with me.

"I gotta run to my room and pack a few more things," I told Mom. "I'll be back in a couple minutes."

As I started upstairs, I glimpsed the living room couch out of the corner of my eye: the couch where Kenny and I so often cuddled and kissed. I remembered the night my mom tossed a pair of shoes down the staircase because she thought it was too quiet downstairs, a subtle warning for us not to let the cuddling go too far.

I walked into my bedroom and sat on the corner of my bed. This had been my room since kindergarten. I looked at the hooks on the back of my closet door. *I hope our bedroom in the farmhouse has hooks like these*, I thought, *hooks to ground me in my new world.*

I started boxing up the clothes that I would no longer need. My new Gibco Diagnostic Sheep Farm job required jeans and sweatshirts, mostly everyday-type clothes, which were a perfect match with me.

I looked down at the sparkling diamond on my finger. It was by far the most beautiful gift I had ever known. I almost didn't feel worthy of such a gem.

I wasn't sure if I felt more like a homesick kid mourning the end of my childhood or a young woman embarking on an adventure. My heart felt light and heavy at the same time.

November 16, 1974, was a crisp, clear fall day with a scattering of golden leaves skipping and dancing across the church parking lot. The sky was a deep brilliant blue as if snow was just beyond the horizon.

Sue Massey

The church was packed for our late-afternoon wedding. I wore a soft white satin dress that Mom and I had created to match a picture I'd torn out of a magazine. The design was simple with a midriff waistline, V-neckline, and lace-cuffed sleeves. When I looked in the mirror just before the ceremony, I hardly recognized myself. A grown woman in white was looking back at me. Like a grass snake, I had shed my childhood skin. The dress made me feel mature, feminine, like someone who mattered. As I turned away from the mirror, I saw a faint shadow, a shadow of the dark, secret friend that followed me wherever I went. I hoped I could leave her behind.

As I walked down the aisle toward Kenny, I thought how handsome he looked in his chocolate-brown tux with his thick, blond, wavy hair, a permanent blush in his high cheekbones, and a smile that went on forever. I looked into his eyes, and he in mine, as we recited our memorized wedding vows, the ones we'd written ourselves. Kenny's cousin sang one of our favorite songs by Crosby, Stills & Nash, "Our House." Kenny was my fire. I was crazy in love with him.

After dancing to my parents' favorite polka band at the local Legion Hall till 2:00 a.m., I thought my feet were going to fall off. It was such fun. Everyone wanted to dance with the bride, and I'd always loved dancing. Afterwards, we slipped into comfy clothes and drove to Madison to spend our honeymoon night. At 3:00 a.m., we crawled beneath the elegant, crisp sheets of the most beautiful bed I'd ever slept in and disappeared into each other's arms.

The next morning, the sunlight cascaded into our suite and woke me. The Inn on the Park, just off the Capitol Square, gave us a stunning view of the lake and the Capitol.

I looked across at Kenny's sleeping face. He looked so happy, so serene, so handsome. I glanced around the room, our clothes in crumpled heaps on the floor beside our bed, and it hit me that I would be waking up beside this man for the rest of my life. The thought shot into my bones like the sunlight that pierced our room. I forced the fear aside with the thought that Kenny would be patient and help me adjust.

We'd taken two weeks off from work. That was an unheard-of break for both of us, but Kenny was determined to take me on a road trip to California and back. I had hardly been out of Wisconsin and dreamed of seeing the ocean for the first time.

I soon realized how much Kenny loved to drive, for hours on end, while I squirmed with pent-up energy after an hour or two in the car. By four o'clock every day, I was ready to find a hotel — with a pool if possible so that I could swim and burn off some energy.

The Rocky Mountains left a huge impression on me, as did the towering redwoods. The Pacific was as majestic as I'd envisioned, but as I stood on the shore of San Francisco Bay listening to the wailing seals and looking out toward Alcatraz, I realized that I wouldn't be swimming in the ocean as I had planned. Not in November. It was chilly, very chilly, but also beautiful. The sights and sounds along the wharf were magical.

By the tenth day of our trip, I was so homesick that we decided to start back early. Driving through a blinding snowstorm and below-zero temperatures in Iowa, the car heater barely kept us warm, and all I could think about was crawling between the warm flannel sheets of my childhood bed in my parents' home.

As we fell into bed together hours later, I thought about all I'd seen of the country and all the places I'd like to return to one day. But coming home was the best part.

Tomorrow we would be spending our first night together in the Massey farmhouse, and a whole new life would begin, a life that I could barely fathom.

Snowflakes drifted down, turning the ground a thin layer of white, each flake unique yet falling from the same cloud, in the same sky.

It was our first Christmas together. Married for a little more than a month, Kenny and I were still in our honeymoon phase. Yet feel-

Sue Massey

ings of separation and loneliness were nudging out my excitement at building our life together. I missed my childhood farm — helping with chores, feeding the calves, working beside my dad.

The first time Kenny walked me through the chicken houses on the Massey farm, I was taken aback by the hens in cages stacked floor to ceiling with long trays of eggs accumulating. There were five thousand hens in each of three houses, filled with deafening squawking, white feathers everywhere, and a thick cloud of dust when the automatic feeders kicked in.

The entire operation stunned me. It wasn't the picture I'd anticipated — so not the Brown Cow Farm of my favorite childhood storybook. When something didn't feel like a fit to me or made me uncomfortable, I shied away from it.

It wasn't as if I hadn't known what I was getting myself into when I married Kenny. I was marrying his parents, a chicken-and-egg operation that the three of them had managed together for years, and a farm that had been in the Massey family for three generations.

Yes, I knew all that before I married Kenny. Still, that first Christmas was hard for me. I think Kenny could sense my trying to fit in and find my place on the egg farm. His Christmas gift to me was a soft, wiggly St. Bernard puppy that I named Tillie. We cared for and disciplined Tillie as if she were our first baby.

I bathed Tillie in the tub every week until one day she hardly fit in the tub anymore. She'd grown into a hundred-pound, lovable, lioness-like giant of brown, white, and black fur. When she sat on the front lawn, gazing out over the valley, she looked like an image I'd seen of the rescue dogs in the picturesque Alps.

Between Tillie, my horse Bojo, house projects, my part-time job, trying new recipes in the kitchen, inviting friends and family for dinners, and growing my first garden, I began to find a home for my creative ideas that both challenged and entertained me.

What I wasn't fond of was the lost privacy. True to her word, Kenny's mom never popped in on us, but a constant string of cars drove by daily, with either farm workers or locals coming to buy eggs. I had always cherished the seclusion of my childhood farm and was used to running around outdoors with skimpy clothes or bikinis in the summer: free as a bird, not caring how I looked, knowing only family members would see me. I now felt as if I were on stage when I worked in our garden, which was on a small knoll where the gravel road looped around the chicken houses. I came to terms with the fact that I couldn't change the scenario. I put a smile on my face and waved, kept a cotton blouse nearby as a cover-up, and lost myself in the warm sunshine, the country breeze, and the feel of the dirt and seeds in my hands as I cared for my little garden plot.

I snaked my way up Highway F through the rolling farmland in my '63 Chevy, the beater car my dad had given me, driving toward my sheep-farm job. I enjoyed the work, drawing blood from sheep for research purposes. I felt a warm connection with the animals and loved being with them.

The car radio played softly as I thought about what the first few months of marriage had been like. The differences between Kenny and me were surfacing. For one thing, Kenny didn't mind clutter; in fact, I don't think he even noticed it. I'd grown up in a picture-perfect setting and felt most comfortable if things were in order. His leaving piles of stuff everywhere began to get under my skin.

In the evening, I would go to bed and wait for Kenny to join me. Instead, I would hear him snoring on the couch downstairs with the TV blaring. It was hard not to take it personally. I eventually realized it wasn't me as much as the fact that he was absolutely exhausted from the hard physical farm work that he put in seven days a week. Still, I felt like his mother going downstairs to shut off the TV and ask him to come to bed. I hated the feeling.

When I came home from work, I couldn't wait to spin together a special supper for us, something I'd been scheming in my head all day. I'd set the table, light a candle, and wait for the back door to open and Kenny's eyes to appear. During my childhood, we always ate at

Sue Massey

5:00 p.m. Kenny's family ate at six, and he wanted that extra time to work, so we agreed on six as our suppertime. However, I never knew when he would show up. Sometimes it was ten after six, sometimes six thirty, sometimes later. The longer I waited, the sadder I felt, and the more it seemed as if I didn't matter. I wondered why he was never late for work but always late for supper. It was as though he were married to the farm.

"Sue, look." Kenny pointed at the hoof marks that trailed off toward the woods. He called this densely pine-covered corner fortress of the farm Purgatory, so thick that sunlight rarely reached the ground. If you wandered in, you might never find your way out.

Blackie was missing. She was the oldest beef cow on the farm. Kenny had noticed she wasn't with the rest of the small beef herd that roamed the vacant pastures after the dairy cows had been sold. Sometime during the night, Blackie had given birth, and we were tracking her to make certain everything had gone OK.

Kenny had walked these field roads since he was a toddler, knee-high to his six-foot dad. I followed behind him.

"Looks like she broke a piece of barbed wire fence along the corn-field — like twenty-five acres isn't a big enough space to give birth?" Kenny trudged along through the thicket. Then he stopped abruptly, holding his arm out to stop me.

"Shh. Listen."

I recognized the soft sound of licking and the low mooing of a mother cow tending a newborn calf. Kenny nodded toward the edge of the cornfield, at a patch of overgrown meadow grass where Blackie was licking her calf, still wet, black as onyx, nudging it and coaxing it to take its first step.

We stood and watched. First it wobbled onto its back legs. Then it tried to steady itself on all four. Blackie stood, patiently waiting for her newborn to find a teat and begin to nurse.

"They're fine. Let's head back. My guess is, she'll bring the new calf back to the barn by nightfall. I'll leave the gate open," Kenny said, lifting his hat and wiping his brow. I caught a glimpse of his jeans; they hung just right, sexy and tight. His shoulders broad, arms as strong as wrenches. I came up behind him and tackled him onto a mattress of meadow grass, took him by surprise, reached for the zipper of his pants.

"Sue, out here?"

"Like someone can see us?"

"What about Blackie?"

"Doubt she'll tell."

In May, six months into our marriage, I arrived early at work to help my supervisor, Bonnie, sort sheep for the day's blood order we had to fill. I was reaching onto a high shelf for some supplies when I felt a shooting pain in my lower back. I winced and sat down on the nearest chair.

"You OK, Sue?" Bonnie asked, squatting down to look into my face.

"I'm fine," I said. But a minute later, another burning pain made me wonder about a urinary tract infection.

Bonnie shot me a serious, mother-like glance, and dialed the Dean Clinic, then informed me that I had an appointment at the clinic in Madison.

A few hours later, I handed the nurse a urine sample and sat shivering beneath a white cotton sheet draped over my naked skin. Everything smelled of sterile alcohol. I lay back, staring at the ceiling tiles, trying to forget the discomfort in my lower abdomen. I figured that the doctor would come in any minute and prescribe an antibiotic, and I'd be off running, and outta there.

A quiet tap on the door, an outstretched hand. "I'm Dr. Mussey," he said warmly. He looked down at my chart and asked me a few questions about my symptoms. When did the lower back pains begin? Had I ever had them before? When he paused, I thought: What are the chances a Massey gets a doctor by the name of Mussey? I instantly liked him. The nurse knocked, walked in, handed him the results of my lab work, and left the exam room.

He swiveled his chair toward me. Gently tapping my knee with my manila-colored file, he said, "Looks like you're pregnant."

I could feel my jaw drop. "But, wait, I just had my period."

"Was it light? It's normal for some women to have a light period during the early weeks of pregnancy."

A baby, oh, my God, a baby.

"You look shocked."

"I am. I thought maybe a urinary tract infection."

"You have that too. I'll give you an antibiotic and some prenatal vitamins and see you in one month. By the way, congratulations." He handed me the prescription and closed the door behind him.

I sat alone, paralyzed for a moment. *A baby, I'm going to have a baby? Boy, do I suck at birth control.* I'd been thinking about going on to school as well as pursuing some other interests. Hmm. Now what? As I pulled on my jeans, I wondered what Kenny would say and how he would feel about the news. What would our parents say? For that matter, how did I feel about this baby news?

I'd always loved kids. As soon as my mom said I was old enough to babysit, I could hardly contain my excitement, and I said yes to every babysitting job that came my way. It was intriguing to watch the little ones interact and develop.

I thought those who had large families were the luckiest people in the world and had looked forward to having one of my own. But this was happening far sooner than I had expected. I was only eighteen. My goodness, I would only be thirty-six when the baby graduated from high school. The whole thing seemed surreal.

I put my hands on my belly. It was hard to believe a new life was growing inside me, a life that Kenny and I had created together. I felt a sense of awe. Beyond that, I wasn't sure of anything.

It started off as a beautiful, crisp December day. I saw pockets of colored Christmas lights being strung along the way as I drove the familiar curvy Highway F toward my doctor's office in Madison. I was seven months pregnant, and this was my regular prenatal checkup.

I was glad that I would be seeing the doctor, because something had been bothering me for the past few days. I was anxious to talk to the doctor about it.

When he asked me how everything was going, I said, "I'm not sure, but something feels different." I placed a hand on my basketball tummy and felt a limb ripple across the surface.

"What do you mean, Sue?" He set my open chart on the desk.

"Well, having never had a baby before, I don't know how to describe it other than I feel pressure."

"Let's take a look. Make sure everything is OK." He draped a white sheet over my legs and pulled out the stirrups as I leaned back on the table. The stiff white pillow crunched beneath my head as I stared at the ceiling squares, counting the seconds until he was done examining me. I heard a faint sigh and looked down between my draped knees to see my doctor's face, which turned from puzzlement to shock.

"Hmm," he said, dropping his eyes, checking again to be sure he'd seen what he thought he had. Then he stood, dropped his latex gloves in the waste bin, and helped guide me to a seated position.

"Is the baby OK?" I asked. My heart thumped loudly in my chest and my breath grew shallow.

"Yes, the baby feels strong and healthy, maybe two pounds, growing nicely. I know you've had your share of urinary tract infections, premature labor, and hospital stays with your pregnancy, but..." and his voice trailed off.

He sat down and looked into my chart, as if scanning for something he might have missed.

"You're scaring me. What's wrong?"

He looked at me, clearly perplexed. "Well," he said, "you're about thirty weeks along, but you're already dilated to seven centimeters. I've only seen this a few times before. It appears you have an incompetent cervix, which means you're unable to sustain a full-term pregnancy."

At first I was too stunned to speak. Then I said, "I'm dilated to seven centimeters? The pamphlet you gave me says that at ten centimeters the baby is born."

"You're right," he said. "That's why you're going to have to take it very easy for the rest of your pregnancy."

He looked down at my chart for a third time, deep in thought. Then he asked, "Sue, have you ever heard of DES, or diethylstilbestrol?"

"No, why? What is it?"

"Back in the fifties, if women had problems sustaining a pregnancy, doctors sometimes gave them DES. It's a synthetic hormone. Later on, doctors discovered that it caused problems in children who were in utero during that time. You need to ask your mother if she ever took DES when she was pregnant with you."

"I know she wanted kids badly and had several miscarriages before my brother was born. I'll ask her." My life seemed suspended in air as I tried to wrap my head around his words.

"Good. Call me and let me know what she says." He shifted in his chair as he wrote down his direct phone number on a business card and handed it to me.

"But what about now? What happens? Kenny and I are signed up for birthing classes but not until mid-January. The baby isn't due until February 14. What do we do?"

"We try to keep that baby in there for as long as we can. The last thing you want is a premature birth. Preemies are twice the work and can have lifelong complications. I know you're very active, and you won't want to hear this, but when you go home you need to put your feet up as much as possible."

"Well, what about work? Can I still work?"

"For now, I'm sending you home and telling you to take it easy. The longer you can sustain this pregnancy, the better."

"Does this mean we'll only get to have one baby? Kenny and I have always talked about a big family, like maybe four." My head was swimming with questions.

"We'll see how things go. In your case, what's recommended is a suture placed around the cervix at about three months, then removed just before delivery. This method has been extremely successful. So, in answer to your question, yes, you'll be able to have more children."

I sighed with relief. My pregnancy had been a stretch of one complication after another: premature labor, a series of urinary tract infections, and a painful vein that throbbed inside my upper leg as the baby grew and pressed against it. At times, I could hardly walk. Maybe this was my body's way of slowing me down.

Later, my mom confirmed that her doctor had prescribed DES for her when she was pregnant with my two siblings and me. Complications of pregnancy and birth were common for DES daughters like me. But my doctor had been right about my ability to have more kids. Each of my five babies stayed in my womb longer than the last, although all were high-risk pregnancies. For my last four pregnancies, I had to have a purse-string suture placed in my cervix, just as the doctor had told me, to minimize the risk of premature delivery. And just like this first time, nothing about any of my pregnancies was easy or routine.

I tried to follow the doctor's orders as much as possible, but it was nearly impossible to spend much time with my feet up. To make ends meet, Kenny and I both needed to work. The only time I could put my feet up was after supper when I would collapse on the loveseat. By the end of my pregnancy there was a little dent in the cushion where I'd planted myself while counting the days until the baby arrived and I was free to run again.

Sue Massey

"Don't push!"

"I have to push!"

I was on the hospital cart, and the nurse was speeding it down the hall as fast as she could.

"Where's Kenny? Kenny!" My head arched, looking backward.

"I'm here. I'm right here, Sue!" I felt his fingertips against my shoulder. Then I saw lights: lights above me, the size and shape of flying saucers. Gowns, drapes, voices, the clicking of instruments, the stinging smell and cold touch of iodine, hands and arms beneath me, lifting, scooting me onto the delivery table.

"I have to push!"

A voice in my ear, coming from nurse Ginny, said, "Push, girl, push all you want, we're ready to meet this baby."

It was December 21, 1975, and Kelli Sue Massey arrived, pink and screaming. There was a bustle of movement: doctors, nurses, a scale. The waves of pain that brought her into the world were beginning to settle, only a pinch here and there. I looked toward the sunlight that streamed into the delivery room. White puffy clouds drifted across the blue sky. I could now have my life back, free from doctor visits and restrictions.

A soft kiss against my cheek, and Kenny's voice was saying, "You did great, Sue. She's beautiful."

"Sweet Jesus, Sue! She's five pounds and one ounce," nurse Ginny told me as she placed Kelli into my arms. "And they thought you'd have a two-pounder — you surprised us all! Great work, Sue."

Ginny smiled as if she'd given birth, and in fact, she'd been there holding my hand, coaching me through as the waves of labor grew strong, peaked painfully long, then grew shallow. Ginny held one hand, Kenny the other, telling me to breathe, pant, blow. It was a team effort. They coached, encouraged, and supported me through. Nurse Ginny's shift had ended two hours ago, but she stayed. She stayed, let me grip her hand until the baby came and with it a joy, a love so intense that the blue sky, the warm sunlight streaming through the windows seemed to dim as I became lost in the glory of a new life, a pink bundle in the cradle of my arms.

Letter from the *Heart*

This wasn't the picture I'd carried in my head.

I shuffled down the hospital corridor in my terry blue robe and matching slippers, an early Christmas gift from my mom. As I prodded open the door to the Infant Intensive Care Unit, a friendly nurse told me to gown up, scrub for two minutes at the sink, and sit in the rocker in the corner.

I walked, eyes cast down, across a blue tile floor so clean it sparkled. When I dared to look inside the isolettes I passed, my slippers grew slow and heavy, and with them my heart. This was far from the row of cute little babes in bassinets I'd envisioned. These babies looked like giant spiders. Their thin skin covered a network of blue and red veins. Everywhere I looked, there were tubes, monitors beeping, syringes, needles, lights, tape, charts, IVs, and little pink and blue hand-knit stocking hats.

I sat down gingerly in the rocker, my bottom sore from delivering the baby. The nurse placed Kelli in my arms.

"She's so beautiful, so tiny. What's this tube in her nose for?" I touched and counted each of her fingers and toes. I watched her chest heave for air.

"She's too weak to nurse. One of the final things to develop in utero is baby's nipping ability, so we tube-feed her. When your milk comes in, we'll tube and feed her your milk. One of the nurses will show you the room where you can use the breast pumps."

"It looks hard for her to breathe." I thought of the newborn calves on my childhood farm. Sometimes when they were born, the amniotic fluid from birth would seep into their lungs, and they would cough and sputter until it was clear.

"Kelli is seven weeks premature. Her lungs aren't fully developed yet. She'll need to be on oxygen until she matures," the nurse said as she listened to Kelli's heart with her stethoscope. "What about baby's dad? Would he like to hold her?"

"He was here during delivery, stayed until I was settled in my postpartum room, then headed home for chores. We farm in Hollandale. It's a fifty-minute drive from here. Because the pregnancy was high-risk, we had to come into Madison. He'll be back this evening. I know he can't wait to hold her."

"That will be perfect. Both of you can get some rest, and Kelli will be ready for another visit." She charted as she talked. "I see by your chart, this has been a long ordeal for you. It looks like you were admitted seven times for premature labor." She glanced up to read my reaction.

"No kidding! This pregnancy has been anything but predictable." Kelli wiggled ever so slightly in my arms. She smelled like baby powder and alcohol where they'd drawn her blood. Her pink skin was covered with a soft down.

A siren exploded, and a stir of activity surrounded an isolette in the corner. My nurse's eyes followed. "Sue, you have to feel lucky. I know you have a long road ahead until it's time to take Kelli home, but she's going to be OK."

My thoughts stopped on "time to take Kelli home."

"Wait, what did you say? Kelli won't be coming home with me?"

The nurse touched my arm, "Even though Kelli has a good weight for her thirty-three-week gestation, she still requires oxygen, and she can take only about an ounce of milk every hour. Her demands are very high right now. You both need time to rest and recover."

"So how long before Kelli can come home?"

She looked at the chart. "Well, rule of thumb is they hope to have baby home by the actual due date, but that can vary greatly."

The actual due date — February 14 — was almost two months away. My heart sank. How could I possibly leave her here for so long?

"See the baby over there?" the nurse continued. "One pound, eight ounces. She's fighting for her life. You're very lucky."

I looked down at the tuft of blond hair around Kelli's pink knit hat. Each breath, the breath we took for granted, suddenly didn't seem so easy. Nothing seemed easy. As I kissed each of Kelli's fingertips, I knew I would carry this moment in my heart for the rest of my life.

I sometimes think about how pregnancy prepared me for what was to come. With all the complications, restrictions, and anxieties, it was impossible not to feel my growing responsibilities for the new life I was carrying. Now, when I remembered my doctor telling me that a preemie was twice the work, I sensed that he had been understating the case. But I had nothing to compare it to. This was all I knew.

I was released from the hospital on Christmas Day. When we brought Kelli home fourteen days after her birth, her sucking ability was still weak. She could only drink one ounce of milk at a time before falling asleep like a tiny bird in my arms only to wake an hour later for more nourishment. Her feedings were every hour on the hour, all day, all night. Kenny helped as much as he could, but he was busy working the farm. Both sets of grandparents helped, but they all worked jobs or farmed, too.

A preemie becomes primarily the mother's responsibility, an obligation she's aware of every second. I knew my life was forever changed. It now belonged to baby Kelli. My days would revolve around meeting her needs and wants.

Raindrops pinged against the window panes like cascading needles as they fell from the sky and turned to ice. I stared out the window but could see nothing but darkness.

It was 1976, and an ice storm had blanketed the southern half of Wisconsin, leaving everyone without electricity for days. Because the poultry houses on our farm had automatic feeding systems, the generators kicked in, and as a result our home had heat. I was so grateful, for I hated the below-zero temps with a passion.

Others weren't as fortunate. Some people were able to burn wood to keep warm, but not everyone had that capability. The situation was dire for those with no way to keep warm.

Sue Massey

Many of Kenny's relatives were in this dangerous situation, so we opened our home to them. Close to a dozen Masseys, including six children, were living in our little house. They slept on our living room floor, conversed, played games, cooked, and ate meals with us. We became one big family with Kelli the center of attention.

Nineteen and a first-time mom, I welcomed all the hands to help hold Kelli. But the complete lack of privacy wore on me. There was one TV for everyone to watch. Feeding everyone was a full-time job: preparing three farm meals a day, washing dishes, and planning the next meal, all while rubbing elbows with extended family. Everyone pitched in, but I felt responsible for the bulk of the work. I felt cabin fever setting in.

Six days into the ice storm, I desperately needed some time away. Kenny's aunt understood how frazzled I was feeling and offered to watch Kelli while Kenny and I took a short drive to Hollandale for groceries and to Blanchardville to see how my folks were doing. At the time, there were no cell phones, and I was anxious to see if my mom and dad were OK.

As we inched our way down the ice-covered roads, I saw firsthand the destruction surrounding us. Trees stood broken and bent under a thick, glistening cloak of ice. Utility trucks with blinking lights and extended ladders were everywhere, repairing downed electrical lines. Except for those trucks, we were the only ones who had ventured out.

Hollandale was a ghost town, silent and sleeping under layers of silver and white. The grocery store was dark and eerie: shelves nearly bare, only a few dim lights flickering. Almost all the basics were gone — no milk, no bread, no fruits or vegetables — but we were able to pick up a few boxes of cereal for the kids.

Leaving Hollandale with our small bag of groceries, we started toward my childhood farm in Blanchardville. Kenny maneuvered his four-wheel-drive pickup down the treacherous curves of Highway F like a pro. I'd always thought of Kenny as a member of the world's best drivers' club. He drove like he lived his life: smooth and skilled, willing to take a risk, but careful and mindful, an extreme problem solver.

The roads had been salted, but the speed at which the rain fell and turned to ice was beyond anything the plows and salt trucks could handle. Our usual ten-minute drive had stretched to nearly an hour as we pulled into Blanchardville.

We found my mom and dad huddled in the basement near the wood stove. Dad had strung wire from the ceiling, and Mom had hung blankets with clothespins in the shape of a box, creating a little room where they sat with a candle glowing between them. A half-assembled jigsaw puzzle rested on the table nearby.

They gathered two more chairs, and we sat and talked about the storm. They asked about Kelli, whom they missed deeply after so many days apart. Mom offered us cookies. She always had a freezer packed tight for just such emergencies. She and Dad were experts at surviving through the long, harsh Wisconsin winters.

It was a comfort to sit with Mom and Dad. When I felt the heaviness of milk in my breasts, I knew it was time to head home. Kelli still nursed often and around the clock, and my body was exquisitely tuned to hers.

The warm March rains finally melted the shield of ice that covered the region.

I was washing windows and pushing them open for the first time that spring when I thought I heard Kelli stirring upstairs. I looked at the green, flower-shaped clock on the wall above the kitchen table. Huh? It wasn't time for her to be up. Our dog Tillie was curled and napping on the rug in front of the screen door. I cracked open the upstairs door and listened quietly to confirm that Kelli was awake. Her cry seemed muffled, somewhat odd.

I climbed the narrow staircase to Kelli's crib in our bedroom. As I turned her over, I was shocked to see her face beginning to turn blue. Panicked, I felt my adrenalin kick in. Suddenly I was a kid on

Sue Massey

my dad's farm, discovering a newborn calf not breathing. I whisked her limp, gasping body up in front of me and shook her gently, then laid her on the bed and quickly massaged her tiny rib cage. Then, I tucked her against my chest like a kitten, and ran toward the sound of Kenny's tractor on the road below our house, yelling his name and waving my free arm.

He shut the tractor off and came running. I looked down long enough to see her cheeks begin to pinken.

"Sue, what's wrong? What happened?" Alarm filled Kenny's face.

I was crying, clutching the baby. "Kenny, I heard a funny noise coming from her crib, and when I went to check on her, she was struggling to get air." I could hardly catch my breath.

"Well, she looks OK now, Sue. It's OK. Let me walk you back to the house. I'll come in for a cookie."

"Kenny, I'm so scared! What if I hadn't gone up to check on her? She might have died." I felt shaken to the core. All my confidence had leaked away, and I didn't want Kenny to leave me alone with her. Though everything was fine, I couldn't stop wondering what I had done wrong. I had placed her, tummy down, on a soft fluffy blanket for a nap. Was she too small and weak to turn her head to the side so she could breathe?

I handed Kelli to Kenny and ran upstairs to her crib. I took the fluffy blanket out of her crib, folded it, and placed it in a dresser drawer along with my shame.

Downstairs, I made Kenny promise never to tell anyone what had happened. I blamed myself, even though Kenny assured me I'd done nothing wrong. It made me sick to think of parents who lose a child to the mysterious SIDS (Sudden Infant Death Syndrome). Preemies are at a higher risk of having SIDS.

I carried the traumatic experience with me for a very long time. I worried constantly that I would find her lifeless in her crib. The thought consumed me until, slowly but surely, she began to grow stronger.

The long, hot, humid days of August arrived. One morning I awoke not feeling well. I looked at the ceiling, as I always did when searching for an answer, and I knew, almost instantly, what felt off. I was pregnant.

I thought of the ordeal that my recent pregnancy had been. It was too fresh in my mind to think of going through it all again. I closed my eyes and wept. Tears of hormonal changes, tears of knowing the long road ahead: the surgery to place a purse string suture in my cervix, the stays in the hospital, the orders to curtail my activity, the months that seemed as if they would never end. And this time it wasn't just me. I now had Kelli to care for as well.

The baby's due date was May 5. When pregnant with Kelli, I'd been hospitalized seven times to stave off premature labor. I was placed on my side and given an IV of vasodilan, which dilated my veins with the hope that the labor would stop. It usually worked, followed by a throbbing headache that felt like the worst hangover one could imagine. This time I was hospitalized only five times during my pregnancy, and the stays were shorter. My body seemed to be adjusting to this thing called pregnancy.

When I went into labor on March 24, the doctors discovered the suture in my cervix had scar tissue that prevented it from dilating. They were within minutes of performing a C-section when Dee entered the world screaming.

Dee spent only a week in the neonatal intensive care unit, a week shy of Kelli's stay before she could come home. Like Kenny and me, Kelli fell in love with Dee the moment she laid eyes on the five-pound, five-ounce bundle. She and Kelli were sixteen months apart, destined to be close friends for life.

We named her Danelle Kimberly. But Kelli would point to her and say "D, D." Thus, her nickname Dee was born, and it stuck.

Sue Massey

CHAPTER 6
Whirlwind

The next few years were a whirlwind of taking care of babies, keeping the household running, and getting used to a new job. My position at the sheep research farm had been a short-term one, and after it ended, I started working four days a week as office manager at the local vet clinic.

One evening after the girls were in bed, I brought up something that had been on my mind. "Kenny, I've been thinking. I sure miss the cows. I miss the milking chores. Is there any way we could fix up the old dairy barn and have a small dairy herd?"

When I'd married Kenny, I'd brought the dream of my favorite childhood book, *Brown Cow Farm,* with me into my marriage. I'd pictured our marriage as a close partnership like that of my parents, working side by side. Instead, Kenny was gone most of the time, and I barely saw him. And I missed my animals, especially the calves with their large eyes and long fluffy eyelashes.

Every morning from our bedroom window, I saw the old Massey dairy barn that had stood empty ever since Kenny's parents switched from dairy to eggs. Whenever I wandered inside, I imagined a restored barn filled with brown-eyed Jerseys and a pen full of calves bawling for their evening pail of milk.

"The barn would be a perfect place for us to keep a few cows," I continued. "We could use the extra income, and it would be ours, Kenny. We'd have something together."

Kenny nodded and replied, "I hear you, Sue, but the barn is in such bad shape, it would be cheaper to burn it and start over. And with the kids, your job, and Bett-Or Eggs, I don't know how we could manage one more thing. Plus the cost of a start-up wouldn't be cheap."

My heart sank. He was right. There was more than enough farm work. But I just didn't feel a part of Bett-Or-Eggs. I wanted something for Kenny, me, and our kids.

"What if we built a shed?" I suggested.

Kenny was silent. He always thought things through before responding.

"Well, what do you think?" Still, silence. "I mean, your parents have been great, but the three of you are out on the farm while I'm in the house, taking care of the kids, and running to Blanchardville to work four days a week. It would mean so much to have a few animals to take care of."

Kenny sighed. I knew what he was thinking: Where do we get the money to build a shed and buy the animals? *It's always the same — no money, stuck and lonely, going nowhere.* There were times I thought I was suffocating inside.

That spring, Kelli was old enough to toddle up the dirt-worn path between our home and the hen house to fetch me a dozen eggs to use in my baking. I could watch her from the kitchen window. She was three, Dee almost two, and I was pregnant with a third.

Easter was special that year. With the hens producing ten thousand eggs a day, I figured a flat or two would hardly be missed. We colored eggs as a family, then Kenny and I created an Easter egg hunt in our house for Kelli and Dee. I had sewn them each an Easter dress to wear to church. Dee now had a wide smile that sprang across her entire face, and the two of them were cute as buttons in their Easter bonnets.

~ꝰ ꝰ

"This chocolate cake tastes like metal," Orval said. Kenny's dad could come across as gruff, but he had a warm side, and I'd grown close to him.

"It has to be the chemo you're on," said Betty. "It's the same cake I've made you for forty years."

I was helping Betty in the kitchen, filling the dishwasher and scrubbing the counters as she stirred together a soup for the following night. Betty had told me the day before that she no longer knew what to fix him. Everything he used to love now tasted vile in his mouth.

It was the seventies, and chemo was much harsher than it is today. It left patients weak, nauseated, barely able to carry on a semblance of a normal life. Even so, Orval got up each day and followed as much of his usual farming routine as he could.

Even before he was diagnosed with colon cancer, Orval was finding it harder and harder to do his daily chores. He'd had several hip replacements and also suffered from emphysema.

From the time I met him, Orval had always seemed old to me, bent from hard work, his face weathered from the sun. Now he was gaunt, his hair gone.

Kenny had a great love and respect for his parents. He would do anything for them. With his dad able to do less on the farm, Kenny stepped in and picked up the workload. The problem was that he already had a full plate of farm chores of his own to do as well. The more Kenny did on the farm, the less I saw of him, and the more I was on my own with the kids.

I often felt like a single parent. I accepted it as part of farming.

It was Wednesday, my day off from work, and I decided to bake some cookies. Our third child, Corey, was just beginning to walk, and keeping track of him added a whole new dimension to the baking, but by late morning I'd finished several batches. These included Kenny's favorites — chocolate-chip cookies, meringue bars, and saucepan brownies — and my dad's favorite, sugar cookies.

I filled the cookie jar, a glass container with a red metal lid. Kenny liked to jingle the lid against the glass like a bell when the jar went empty. It always made me laugh.

I packed the rest of the cookies and bars into a basket. "Ready for our cookie deliveries?" I asked. The kids responded with excitement. We often followed this routine on Wednesdays, and they always enjoyed it.

First we followed the sound of Kenny's John Deere tractor and met him for a cookie-and-lemonade break in a pile of meadow grass beside the cornfield. After munching on still-warm cookies beneath a blue sky, the sun reflecting off the river nearby, the kids and I headed to Blanchardville.

Our next stop was my grandparents' house, where we dropped off a variety of cookies. Time was growing short, and I still wanted to stop at my parents' house, so we only visited for a while. I was kissing my Grandma Gunhild good-bye when she slipped a Kleenex tissue into my coat pocket.

"Grandma, no, that's not why we come to see you."

"Hush now. I have more of those where that came from." Her large brown eyes reflected her genuine kindness.

I knew there was money in the tissue because she had done this before. I was both grateful and embarrassed. I shook my head, "Grandma, no." I wanted her to take it back, but I knew it would do no good to protest. If she made up her mind, there was no changing it.

As I backed out of her driveway, I looked down at the crumpled Kleenex with a twenty-dollar bill sticking out. At that moment, it felt like a hundred dollars.

I turned up the hill toward my parents' house. In back, the kids were arguing over who would get to carry in the plate of cookies. White cumulus clouds were forming and lifting above the horizon. One looked like an angel, and I was sure she had put that twenty-dollar bill in my pocket, for I had two dollars to my name, and now I could stop and buy milk, sugar, and butter on the way home.

Sue Massey

"Corey, put the stick down," I said. I was watering the bed of shasta daisies just outside our kitchen window, a tiny cutting garden with poking heads of white blooms on twig-like stems that graced the vase on our kitchen table all summer long. Blu, the little blue heeler pup that I'd given Kenny for his birthday, was happily chasing the stream of water as if it were a toy to catch. He'd crouch forward, biting and barking at it in pretend fury.

Two-year-old Corey was playing with a stick and suddenly whacked Blu on the head. "Corey, stop. We never hit animals," I said, moving quickly to take the stick away from him.

I was too late. Corey lifted the stick and struck Blu again, this time in the face. The dog lunged and, with sharp puppy teeth, caught Corey in the face. Blood spilled everywhere.

I dropped the hose and fell to my knees, wiping the blood with my shirttail to see how severe the wound was. Blood was spurting from his eye. I knew immediately he would need stitches. I swallowed my fear, trying to stay calm for the kids. Corey wiggled and held his bleeding eye as I scooped him up and ran toward the house.

Kelli and Dee had been playing in the sandbox nearby. They'd seen the commotion and were now standing beside me with fear in their eyes. How could such a lovely, peaceful moment in the early summer sun turn so wrong?

"Get your dad. I need to grab my purse and some clean towels and take Corey to the hospital. We'll drop the two of you off at Gram Betty's."

We all scattered. Soon Kenny and I were in the car, speeding our way up the country road, a twenty-minute drive that felt like an eternity, toward the hospital emergency room. Corey was sobbing, nose running, tears flowing, blood everywhere, squirming uncontrollably with the pain as I tried to hold him close and keep pressure on his gaping wound. His blood covered us both. Kenny's eyes seesawed between the road and the passenger seat where Corey crouched in my arms.

Inside the emergency room, the medical team took over. The nurse lifted Corey from my arms and told him they were going to make everything better.

The doctor came in and introduced himself. As he talked to us, I saw the nurse putting Corey's arms in a pillowcase behind his back so that they stopped flailing.

"Hold him down now," the nurse told Kenny. "Talk to him. This will be the worst part of the procedure, injecting the open wound on his eyelid with a numbing solution so we can stitch it up."

Corey's crying escalated to a scream. I felt my knees weaken. The blood drained out of my head, and I thought I was going to faint.

A nurse grabbed my arm. "Are you OK? Do you need a chair?" When I stared at her in wide-eyed silence, she led me toward the door. "Here, come with me."

I was five months pregnant with our fourth baby. The audible pain of one of my own sent me out of the exam room and down the hall as far as I could walk until his cries disappeared into the hollow corridor of the hospital.

Back home, in the days that followed, Corey's eye swelled up like a puffer fish and became a deep black and blue. After two weeks, it turned an odd cast of yellow, and the swelling disappeared, with only a thin line of scar tissue remaining.

Through the years, as Corey grew, the scar lightened and disappeared into the crease of his eyelid. He was very lucky. We were very lucky. I had feared that he might need plastic surgery, but he didn't. The doctor had done a fantastic job stitching up his eye.

There's something about scars. They can be noticeable reminders of trauma, and a glimpse can send you back to that horrific moment when the world stopped ever so slightly. Then there are the scars within, the hidden ones that reappear from nowhere so quickly they can take your breath away. Life is a series of wounds and scars; the secret lies in how we choose to cope with them.

Sue Massey

"Sue, what did the doctor say?" Kenny's head poked over the swinging gates that hung between the kitchen and laundry room.

"That I have to have surgery. Just a day, an in-and-out procedure." I wiped my hands on a dish towel and walked toward him. The kids were watching a nature show on PBS.

"Really? Did he say why your voice has turned hoarse?"

"He asked if I'd recently had a bad cold. He said it looked as though I'd begun to hold my breath when I talked, probably from a stuffed-up nose." I followed Kenny into the laundry room.

"I've never heard of that before." He glanced at me as he scrubbed the grime and grease off his hands in the laundry sink. They were permanently stained.

"Me neither. He said my not breathing when I spoke has caused nodules to form on my vocal cords. He said he'll put me to sleep, take them off, and I'll be fine."

"Thank goodness it isn't anything worse." He dried his hands on the towel and tossed it over the hook.

"I know. Here's the part you're gonna love. I'll be on complete voice rest for two weeks, then probably need speech therapy to learn to breathe and speak correctly again."

"You can't talk for two weeks?"

"Nope, not a word. Can you imagine?" I laughed at his expression. He looked almost speechless.

"Wait, does he know you have four small children?"

Our fourth child, Maron, had been born recently. She may have been the fourth, but she was my first full-term baby. In the hospital, the nurses all thought she was my first because I wouldn't stop holding her, caressing her plump little face, her open eyes, her perfect everything. She was a joy beyond words.

I glanced at Maron, now sleeping in the small crib in the corner of our kitchen. Our oldest, Kelli, was six, Dee was four, and Corey — our only boy, who already consumed far more time, effort, and energy than the three girls put together — was two.

I nodded. "I know, and a husband who typically works twelve-hour days — oh, and then there's the fact that I answer phones four days a week at the Veterinary Clinic. It should be interesting."

When I came home from the hospital procedure, I had no voice. In the days that followed, I vowed that I would never take my voice or any of my senses for granted — ever.

I'd talked to the kids beforehand about how we would handle the situation. Kelli could read, so I wrote things on a notepad, and she passed my messages on to the younger kids. If I needed to get their attention for dinner or bath time, I snapped my fingers, rang a bell, or clapped my hands, and they came running and giggling at the silliness of our predicament. During mealtime, if someone was out of line, I tapped their wrist or reached under the table and squeezed their knee. I was so glad it was only temporary.

When I began speech therapy, I was floored by how difficult it was to coax out the words. After each session, I went home and practiced, trying to form words. Sometimes only half a word would emerge. At times I wondered if I would ever speak fluently again. But like so many things in my life, I was forced to swim or sink, and before I knew it my speech had fully returned in the fast-paced stream of life, of earning a living and raising a young family.

Not long after, Corey was diagnosed as having a slight speech delay and was placed in speech therapy. Every time I picked him up from a session, I cheered him on for all his hard work. To this day, Corey's eyes are focused on the lips of whomever is speaking. It has made him a great listener, and listening is an art in itself. The two of us are not only connected by the constant road trips and challenges of speech therapy but also by our special understanding of what a gift it is to be able to speak.

"Corey, enough." I glanced over as he squeezed the honey bear with both hands until the pile of honey was larger than the mound of oatmeal in front of him.

Sue Massey

I leaned across the table with a spoon, scooped half the honey off, and drizzled it onto Maron's bowl of oatmeal. Corey tested me from sunup to sundown. I had an inkling that something about his development was slightly different, though I couldn't put my finger on it. That growing awareness hung in my head like a chrysalis that I kept watching, wondering what would emerge. I kept telling myself that Corey was going to be like *Leo, the Late Bloomer*, a favorite bedtime storybook we read together, but something deep inside told me it was more than that.

Children had always intrigued me — how differently each grew, at their own pace and when they were ready; how with words of encouragement, they seemed to open like a flower, one petal at a time until they were in full bloom. I loved seeing their differences emerge. But there were little signs that Corey was unfolding in a way much different from what seemed within the norm.

The kids finished their oatmeal, darted outside, and climbed onto their trikes to whirl around the small concrete pad beneath our front porch. The back door opened and closed as Kenny came in to microwave a "hotdog to go." That was so him: a flash in and a flash out.

As I rinsed the last Corelle breakfast plate, I caught a glimpse of Kenny scanning the fridge for ketchup and mustard — his long blond tangled 'fro, smudges of grime and grease on his worn jeans, his muscular chest beneath a faded T-shirt — and all I could think was: too sexy.

I reached for the honey bear jar still on the counter and squeezed a sticky drop onto the tip of my finger. Kenny turned my way, and I pulled him close, placed my fingertip with its drop of sticky sweetness into his mouth. Then I kissed him and whispered in his ear, "Hey, Papa Bear, don't suppose you could squeeze Mama Bear into your busy morning, could you?"

His cheeks blushed, sweetly surprised. That was exactly how I rolled — a little naughty, a little nice. I took his hand and led him toward the tiny bathroom just off the kitchen. On the way, I glanced out the window at the kids; they were fine, still playing. I locked the door, unzipped his pants, lifted myself onto the vanity counter, wrapped my legs around him, and felt the pleasure of his warmth, our closeness, suspend us for a brief moment in time. I whispered in his ear, "Baby, you know I love your sweet honey."

Kenny and I each climbed a ladder to hang the sign on our new shed. In large, colorful letters, I had hand-painted the sign — Ewes View.

I was thrilled. After numerous discussions, we'd found a way to make *our* shed become a reality. When Kenny was in on an idea, he poured his soul into it.

Kenny, problem solver that he was, had managed to erect the shed at the lowest cost possible. He had cut trees from the part of the farm he called Purgatory, in woods so far back that only he knew how to reach them. Then he had found someone to mill the trees into beams, rafters, and boards, and some local guys to help him with the building. He was always helping other people, so they lined up to repay the favor whenever they had a chance.

Kenny and I were both so proud of that shed. Together, we'd chosen the spot for it — a beautiful area overlooking the Pecatonica River.

While working at the research farm, I'd fallen in love with the sheep. Now I hoped we could have a small flock and sell the extra lambs for breeding. I could hardly wait for the western sheep we'd ordered to arrive. But when they finally did, they were infested with lice. We dug deep into our pockets to buy medication to treat the infestation. However, the lice had already taken a toll on their health. I realized that we'd probably never get them up to breeding weight, despite all the lush pasture land we had. We had trusted the man who sold us the sheep, and we'd been taken. That night, I felt heartbroken as I crawled into bed.

We also bought some calves to raise and sell as springers (first-time pregnant dairy cows ready to join a milking herd). The market price was $900 apiece, and we thought that would be a great way to earn extra income. But by the time the springers were ready to sell, the market price had dropped to $500 apiece, and we lost money on the endeavor.

One morning, I opened the door to my little clutch of half-grown ducklings to find them lying scattered on the floor, every one of them dead. The weasel had made its way up the river bank and sucked the blood out of each of their necks. I slammed the door shut and with it my piercing sorrow.

I walked back to the shed and sank onto a lone bale of straw. I gazed at the corner of the shed where Kenny was planning to build Bojo a stall, like the one my dad had built on my childhood farm. With so many other projects demanding Kenny's attention, the boards lay in a pile waiting to be assembled as Bojo grazed in the pasture below. When the kids and I wanted to ride him, we'd tie him to a fence post to saddle him, hoping one day that he'd have his own stall in which we could groom him.

After that, I drew closer to our home, our yard, and the kids, the only spheres where I felt I had some sort of control. The kids and I would wander down to the river, select pebbles, and toss them in, watching our reflections ripple and disappear. Sometimes I didn't even recognize the person looking back at me. Who was she? Mom of four just didn't seem to be enough. I would look to the sky and wonder what my future held.

I helped the kids build forts using empty boxes. Or we'd gather sticks and build teepees out behind the garage. I tried to add as much fun as possible to our days, but still something was missing. The stirring inside my head never settled. I could almost feel the drops of my creative being evaporating from my skin. I was living and being strangled in the same breath. I was sure that I had more to offer than growing babies and turning out three meals a day, but what? Where, I wondered, was my place in this world?

With each pregnancy, I carried the baby closer to term. Kelli was seven weeks early. Dee arrived two years later and was only six weeks premature. Two years after that, Corey came three weeks early, and then two years later Maron was born only one week before term. With each pregnancy I had fewer complications. I joked that my body decided to join my team rather than fight against us.

We had always talked of having four babies, and when I discovered I was pregnant for the fifth time, I cried. The timing couldn't have been worse. There had been a drought, and most of the corn crop had been lost. Money had always been scarce, but there was a growing feeling of doom that hung in the air. A doom we didn't talk about.

I thought back. I knew when it had happened — too much wine followed by a wild night of careless passion, too inflamed to consider consequences and reach for any kind of birth control. I was a calculated planner, but sometimes my emotions took over and completely overwhelmed my intentions.

Despite the poor timing, my fifth pregnancy was the silver lining in the gathering gloom of financial worry. It gave our family something to look forward to. A new life, a new baby would be joining our family. It was the light in the days that were beginning to darken with anxiety.

"What's a quiche?" the kids asked in unison, all seated around the kitchen table in front of their empty plates, eyes on me.

I reached into the oven with potholder mitts, lifted out a bubbly, golden quiche, and set it on a hot pad in the middle of the table. Pulling the mitts off, I sat down and told them that a quiche was a pie made with cheese and eggs rather than fruit.

"We need to let it cool a few minutes before I slice it," I said. As I spread peanut butter on some bread and passed a slice to each of the four kids, I felt the hard ripple of a knee or arm beneath my rib cage.

There was something about this pregnancy that made me uneasy.

Sue Massey

It wasn't anything like the first four. I could hardly move, or breathe; this baby had taken over my entire abdomen.

My due date was in seven days, and the house was brimming with the excitement of meeting our new baby. The kids had helped put sheets, pillows, and soft, stuffed animals in the little wooden crib that sat in a corner of our kitchen, the hub of activity in our home.

"A quiche is a fun dish to make and eat," I went on to explain. "It has lots of eggs, cheese, milk, and seasoning in it — all really good things to help you grow big and strong."

The kids grabbed their forks, anxious to try a piece. To myself, I thought: Quiche is what a mommy makes for a brood of hungry kids when she lives on a farm with fifteen-thousand laying hens, is way past due for a grocery run, the checkbook balance is on minus ten dollars, and their dad is working late.

I watched the kids devour the quiche. I had to grin, thinking about the time my friend's boyfriend looked up at a young waitress, pointed at the menu, and said, "I'll have the quickie," and she replied, "I'll bet you would like a quickie, but, sir, that is a quiche."

The kids wiped their plates clean, except for Maron, who always left a bite or two of everything we put onto her plate. We had a rule at the table. They had to try a small bite of everything. If they liked it, we wanted them to say so. We figured the kids would be less skeptical of something new if one of their siblings vouched for it. If they didn't like it, they could leave it on their plates, but they weren't to grumble about it. We discovered early on that if one didn't like something, then the whole bunch would put their forks down. There wasn't time or space for negative thoughts in our house. We already had enough challenges weighing us down.

As I bent to stack the empty plates, the sensitive vein in my groin throbbed. The pain had increased with each ounce that the baby grew. I could hardly stand unless I leaned over to shift the baby's weight.

I was thrilled that at last I had a baby who was willing to remain inside me for nine whole months. But, in the back of my mind, I knew there was something else different this time around.

The sky turned an ominous slate gray. The air was so humid, still, and heavy, I could scarcely draw breath. Sitting on our little porch, I watched the kids kick a ball back and forth across the lawn beneath the maple. Warm droplets of sweat trickled down my face, and I wasn't even moving. An eerie feeling stirred inside me. I thought of the many times I stood as a child looking out the lower barn door toward the horizon, watching the storms roll in. The sense of excitement and anticipation I usually felt was missing now. Instead, I had a feeling that something really bad was going to happen.

As night descended, a string of bats flew out of the attic vent, and the kids started screaming and counting them at the same time.

"OK, gang, time to clean up, brush your teeth, and hop into bed," I called to them.

Just after midnight, I awoke, baby kicking, the bedroom windows open, curtains hanging limp in the choking heat with the ominous calm still surrounding me. The only sound was that of a little fan that sat on our dresser and the soft purring snore of Kenny beside me. I went to the window and looked at the sky. Parts of it hung like heavy balloons filled with water, and parts were gray, then a glowing pink. It was a sky I had never seen before. Through the stillness, I began to hear tornado sirens going off in neighboring towns — Hollandale, Blanchardville, Barneveld; they seemed to be coming from all directions. I woke Kenny.

"Listen — tornado sirens. Should we wake the kids? Take them to the basement?" I knelt on the floor and leaned into the open window to look outside. Even the white pine was still, as if bracing itself for what was to come.

Kenny gazed over my head out the window with a slight frown. "That doesn't look good. I think we'll be OK, but somebody's gonna get hit hard." We crawled back beneath a sheer cotton sheet in the sweltering heat.

Sue Massey

Around 1:30 a.m. the sirens stopped, and I fell asleep. At 5:00 a.m. Kenny's alarm went off, and I heard him get dressed and drive off into the pre-dawn darkness.

Half an hour later, the phone beside the bed rang. When I picked it up, Kenny was on the other end, sounding shocked.

"Sue, oh my God, I just drove through Barneveld. It's gone. Literally gone. The entire town is flattened. I've never seen anything like it in my life."

His words siphoned the air right out of me. Barneveld was the quaint little village that neighbored ours. We often drove through it on our way into Madison.

"It looks like a bomb exploded, not a single building or tree left standing, power lines down, emergency vehicle lights flashing everywhere, complete bedlam, people dazed and digging through the rubbish."

"Oh, Kenny, that's awful, and way too close to home."

For a week, officials asked everyone except cleanup crews to stay away from the ravaged area. Our two oldest were Girl Scouts, and they helped one afternoon as part of a cleanup brigade. They came home struggling to make peace with something beyond what they'd ever seen, or imagined, so close to home. The stores we had frequented were now gone — part of the sea of rubble stretching from horizon to horizon. The water tower stood like a lone soldier looking over a war zone. Townspeople foraged through the rubble for scraps of their lives, now strewn for miles.

Anyone who sees a devastation of that magnitude is forever changed. It took years and many hands to put Barneveld back on the map. There were many wounds to heal, scars that would last forever. Nine died and nearly two hundred were injured in the tornado, and the cost of damage was in the millions.

The newly built town was, many people believed, far better, stronger, and more modern than before — and the community far, far more closely knit. Sometimes a crisis leads to something more durable, even if it's not what we would have chosen. But after losing everything you've known, without even a signpost left to point the way, it takes time to mourn the loss, stagger forward, and build a bridge to the other side of trauma.

"You were making doughnuts at 3:00 a.m.?"

Mom raised a puzzled eyebrow at me as she folded the kids' belongings into their four overnight bags.

I was in a flurry, trying to find my purse. "Mom, I was so uncomfortable with the size of this baby, I couldn't sleep, eat, or breathe, so I went to the kitchen, stirred up a double batch of doughnut dough, put it in the fridge to cool, and went back to bed. Maybe I was nesting. I don't know. Next thing I knew, I woke up in a puddle of warm water. I've never had my water break at home before. I swaddled a towel beneath me and reached for the phone to call you."

Feet were scrambling in all directions as I tossed our sheets and towels into the washer, added soap, and hit the "on" button. A labor pain made me stop to breathe through it. With each contraction, the intensity was growing.

Just before heading out the door, Mom opened the fridge, pulled out the bowl of chilled dough, and said, "Here, the kids and I will fry up the doughnuts."

"Thanks, Mom," I managed as the pain lessened. The kids headed for Mom's car. They would be staying with my parents till the new baby came home.

Kenny helped me into his car and took off like a shot. Just before we reached the outskirts of Mount Horeb, he turned to me with the fear of God in his eyes.

"Sue, please don't be mad at me, but when your water broke, I called and asked the ambulance to meet us at the Mt. Horeb bank to transport you to the hospital." He turned away, not wanting to see my fiery reaction.

"What? Please tell me you're joking!" A pain took my breath away.

"No. See, you're in hard labor. That's not supposed to happen at

Sue Massey

home when you have a suture in your cervix. You'll just have to be mad at me, Sue. I knew if I told you, you'd refuse."

"Yeah, well, I'm mortified. I hate this sort of attention. I'm just fine. Ahh, I can't believe you did this! I'd rather have you beside me, and now I'll be with strangers in an ambulance while you follow along in the car." I clenched my hands, so upset that I felt like pulling my hair out.

Kenny pulled into the parking lot, where red ambulance beams were ricocheting off the bank building. The crew helped me onto a stretcher, covered me with thick blankets, and rolled me into the ambulance.

I felt scared and helpless, a blood pressure cuff on my arm, warm cloth on my head, medical equipment all around me, and the sterile stench of alcohol hanging in the air. *This is about as far from natural childbirth as one can get*, I thought. Then a wave of labor reminded me to count and breathe through the contractions that were becoming stronger by the minute.

The drive from Mount Horeb to Madison, usually a half-hour trip, took fifteen minutes in the ambulance, siren blaring. It seemed like an eternity.

Our parents waited all day to hear about the baby, but their phone never rang, and their worry grew.

I was on the delivery table when they discovered the baby was in breech position. Now I knew why I'd been so uncomfortable. The baby's head was up in my rib cage. I couldn't budge her from my pelvis. When I heard someone say "emergency C-section," I was beyond ready for them to put me to sleep; the pain was searing. I remember asking the doctor for a bikini cut in a hard-to-believe moment of foresight, because I'd seen my mother's huge C-section scar, and I felt such freedom when I wore a bikini.

The next thing I remembered, I was opening my eyes to see Kenny holding the largest pink bundle I'd ever seen — almost twice the size of our first-born Kelli. Kenny placed eight pounds, two ounces of Naomi Rae Massey into my arms, and the world fell away in the blissful delight of holding my newborn. She was perfect in every way: chubby cheeks, rosebud mouth, large eyes trying to see me, and a mop of dark hair. I buried my nose into the powdery fresh scent of baby.

The second evening after Naomi was born, my parents brought the four kids to the hospital to meet their new sister. The kids climbed on the bed, held the baby, touched her fingers and toes, played in the corners of my room, checked out the cards and flowers, and watched TV, until my mom said I looked tired and it was time for me to get some rest.

I had lost a great deal of blood during the C-section. After the kids filed out, kissing me good-bye one by one and patting Naomi's head, the nurse came in and hung a unit of blood. With each drop that filtered into my vein, my temperature plummeted. I began to shiver, my teeth chattering. Kenny, who was putting on his jacket, preparing to leave, looked horrified and ran to get a nurse as I pleaded for him to take the needle out. I knew something wasn't right with the blood transfusion. I was weak, terrified, falling into shock. I believed I was about to die.

A panicked nurse arrived, removed the pint of blood from my arm, and wrapped me in piles of warm blankets. When she came with a second unit of blood, I shrank away in horror, shaking my head.

She reassured me that this would be a perfect match, that a rare antibody in the previous blood must have caused my reaction. I wasn't sure, but I gave her my arm and asked Kenny to stay until I felt better. He sat beside me with Naomi in his arms, holding my hand. By nine o'clock, I sensed I would be OK. He kissed us both and told me he'd be back the next day.

I had spent so many nights in the hospital over the years with all the pregnancy complications that I could recognize Kenny's footsteps coming down the corridor long before I saw him. I knew the sound of the snack cart, the meal cart, what times the nurses changed

Sue Massey

shifts and doctors made rounds. I knew the names of the doctors paged, what each code meant, and what all the medicines and machines were used for. I knew the life within the walls of the hospital. But this time, when I walked out those heavy swinging doors, I would not be back. Naomi was our final and forever baby.

The back door opened and banged shut, and Kenny appeared in the living room. The kids were playing on the soft, blue shag carpet that gave new life to the old farmhouse floor. Mom and Dad had helped us lay the carpet, paint, panel the kitchen, even lay remnant ends of linoleum in two of the rooms — touches that made Kenny's old childhood farm home feel like ours.

Kenny's arms spanned wide around an empty refrigerator box. "Ma saved this for the kids to play in," he said as he tossed the box in the middle of the room. Like iron filings to a magnet, all four kids were on it. "Guess their old refrigerator took a dive, so this box is from their new one."

I was sitting in the rocker, nursing Naomi. Kenny lingered, which wasn't like him. He usually grabbed a mustard and ketchup sandwich and was out the door.

"What's up?" I asked. He seemed to be trying to gauge my mood, see how my morning had been before opening a sensitive topic.

"Well, Dad just told me that I better start to look for a permanent job off the farm."

"What? You're kidding, right?" Naomi's fingertips caressed the nap of my green vest as she nursed.

"No, I'm not kidding. Do you think I'd kid about something like that?"

"Kenny, tell me more. What did your dad say?" Pulling information from him was like trying to pry the lid off a dried paint can that had been sealed for years.

"Dad said that after last summer's drought, the corn yield was so low, they've had to buy corn for over a year now. And corn prices keep going up. So there's a huge feed bill they haven't been able to pay, and it's getting bigger every day."

"What, for over a year? And I'm just hearing about this now?"

"Well, yeah, that's right."

"So what does that mean? How high is the feed bill? What's your dad's plan?"

"The bills are approaching a hundred thousand dollars, and there's no way we can pay them off. Egg prices have sunk so low that we're losing money on every egg we sell. Dad says they have no choice but to shut down the egg business. So I need to find a job, and right away."

"Just like that?" I patted Naomi on the back for a burp, set her on her little quilted blanket on the floor, and glared at Kenny.

"Yeah, just like that!" Kenny turned to walk away, as he did every time we broached an uncomfortable subject. He hated conflict and avoided it at all cost. Kenny's parents were the same way, and I guessed that's why they hadn't brought up the issue of the mounting feed bills. They probably thought the problem would resolve itself over time, as their farm troubles always had in the past.

I was horrified to think that our farm had been sinking into debt for more than a year and this was the first I'd heard of it.

"Wait! So what does this mean? Do I start to pack? Do I look for a better paying job, five days a week rather than my current four? And what about you? How do you write a résumé when you've been self-employed on your farm your entire life?"

"Sue, I don't know, but I gotta go. Dad's waitin' on me."

"No, Kenny, you're not coming in here, turning our world upside down, and walking outside to do chores!" The anger I felt inside scared me.

"Sue, not now. It's not the time. We'll talk later."

"With you, there's never a later!"

I handed Naomi a rattle and followed Kenny into the kitchen so the kids couldn't hear.

Kenny was already opening the back door. When I realized he was planning to leave without answering any of my questions, I exploded. "Fine, go do your chores, and you know what? I'm going to start packing! I'm not waiting for someone to kick us out of our own home."

Kenny turned on a dime, fire in his eyes. "Sue, we are *not* moving! They'll have to drag me off this farm! We're not leaving!" The door slammed behind him, so loud I thought the window would break.

I turned and walked back to the living room. I was furious.

"Mommy, is everything OK?" Kelli peered from behind the cardboard box.

I took a deep breath, tried to calm my anger and pull back the tears. "It's OK, Kelli. Sometimes mommies and daddies don't always agree on things, and that's OK."

I plopped down in the rocking chair. It infuriated me when Kenny shut down, refused to discuss a decision that involved both of us. I wanted to openly discuss things and come to a decision, a compromise. This situation reminded me of his reaction when I suggested he get a vasectomy. There was no discussion. He refused to do it. Subject closed. So I had a tubal ligation. It didn't seem fair.

I rocked back and forth, back and forth in the chair, and stared out at the bluff, out at the shed we had built, and wondered what our future would be. Or did we have a future? For the first time ever, the thought of a separation crossed my mind, and it seemed so foreign a thought that it frightened me. Then, I looked at the kids, lost in their make-believe world. I loved to watch them interact and learn from one another. The older ones learned patience and kindness as the young ones discovered new things.

I tucked my hands inside the pockets of my green vest, searching for answers and solace. I tried to imagine leaving Kenny and wondered what it would be like. Where would I live? How could I manage? I already felt like a single mom when Kenny worked long hours seven days a week. Would life be worse if we chose to move in separate directions? I tried to remember the last time he made love to me. Had it been a week? Two weeks? Maybe it was the financial stress that was changing us both, making us people we hardly recognized. I had felt for a while now that something was wrong, but whenever I asked Kenny or his parents, they always insisted that everything was fine.

I rocked, thinking over what Kenny had told me. It sounded like a stretch of irreparable circumstances — the drought, the bad corn yield, the rising cost of feed for the chickens, plummeting egg prices. It didn't seem as if things would improve any time soon. A knot formed in the pit of my stomach.

Kenny's parents wouldn't be shutting down the egg business unless things were truly dire. With no income and steadily increasing debt, the next inevitable step would be foreclosure on the farm itself.

That's the thought I couldn't wrap my mind around. I'd heard of other farms going bankrupt and being repossessed, and it always made me sick to think what those families must be going through. It had never occurred to me that it could happen to us.

If the farm was foreclosed, Kenny's parents wouldn't have to leave their house because they'd zoned it separately from the egg corporation. But Kenny and I would lose our home, our livelihood, our dream of raising the kids in the country.

The future looked just as scary either way — if I stayed with Kenny or if I left. I couldn't picture moving into town, away from this beautiful farm that had been in Kenny's family for eighty years, with the river where the kids and I tossed pebbles, the bluffs that wrapped their towering arms of beauty around us, and the wide open meadows that waved with blue stem grasses. I could not imagine having to leave our farm, the beautiful shed we'd built together, and the house we'd grown to love and call our own.

My mind surged with questions. The kids — what was best for the kids? Was there any way I could protect them from the rupture to come, to keep from tearing their lives apart? If we had to leave the farm, where would we go? If we could no longer farm the land, what would we do? Kenny and I were country through and through; it was sewn in the very fabric of our DNA. It was what we loved. It was all we knew. If we had to leave it all behind, what would become of us?

Sue Massey

1. Johnson Family Farm, oil painting by Sue (Johnson) Massey, 1974. 2. Building forts, brother Bruce, sister Sandy, and me. 3. Pecatonica Dam (Blanchardville, WI).

4. *Brown Cow Farm*, my favorite childhood story book. **5.** Lucky, my first fair calf.

Sue Massey

6. The guy in my dreams (Kenny). **7 & 8.** November 16, 1974, our journey begins. **9.** Kenny's family.

10. Our first home on the Massey farm. **11.** The building of our shed (Kenny and Dee). **12.** Back in the day, my grandpa George farmed land adjacent to the Massey homestead.

PART II
INTO THE FIRE

Yesterday is ashes.
Tomorrow is green wood.
Only today does the fire burn brightly.
~ *Eskimo Proverb*

CHAPTER 7
The Envelope

I didn't leave him. I thought long and hard about it. Then I decided to stay, make the best of things, and keep the family together. I knew I couldn't expect Kenny to change, and I would have to accept the parts of his personality that frustrated me. When I weighed the pros and cons of our relationship, I knew he was still the guy meant for me.

Maybe, by some miracle, things would turn around and we wouldn't have to move after all, although I couldn't figure out what that miracle might be. Even if egg prices suddenly increased, it wouldn't help us now. Kenny's parents had already closed Bett-Or Eggs, and the leased hens were being trucked in cages off the farm. And a hundred-thousand-dollar debt wouldn't magically disappear, no matter how hard I wished it would.

Still, Kenny and his parents were so stoic about the situation, moving through each day with such fortitude, that all I could do was follow their lead. Yelling, crying, or protesting would do no good. It seemed that my only option was to carry on with my daily duties — to bury the pain, to endure. So that's what I did. Every day, I pushed the fear down so deep that I couldn't feel it.

Sue Massey

Kenny had been receiving a monthly salary from Bett-Or-Eggs, with our farmhouse rent deducted from his earnings. Now that Bett-Or-Eggs was closing down, Kenny stopped receiving a paycheck.

There weren't many jobs in the rural area and, as I'd feared, it was hard to create a résumé for Kenny when he'd always worked on the farm. He was a sharp guy who had vast experience with improvising and calculating, with nothing to show on paper.

But he was an ambitious problem solver and within days had landed a welding job from a friend who owned a prefab company down the road. The work was close to home, and he enjoyed the environment and being able to apply his welding skills. It allowed him time to tend to a few chores on the farm and spend time with the kids.

Eventually, a friend of a friend told Kenny he'd heard of an LTE (limited term employment) position available, working for the state. It was in the farm labor division of the University of Wisconsin in Madison and sounded like a perfect fit. Kenny would be working outside all day, planting, plowing, mowing, engaged in many of the farm chores he was already used to doing.

There was one hurdle, however: He had to pass a written exam.

"Well, how'd you do?" I asked when he returned from taking the test.

"Ninety-nine. I missed one." He set down his cap and emptied his pockets onto the counter.

"That's sick," I teased him. "How you can ace an exam like that is beyond me. You were bored in school, rather be outside farming, yet you can take a test like no other. Good for you, babe. Wish I could do that. Soon as I hear the word 'test,' my brain freezes. Instead of focusing on the questions, I worry about how much time I have left. Was your exam timed?"

"Yes, but there was plenty of time." He reached for a glass from the cupboard and gulped down two glasses of fresh farm water from the tap before heading back out.

"Dad, where you going? Can I come?" Corey looked up, holding a toy tractor and wearing his John Deere cap. He was Kenny's shadow. Wherever Kenny was, Corey wanted to be.

"Getcher boots on, buddy. We need to check the fence down by the bridge. Saw one of the beef was out on the road." Kenny tapped the lid on Corey's cap down below his eyes.

"Dad." Corey yanked it back up so he could see.

Kenny got the job. Thus began a string of jobs with the state, a fifty-minute drive into the city of Madison. Not great pay, but the benefits were huge. Dee was prone to getting pneumonia every time she came down with a cold. Then there were the ear infections, accidental falls, plus all the usual illnesses kids come down with. What would we have done without the great health insurance benefits provided by the state?

When his limited-term position ended, Kenny took a janitorial job at the Memorial Union Library on the Madison campus. He worked the night shift, which took a huge toll on our marriage.

I was glad he had a job, but I hated the fact that it was the graveyard shift. I grew to dread the moment each evening when he reached for his hat, kissed the kids and me good-bye, and headed out the door into the darkness. I would usually nurse Naomi before reading the kids a book and tucking them all into bed. Then I would pack five lunches and set out outfits, jackets, shoes, and backpacks all in a row on the couch, so we could hit the floor running in the morning.

Kelli, now eleven, offered to give Naomi a bottle if she woke in the night. She wanted to help in any way she knew how. She and Dee, being the oldest kids, were a huge support in keeping our little raft afloat.

The farmhouse was drafty and cold. To save money, we burned wood in the old woodstove as much as possible. We all pitched in to feed the fire.

When Kenny arrived home at 7:00 a.m., the kids and I were long gone: three to school, two to the sitter's, and me to work. The last chicken house now stood empty, but Kenny had one last crop of corn to harvest. After I got off work, picked the kids up, and began supper,

Sue Massey

Kenny would come stumbling sleepily down the stairs, and I knew he'd worked at farm chores too long and only had half-a-tank of sleep. At 8:00 p.m., after a quick supper, he would ride-share into Madison for his next shift.

At night, when my head finally hit the pillow, I would lie on my back, searching for clues to what we were supposed to do. Alone, with no one to hold, the arms of worry embraced me. I liked having a plan in place and felt anxious when I didn't know what was coming next. Now the whole future was like the Atlantic, a vast sea of the unknown.

I would watch the numbers on the alarm clock flip. One o'clock, two o'clock... I needed to get to sleep, but it would be six o'clock and time to get up before I knew it, and I was on my own with these kids. It was like a long black tunnel with no light at the end.

One brutally cold afternoon, after church and Sunday dinner, the kids and I climbed into our beds to read and nap. Kenny climbed the hill to check the water pipes in the empty chicken houses in case they'd frozen in the ten-below-wind-chill temperature.

As I lay alone in our bed, I could hear the wind howl and beat down upon our little wooden farmhouse. Then I heard a weird noise that sounded like water dripping inside the chimney, which towered from basement to roof behind the headboard of our bed.

Something felt very wrong. I looked in on each of the kids. They were all sleeping peacefully.

I took the steps by twos, hurrying to see if everything was all right downstairs. The living room looked fine, so I moved toward the dining room to check on things there.

The instant I opened the dining room door, flames flew across the ceiling toward me.

I slammed the door and leaped back up the stairs. "Fire!" I screamed to the kids.

I grabbed Naomi from her crib, herded the other kids down the stairway into the back room beside their cubbies, and grabbed their jackets by the handful. They were scared and crying but did exactly as I said. Kelli and I guided the younger kids out the back door, and as she put their jackets on, I ran to call Kenny on the chicken house phone, then dialed the local fire department, and within minutes they arrived.

It was a chimney fire. Because Kenny was a volunteer on the Hollandale Fire Department, the other firefighters tossed him his jacket and boots and he disappeared into the hosing action along with them.

Fortunately, the house had little damage, except for the smell of smoke and a heavy film of black soot that lined everything. We were shaken, but fine.

There was no washing the soot off the walls. A professional cleaning company had to come in. We were grateful to have insurance to clean up the mess. Some of the cross-stitched pictures that I'd sewn for each of the kids were history, but we were able to save most of our family photos, the scrapbooks full of our most precious memories.

But the important thing was that the kids were all OK. I was so thankful for that.

I'd always felt drawn to the mystery of fire and loved the warmth of its flames, but that experience left a mark on me. Sometimes I would wake at night in a sweat, thinking I heard crackling in the walls. I would get up and check each of the kids, make certain they were safe.

As Kenny continued to work the graveyard shift, we lived increasingly separate lives. We rarely saw one another. I became the disciplinary voice because I was the one with the children. I grew more and more weary and lonesome.

Lying alone in bed, night after night, unable to sleep, I would relive the whole afternoon of the fire in my mind. What if I had fallen asleep that day, too? I remembered how tired I'd been, how easily I might have drifted off. What if I hadn't heard the faint sound that had, for some reason, alarmed me? How chancy life seemed sometimes.

Early the next fall, I received another shock. I'd been taking Corey to speech therapy religiously, and his speech did improve. But I had a deep sense that there was more to it. Something wasn't right. And it

Sue Massey

wasn't just because he was a boy and I was used to girls, as many of my friends and family told me.

Discipline was more than a daily, or hourly, challenge with him: It was a moment-by-moment trial. While most children learn by connecting unacceptable behavior with unwanted consequences, Corey didn't seem to equate the two. I had to apply the same consequences over and over, and still he kept doing what I'd told him not to do.

Sometimes it felt as though he consumed every ounce of my energy. He seemed to crave constant attention, and it didn't matter whether that attention was positive or negative. I felt constantly bridled with guilt for all the time and effort I directed toward Corey, wishing I could spread myself more evenly amongst all five. The girls were equally important to me, but Corey soaked up my time from the instant he woke to the instant he fell asleep.

Then, at one of our many doctor's appointments, we were sent to a new physician, who tested Corey extensively and diagnosed him with ADHD (attention deficit hyperactivity disorder). I began to read everything I could get my hands on about ADHD. I sought help from specialists and learned that kids with ADHD have short-term memories and need a different approach to discipline than most children. It was comforting to finally understand his differences. It tempered my frustration when I found myself repeating the same thing dozens of times in ten minutes. It deepened my compassion to know he wasn't misbehaving out of defiance, that he truly did want to be a good boy. He was trying with all his might, but desperately needed help, guidance, and a very firm and loving hand.

We talked as a family about Corey's challenges, and the girls were understanding and patient with him. Together we learned that sharing the burden of a special-needs child meant we also shared the joy of his hard-won accomplishments. Corey helped us learn to revel in the smallest of victories.

Much as we all loved him, the need to be on constant alert with Corey was wearing. My concerns about him were layered onto the financial strain that was now a persistent buzz of anxiety in my head.

It was a sunny autumn Wednesday, my day off work. I'd just picked up the kids from school, and they were playing in their sandbox while I pulled weeds in the garden. Our heads all turned to the sound of a car pulling up by our garage. It was a sheriff's car. I walked down the hill to meet it.

"Are you Mrs. Kenneth Massey?" The sheriff's formal, tan uniform took me aback.

I glanced back at the kids, who stood like little soldiers, motionless, watching.

"Yes, I'm Sue Massey."

"By law, I'm required to deliver these papers to you in person." The sheriff handed me an envelope, pointed at an X for my signature, turned, got back into his squad car, and drove off.

I climbed back up the hill, sliding the envelope open with my finger.

"What was that about? " Kelli asked.

"Don't know yet," I told her. "It's something legal. Let me take a look and see what it says."

Five pairs of eyes were glued on me, waiting for my reaction. I scanned the letter until I saw the date at the bottom of a lot of legal jargon.

On October 24, 1985, at 10 a.m., the Massey farm will be sold at auction unless outstanding debt is met before that date.

I could barely breathe. That was only a month away.

"Ah, it's some legal paperwork regarding the farm. Nothing to worry about. Here, back to building that sand castle. I'll run inside and get some milk and snacks. Be back in a minute."

I walked inside, on the verge of tears, wanting to scream in utter anguish, tear the letter into a zillion pieces, and flush it down the toilet.

Sue Massey

I knew that I couldn't. Instead, I tucked my feelings away along with the envelope. I'd show Kenny the letter when he got home from work.

Pulling a smile onto my face, I walked out with a little tray of Dixie cups filled with milk and a plate of graham crackers layered with peanut butter frosting. The kids crowded around the picnic table and began to grab and gulp as if famished.

"That was scary," Dee said. "Never saw a sheriff's car in our driveway before."

"Hope it's the last time, too," I answered. I took a deep breath and explained, "By law, some documents have to be delivered by the hand of a police officer. Otherwise, someone could say we never got it. This way, they get a signature showing that we received the legal papers. First time I ever signed for papers, so it's new to me too."

The kids seemed satisfied with my explanation. "Race you to the slide?" Maron challenged Dee as she set her half-eaten snack back down onto her napkin. She was our little bird eater. She never finished her plate. Kenny and our dog Tillie were our garbage cans; they would clean up the kids' leftovers. Nothing went to waste.

"Good job, gang! I'm going to run in and get something started for supper, maybe light the little grill and cook burgers." I started toward the house with the empty tray and cups in one hand and the weight of the world on my shoulders.

CHAPTER 8

Flame, Wind, and Stars

Winter came early that year. The wind whipped and corkscrewed snow castles everywhere.

Despite the cold, I bundled the kids up, and we went out to play. We fell backwards into the snow and made a family of snow angels. Corey threw snowballs to irritate the girls, and when they'd had enough of his pranks, they tackled him and pressed his face into the snow. Naomi was strapped into her toddler sleigh, giggling at her siblings. With frozen cheeks, our noses dripping with melted snow, we all agreed it was time to go in.

While they kicked off their snowsuits and boots, I threw in a load of laundry and started cocoa in a kettle on the stove. When it was on the verge of boiling, I called Kenny, who was fixing a leak in the bathroom.

He was, thankfully, no longer on night shift: That arrangement had nearly cost us our marriage. He was still working for the university but now in a day-shift, grounds-related job that kept him outside, the way he liked it. In addition, he did welding jobs at the nearby shop whenever he could. We were always scraping by.

We all sat around the table and drank from steaming mugs. Kelli counted and passed out one chocolate chip cookie to each of us.

As they finished their snack, I filled the tub with hot water, and Kenny and I settled into our bath routine. All five hopped into and then out of the tub like an assembly line. Draped with towels, they headed toward their dad. Kenny fluffed their hair and clipped a hundred little fingernails and toenails before zipping them into their footed pajamas. I threw some wood on the fire and grabbed a storybook. Then I tossed a load of dried towels onto the dining room floor, and the kids sprang into the heap as if it were a pile of snow to play in.

"Everybody, fold a towel, and we can read a book as soon as this load is folded," I said. They made a game of it. First they spread the towels out and sprawled on them as if lying on the beach in the warm sun. The sight always made me smile. Then, corner to corner, each of them folded a towel, placed it in a pile, made a stack in the corner, and scampered up onto the couch to read a book together.

After I'd finished the story and tucked them into their beds, I did some housework and checked over my plan for the next day. I had so many calendars and lists going that I'd started making lists of lists. I had a color for each kid so that with just a glance at my calendar, I knew who had to be where, for what, and by when. Then I pulled out my checkbook and basketful of bills. Money was so scarce that I could only manage partial payments, and sometimes not even that.

We had managed to arrange a delay of the farm auction. But the reprieve had only put off the inevitable. The farm was now scheduled to be auctioned off on March 4, and we knew there was no way to postpone it any further.

After the sheriff delivered the official notice that our farm was going to be sold, Kenny had agreed that we needed to sit down with the kids to explain the situation. We knew the news would spread quickly, as it always does in small towns, and we didn't want them to hear from someone else that we might be moving.

"For now, we're taking it one day at a time," I told them. "I don't want you to worry. No matter what happens, it will be all right as long as we're together. The love we have for one another as a family is never going to change."

In the days that followed, I tried to keep to our usual routine as much as possible, with all of us having meals together, baking cookies, and making time for homework, bath time, and bedtime stories, followed by nighttime prayers. It seemed that if we didn't dwell on the problems, neither did the kids. They were lost in their own world of play.

I had always dreamed of raising my children on the farm. More than anything in the world, I wanted them to have the experiences I'd had, growing up on the land, immersed in the elements. Now that dream was fading by the day.

I turned the burner to high; it matched the flame within me. I was always running on all cylinders. I had to. From the minute my toes hit the little woven rug beside our bed, I'd better be a blaze of energy. Every morning was a juggling act with five balls constantly hovering in the air. The balls were ages one to ten.

Lay out five outfits, prepare lunches, find backpacks, make eggs for breakfast, make sure teeth were brushed, fill the crockpot with spaghetti sauce for supper, start a load of laundry, and finally fly out the door, taking three to school and two to an in-home daycare, where the other three would be dropped off after school was over.

That day didn't seem much different from any other. After my shift as office manager at the small veterinary clinic in Blanchardville, I ran into the grocery store, grabbed milk, picked up the kids, and whirled home to my next shift of work, the household. The ten-minute drive home was filled with laughter and details from everyone's day: who did what and when. It was the perfect time for me to transition from the office to the home front.

We pulled up to the little one-car garage that stood beneath a towering oak. As soon as I parked, seat belts unsnapped, the car doors flew open, and the kids sprang out and lugged their backpacks single file up the narrow walk. I unsnapped Naomi from her car seat, tossed my bags over my shoulder, and held her hand as we toddled

Sue Massey

up the walk together. One thing about having five children: Once they learned to walk, they became very independent, as there weren't enough hands and arms to carry them all.

Naomi was on my hip as I turned on the heat under a pot of water for the angel hair pasta. Dee was unloading the dishwasher, Kelli was setting the table, Corey was playing with tractors and asking for his dad, while Maron was showing me the pictures she'd drawn at the sitter's. The kitchen was filled with excitement: the clanging of dishes and silverware, the setting of the table, the chattering of the children. This was my world.

I lifted the crockpot lid to give the spaghetti sauce a stir. The aroma of garlic, basil, oregano, and tomatoes filled the kitchen, teasing all of our appetites. I was always thankful to come home to a meal in the crockpot. It was one less thing to figure out, and the scent of home cooking reminded me of my mom's amazing suppers — the snug comfort of always being cared for.

My head was in a constant state of planning and organizing. Timing the garlic bread to come out of the oven as I drained the pasta, I wondered if Kenny would be on time for supper or if the kids and I would start without him.

The phone rang, and Kelli answered it, "Hello, Masseys'."

She handed it to me, mouthing that the caller had asked for me.

"Hello. Yes, this is Sue Massey. I won? What did I win? I was the national winner?"

Setting Naomi down so she could color with Maron at the kids' table, I pulled the phone cord into the bathroom so I could hear better. I listened carefully, then managed to mumble some sort of a "Thank you" before I hung up.

The back door opened and banged shut.

Kenny came in, and I leapt into his arms.

"You aren't going to believe this. *Farm and Ranch Magazine* just called and said I won their contest!"

"Wow, what contest? I didn't know you entered a contest." Kenny was his usual calm, collected self as I bubbled like the pasta water about to boil over on the stovetop.

My mouth had trouble keeping up with my words as I rushed to explain. "They had a Forty-Hour Week Contest. They launched it in conjunction with the song 'Forty-Hour Week.' "

Kenny nodded to show that he knew the song. Recorded by the country music band Alabama, it was a huge hit, at the top of the charts.

"They asked people to send in the number of hours they thought a farmer worked in a week. A woman in Kansas kept track of her husband's hours during wheat harvesting season and discovered that he worked ninety-six hours and sixteen minutes a week. So whoever was closest to that number won the contest. And it was me! I estimated ninety-six hours and fifteen minutes — only a minute off! Can you believe it?"

"That's amazing. How did you come up with that number?" Kenny took his hat off and hung it on the hook beside the back door.

"Here's what's really weird, Kenny. When I saw the contest in the magazine, I tore the page out and set it with the bills to fill out when I wrote checks. Late one night, when I went though the pile, I threw the contest entry page in the trash with all the junk mail. I just didn't feel like dealing with one more thing.

"Then, a voice inside me whispered to try. So I reached in the wastebasket and took the entry form out, sat for a moment with the calculator, and figured it backwards. Whenever you were planting or harvesting corn, the only time you weren't working was when you were asleep. So I added up the hours you slept, subtracted that from the hours in a week, and came up with ninety-six hours and fifteen minutes. I wrote it on the entry form, dropped it in the mail with the checks, and totally forgot about it. You know me, I'm always tossing ideas into the wind. Some of them land and take root, and some just float on by."

"What did you win? What's the prize?" Kenny was beginning to smile.

"Oh, yeah, get this. They're flying the two of us to the Kansas State Fair to meet the band Alabama in person. We'll have backstage passes after their concert. How cool is that?"

I wrapped my arms around his neck. "I'm so excited. What do you think?" I kissed him and ruffled his hair.

"Sounds great. We could use a short vacation. When do we leave?" Kenny was like his mom, always ready for a road trip or an adventure.

"Two weeks from today. Isn't it incredible? I can't believe it. What are the chances?"

"What about us kids? Where will we go?" asked Dee, her eyes wide with wonder.

"I'll check in with Grandma Johnny and see if she can keep you."

"Yay! I can pack my own bag," said Corey, beaming with excitement. "I'll get to drive Grandpa's tractor with him."

That night, I had a hard time falling sleep. I couldn't believe how quickly everything had changed. It was as if a grenade had been tossed into the middle of my life of endless routine.

At the time, I had no idea where the pieces would fall.

The trip was a burst of firsts: first time we ever flew, first time away from the kids for more than a day, first time we met a famous band in person.

The next few days flashed by like a meteor. The highlight of the trip occurred at a press conference before the concert.

The Alabama band members were at the height of their career and would go on to be voted entertainers of the decade. (Wikipedia calls them "undoubtedly the most successful group in the history of country music, releasing over 20 gold and platinum records, dozens of #1-ranked singles, and selling over 73 million records.")

I was thrilled when Alabama's lead singer, Randy Owens, came up to us, introduced himself (as if he needed an introduction), and shook our hands. With a soft Southern drawl and dark, handsome good looks, Randy was country born and raised, and he and Kenny instantly bonded. They shared stories, laughing and shooting the breeze like a couple of farm boys at the local co-op.

Then Greg Fowler, the band's PR manager, came over to greet us. His Alabaman accent was even more pronounced than Randy's. It was a delight to listen to the three men banter with such ease. After a few minutes, Greg told Randy it was time to set up for their concert.

Before he left, Randy leaned toward Kenny, "How's farming in Wisconsin?"

"Not good," Kenny replied in one of his usual understatements. If Randy had asked me, I would have told him the truth — "horrible," "devastating," and "sad beyond words." But I could see Randy knew. Deep down he knew.

Randy shook our hands and told us to "hang in there, and please stay in touch."

His brown eyes were sincere and genuine. He meant it.

The crowd stood and roared when Randy and his band took the stage. Our seats were so close to the front that I could see the buttons on Randy's shirt as he belted out one top-ten ballad after another.

Before playing their hit song, "Forty-Hour Week," Randy told the audience about the Forty-Hour-Week Contest and how I'd won it by estimating that the average farmer worked double a forty-hour week and then some. He dedicated the song to me and to farmers everywhere.

The audience went wild.

I closed my eyes as I listened to the band play while Randy sang. The bass vibrated through the bleachers in a way that seemed to rock my soul. I didn't want the moment to end.

Yes, I missed the kids terribly. But I didn't miss the rest of it — the daily feeling of despair and doom that had become our life on the farm. I pushed away all thoughts of the imminent loss of our farm and submerged myself in the musical magic of the evening.

For two hours, we sang along with Alabama's songs, danced in front of our bleacher seats, and cheered along with the rest of the crowd. Alabama was known to put on an amazing concert, and it was all of that and even more.

When the lights dimmed, Kenny and I made our way backstage where only a handful of guests were permitted. There was a guard as big as a gorilla guarding the gate. He glanced at our passes and motioned us forward.

We spent another glorious hour in the backstage area as we chatted with each of the band members, all very nice and easy to talk to, and shared a Coke beneath a clear sky filled with a field of sparkling stars.

As we walked back toward our rental car, Kenny and I held hands and stared up at the moon. It was a mere tilted sliver in the sky.

The next evening, we were home. I was never so happy to see the kids. As I hugged and kissed them, I thought to myself: *No matter what happens, even if we do lose our home and our farm, I still have the most precious thing in the world.* How lucky I was to have this beautiful family, my blond, blue-eyed munchkins.

My mom and dad had treated the kids like royalty. They were still telling stories and asking about our trip as we tucked them into bed.

Long after everyone else was asleep, I went to the kitchen and sat down at the table. The house was dark and quiet. Only a soft wind blew through the white pine out back, and through the kitchen window, a shaft of light gleamed against the side of the corn dryer.

My mind was still playing through images of the fantastic experience that Randy and his band had given us. I decided to write them a thank-you letter.

As I began to write, something strange happened. It was as if my heart opened and spilled out onto the paper. Feelings I didn't even know existed inside me, words I'd never said aloud, tumbled out. What began as a simple thank-you note became a cry of anguish about the uncertain future that we and all farmers faced as we stood on the brink of losing everything, everything that meant so much to us.

After I signed my name, I was too exhausted to reread the letter. I decided to sleep on it. I fell into bed and into dreamland.

In the morning, after the older kids were off to school and Maron and Naomi were playing quietly together, I looked over the letter. It certainly had taken a different path than I'd planned. But I thought it captured the reality I'd been struggling with for so long.

I remembered something that Randy Owens had mentioned when we talked to him at his concert. He said that his band would be performing at the upcoming Farm Aid in Champaign, Illinois. Willie Nelson was spearheading the event, which was to showcase a line-up of top musicians. The idea for Farm Aid was sparked earlier in the year by Bob Dylan's comments at Live Aid that he hoped some of the money would help American farmers in danger of losing their farms. Farm Aid was getting tons of publicity in the national news.

Maybe my letter would shed some insight into what farming meant to folks like us, I thought. "Farmers aren't looking to get rich," I'd written, and that was certainly true. All we wanted was to make a decent living and pass on our love for the land to the next generation.

I stuffed the letter into an envelope. At the last minute, I decided to enclose a few snapshots of the kids because, to me, uprooting the children, depriving them of the future we'd built for them, epitomized the trauma we were facing.

I bundled Maron and Naomi into the car and drove twenty minutes to the Mount Horeb post office. Handing the clerk the letter, I asked how much it would cost to overnight it.

When she said "ten dollars," I hesitated. Ten dollars was all the money I had in my pocket until payday at the vet clinic, which was several days away. I mentally scrolled through our kitchen cupboard, recalled the gas gauge was on three-quarters of a tank, and decided we could make it. Then I reached into my pocket and gave her my last ten.

After leaving the post office, I went on with my day and didn't give the letter another thought.

Sue Massey

The next day, when I answered the phone at the vet clinic, I was greeted by a familiar Southern voice. "Hey, Sue."

It was Greg, the PR guy we'd met in Kansas.

"Hi, Greg. What's up?"

"Randy just received your letter, and it blew him away," Greg said. "He would like your permission to use it during Willie Nelson's Farm Aid concert."

The phone fell silent as I tried to imagine how they would use my letter for Farm Aid.

"If you agree, we'd like you to overnight us a few more photos of the kids and the farm. Send them postage due, and we'll pay. We're hoping to produce a video with a montage of your pictures and run it while Randy reads your letter on the air."

I was still reaching for words when Greg went on, "I do need to caution you about the power behind national TV. The exposure can be both good and bad. But I believe your letter will help other struggling farm families and draw awareness to their plight as well. Why don't you talk it over with Kenny and get back to me? We'll need you to sign some legal papers."

"OK, I'll call you," I said.

"You know, Farm Aid is less than a week away, so we need to move quickly on this. I think your family photos will put a real face on the problem. Who knows, it might even help save your farm."

The minute I set the receiver down, a farmer called the vet clinic with a cow down with milk fever, and I sprang into action, radioing the vet with the emergency information. The bell on the door jingled, and a couple of farmers walked in to buy medicine and pay their bills. I didn't have time to think much about Greg's request until I'd picked up the kids and was on my way home. When I pulled into the drive, I was never so glad to see Kenny walking around the side of the house.

As the kids raced to play on their swing set, I ran toward Kenny and recounted my conversation with Greg. "What do you think we should do?"

He lifted his hat, ran his fingers through his hair, and I knew he was deep in thought, pondering all angles. "What did you write in that letter?" he asked.

"It's crazy. I didn't keep a copy. It began as a thank-you note and turned emotional. I don't remember exactly what I said. I sent a few pictures of the kids, and maybe that's what gave them the idea for the video. I never dreamed something like this would happen. Kenny, I'm as shocked as you are."

"Well, it's your letter. What's your feeling about having Randy read it on TV?"

"Honestly, I don't know what we have to lose," I said.

"I wish I knew what was in that letter," Kenny mused, looking into the distance. The sun was beginning to lower, the wind barely there. Behind him were the bluffs and knoll where we'd planned to build our dream home someday.

"I remember that writing the letter seemed like an out-of-body experience. But the next day, when I reread it, I felt that it made an important point about how much farming means to us."

Kenny nodded. "Well, if you feel OK with it, it's fine with me."

"Great! I'll give Greg a call. He needs me to overnight him a few more pictures. Can you watch the kids while I run in and grab a handful from the scrapbooks? I'll mail them tomorrow on my way in to work."

The next day as I stopped by the post office, I thought about the video taking shape, and I started to feel a nervous excitement. There was something about the art of putting words and pictures together to tell a story that had always captivated me. I thought about Greg's tight deadline: Would they be able to pull this off? If so, what on earth would it look like?

Sue Massey

CHAPTER 9

Letter from the Heart

Watching Farm Aid on TV was unlike anything I'd ever experienced.

Although it was an instant success and became an annual event, this was the very first Farm Aid, and the hype was unbelievable. The highlight was Randy Owens and his band. When they took the stage, the result was complete mayhem.

When the applause died down, Randy said he had a letter he wanted to read, a letter that "said it all." The crowd hushed as Randy read the words I'd written in the depths of that fateful night.

Dear Alabama,

After returning home from your concert at the Kansas State Fair and hearing about your involvement with Farm Aid, I felt compelled to write. My husband Kenny is a third-generation farmer. We're facing an approaching auction to sell off our farm unless we can pay our overdue bills. Words can't relate how destructive this can be. One's self esteem drops to rock bottom with feelings of failure. The stress can be hard on a marriage and devastating to the kids.

Letter from the *Heart*

133

Our family story is probably similar to many other farm families. In 1968, the farm was debt-free. Kenny's father switched from dairy to egg farming. Prices had their ups and downs, but soon the bills were paid and things looked fine. Then suddenly prices dropped drastically and stayed down for too long. Kenny's folks struggled with increasing feed bills and expenses, hoping for the market to return. But after eighteen months, the feed bills had grown so high there was no more hope. So we reluctantly stopped production.

Now all that's left are the bills. We're faced with a forced sale of our farm.

Those are the awful facts. But then, there are the feelings. It's the love for one's land. And if you asked Kenny what he'd like to do for the rest of his life, I'm sure he'd say: Be able to farm.

Farmers aren't looking to get rich. It's the simple things they love and understand. Raising crops and watching the kids grow. Being close and being together with the family, sharing the fruits of our labor. Memories and experiences that will last a lifetime.

Ken has been forced to work for the state to support our family of seven. He drives two and a half hours to and from work. This increases his appreciation and love for our farm.

This is a plea for help from our young family in its struggle to hang on. Please forgive us for asking, but we are at the point of desperation. The forced sale is approaching within eight weeks, and time is of the essence.

Please take a moment to view the photos that I have enclosed so you can envision our love for the land and what farming means to us.

With kindest regards,
Sue Massey
Hollandale, Wisconsin

Sue Massey

Randy's eloquent delivery, each word carefully articulated and dense with emotional despair, lent weight to the simple message I'd written. As he spoke, pictures flashed across the screen in vivid color — the children playing in an egg crate, me riding Bojo, Kenny and the kids building our shed, the whole family in front of our farmhouse. One by one, the pictures told the story of our life together on the farm. Randy's voice, the letter, and the innocent faces of the children all played across the screen like a down-to-earth drama at a movie theater. Even I stood in awe, as if watching someone else's life.

Afterwards, still stunned, I thought the audience would never stop cheering. I glanced at both sets of our parents, who were sitting on the couch. They were as amazed as I was.

Corey, seated in front of the TV, turned and said, "Mom, did you know we were gong to be on TV like that?"

"Well, not exactly. I didn't know what to expect."

And the phone rang... and rang... and rang. I hadn't understood what Greg meant by the power behind national TV, but now it was becoming clear, as sharply clear as the constant ring of our telephone. I soon realized our world as we knew it had been forever changed.

As I turned the ignition key off, Kenny's eyes appeared in my car window. The look on his face was one I'd never seen before. His cheeks were pale, his smile gone, his eyes filled with fear.

"Thank God, you're home! I don't know what to tell these reporters. They all want the story. I kept telling them you'd be home from work soon."

"Like I know what to say?"

"You always know what to say."

"Right." I was not convinced. Not this time. I grabbed my purse and slid out. "I've got Naomi and the diaper bag. Can you help Maron?" I crawled into the back seat. "Here, sweetheart, let Mommy help you."

As I unsnapped the buckle of her car seat, Kenny opened the door opposite me to unbuckle Maron. "Kenny, wait. When can we talk?

We need to figure out what we're going to say."

"Sue, you'll handle 'em. I know you will. I'm not worried."

"Right, I'll handle 'em."

I swung the diaper bag over my arm and lifted Naomi onto my hip. Our front yard looked like something out of the movies with satellite trucks, media vans, and press everywhere.

"Sue, Sue Massey, have you got a minute?" "Sue, over here," "Sue, can I talk to you?" "Mrs. Massey, I'm Rick with NBC News." "Sue, John with the *Journal*. Couple questions for you."

My name was being called from all directions as the postal truck drove up and the rural carrier stepped out and handed me a large carton stuffed with letters. "Won't fit in your box, Sue," he said, as he turned and drove off.

Nothing in my life could have prepared me for what was happening. I had no worldly experience — certainly not with the paparazzi.

Someone shoved a microphone in my face.

"Please, give me a minute. I need to settle Naomi inside first."

"Mommy, look." Naomi pointed toward the road where the school bus had slowed. Out filed our other kids as the voices of the children on the bus filled the valley.

Right. I'll know what to say. I can do this. Let's see: There's supper to make, a diaper to change, laundry to start, homework to tackle, lunches to pack for tomorrow, and it would be great to hear about my kids' day. Where do I fit in the interviews and open that pile of mail? Hmm...

"Sue, this young man would like to ask you a few questions. This is Paul from the *Tribune*," Kenny said as we walked into the house together. The phone was ringing, the answering machine full. I set down my purse, and the kids headed to the kitchen. *Wait, what are all these people doing in our house?* The living room looked like a movie set with lights and cameras everywhere. Breathe, Sue, just breathe, go with the flow, I told myself.

"Mom, we're starving. What are all these people doing here?"

"Kelli, can you get down some cups for milk? And there are cookies in the cookie jar." I turned toward our oldest. "No more than two or it'll spoil your supper. I'll be in the living room if you need me. You can turn *Sesame Street* on while you kids snack. Thanks, Kel."

The photographers' floodlights were warm as Kenny and I sat down on the couch. Someone pinned microphones to our collars. I'd always been intrigued with movies and TV production and wondered how it all came together. *If only I could stand back and watch instead of being in the center of it all. If only my brain felt sharper, not so foggy and besieged.* I noticed that the national media people trumped the local media. It seemed like an unspoken rule they all respected as they hung out waiting for their turn.

"Mrs. Massey, let's begin with you. I'll let you know when we're about to tape. Just ignore the lighting and sound guys. So tell us exactly how this all began: your involvement with the band Alabama, your letter, Farm Aid, and we'll finish up with the reaction since your letter aired on national TV."

The interviewer's voice continued as other guys measured the distance from our faces to the camera, then adjusted the lights and light reflector screens. "Testing, one, two, one, two, testing, check, sounds good." If I could set aside the fact that I had to speak, the entire process was captivating.

As the interviewer scanned his notes, I noticed a pair of tiny blue eyes peer beneath the stand that held the camera. "Corey, don't even think about it," I said. "We'll be done shortly, Please, play with your sisters until supper."

I glanced out the window at the gang of press waiting to interview us. It looked twelve deep. This could take a while. It might be a frozen pizza night.

At eleven o'clock, I turned the lock on our front door, wishing I could leave it locked for days and just hide out here within the walls of our home, here with our little family. As I collapsed into bed, I realized that somehow we'd done it. The kids were fed and in bed, thanks to Kelli. Everything on the list was done, and every inch of me was tired. The parade of questions and answers marched through my weary head. I rethought everything I'd said, hoping I'd said the right thing. I wondered if tomorrow would be quieter. Maybe I'd have a chance after work to return some of the phone calls.

Each reporter had repeated the same series of questions, and I wished we could have addressed them as a whole to save time. That was my mommy brain talking. I was programmed to think in terms of how to simplify.

Cards and letters jammed the mailbox that stood like a worn-out soldier at the end of our gravel drive. Piles of mail overflowed all the tables in our living room. Between press interviews, phone messages to return, five children under the age of eleven, and work and school schedules to meet, we had set the mail aside until we could break loose to open it.

I thought of how Greg, Alabama's public-relations agent, had warned me about being on national TV. He hadn't been kidding when he told me how powerful such exposure would be. It had been a stampede that bolted us out of our tiny corner of the world.

Trying to make sense of it all, I told Kenny the two of us had to sit down and sort through the mail. That was one thing that would bring a semblance of order back into our lives.

With the kids tucked in bed, Kenny and I began opening the trays and boxes of letters. For a moment, all was quiet as we slit open envelopes.

Then I gasped. "Kenny, look!" I held up a check for $250 as I read from the letter: "I was so touched by your heartfelt words and the pictures of your family on TV, I would do anything possible to help you save your farm."

His face mirroring my disbelief, Kenny held up another check. "My God, Sue, this one's for $100," he said.

As we continued to sort through the mail, we found more checks, some cash, many words of encouragement.

"Here," I said to Kenny. "Why don't you pass me all the ones with

Sue Massey

checks or cash inside. I'll write the amount on the envelope. That way, we'll have separate piles and records of everything."

"Good idea," he said. "But, Sue, what are we going to do with all this money? It just seems — "

He made a gesture of helplessness.

"I'm not sure, Kenny. I have no idea what to do. Never in a million years did I think something like this would happen."

"We have to make a decision." Kenny looked as much at a loss as I felt.

"Let's put the decision-making aside for now and concentrate on organizing this mass of mail. Once we see what we have, we can talk about what we should do next."

"That makes sense," he agreed and turned back to the heap of envelopes in front of him.

Hours passed, and the enormous piles began to lessen, look more manageable. The stacks of envelopes with checks inside rose steadily higher. We had started another pile of letters from people who didn't send checks but instead offered us money or said they could arrange low-interest loans or had other ideas for ways they could help us.

For the most part, we were silent, but occasionally we read each other snippets of the letters. "Here's one from a woman in Vermont who used to be a dairy farmer," I said. "She writes, 'My husband and I lost our farm years ago, and I've still found nothing to give me the feeling of worth that farming did — nothing that brings me as close to my husband or makes me feel as alive. It's been hard, but we're getting through it. The main thing I want to say is this: Lean on each other, love one another, remember your strengths. Carry those strengths into the future rather than letting the sorrows weigh you down.'

"She is so right, Kenny. We have to focus on us and the kids. We need to stay strong."

"What a wonderful letter," Kenny said. "It's so encouraging."

I nodded and turned back to my stack.

There was a small secret pile of letters I was keeping on the side and not sharing with Kenny. Those were the harsh, hurtful ones —

like the woman who spewed words onto paper, criticizing us for having five children. "What were you thinking? What if everyone had five kids? The world would be grossly overpopulated! Stop your complaining and get on with life!" Or the postcard that shrieked, "I am so sick of your whining! Instead of begging for a handout, why don't you go to work? Society doesn't need any more lazy slough-offs, and I'm sick of hearing about your pitiful woes."

Those words jabbed at me. How could people judge us when they didn't even know us? Why would they leap to conclusions so far from the truth? I wished I could explain to them that all we ever dreamed of was to create a large, loving farm family that earned a living off the land.

At midnight, we could take no more, set the piles aside, gave each other a "to be continued" look, and climbed the stairs. Lying in bed, I looked at the moonbeam that sliced through the bedroom window as every letter, every card streamed through my head as if on replay. Messages from all walks of life: blue collar, white collar, famous people, poor people, people in prison and the armed services, all races, all states, even many from overseas.

I tried to calculate in my head how much the checks added up to and then gave up, deciding to wait till I had a paper and pencil. But was this really the solution? Accepting money from strangers? Something about it didn't feel right to me, and I could tell Kenny was bothered by it too. Even if we accepted the money, wouldn't we be faced with the same economic problems next year, or the year after? No matter what family farmers did to try to stay afloat, it seemed they were doomed to go out of business as the huge farm conglomerates took over and the weather directed their future. And did we have the energy and will left to fight? We had five young children to care for, and the farm had fallen into such disrepair. It would take a ton of money and energy to turn it back into a viable, revenue-generating family farm. When I couldn't bear to think any more, I decided to pray for an answer, hoping that when I woke I would know what to do next.

Sue Massey

CHAPTER 10

Decision

It was a plain white, business-sized envelope with no return address. I slit it open. Inside was a one-dollar bill with a handwritten note:

I wish I were in a position to send more to help save your farm. You have drawn attention to the emergency situation of our nation's family farms, the bread basket of our country. You are a symbol of what America is made of. Please accept this dollar as a small gesture of my gratitude. I did not include an address, for it is a gift that does not require a written thank-you. Perhaps one day, when you are in a position to do so, you will think of me and help someone else in need.

–Sam

I sat back, contemplating this powerful act of kindness. Someone who could spare only a dollar took the time to wrap and mail it to Ken and Sue Massey, Hollandale, Wisconsin.

I promised myself I would never forget Sam's simple gesture. I vowed to pass it on, just as he suggested. There would be no strings attached, no acknowledgment needed, for it would be a gift from my heart.

I looked down at the basket of cards and letters yet to open. The torrent of mail had slowed, but we still received a few more letters every day. Each touched me in a way I knew I would always remember.

Today was Saturday, and as soon as Mom arrived to take the kids for the day, Kenny and I planned to open the remaining letters and decide what to do with the checks. I'd been going back and forth in my mind but was no closer to a decision. I hoped that talking to Kenny would clarify things.

Kenny's parents had told us it was our choice whether to use the checks to try to save the farm or send the money back. I knew they would love for us to accept the money. They would do anything to keep from losing the farm that had been in their family for generations.

I was still holding the dollar bill in my hand, staring into space, when Kenny came in to tell me Mom had arrived. I folded the dollar back in its envelope and went outside to say "hi" and help her pack the kids into the car.

"Thanks so much, Mom," I said. "We have a tough decision to make, and we need a little quiet time to reflect."

"We have big plans for the kids. Maybe a picnic," she said. The kids were lucky; no one could create a picnic like my mom. "I'll see you this evening after milking chores."

Back in the house, Kenny and I sat across from each other at the table. At first we opened letters silently, lost in our thoughts.

An hour later, Kenny sighed. "I don't feel any closer to knowing what to do with this money."

"Here," I said, grabbing a notebook and pen. "I'll make a list of the pros and cons."

"OK," he agreed. We moved the letters off to the side.

"It feels as though some of these people tucked pieces of their hearts inside the envelopes, doesn't it? It seems rude to even think of sending the money back," I said. "But if we keep it, we have to make sure it will go toward their wishes."

"There's no doubt that lots of people are rooting to save our farm,"

Sue Massey

Kenny said. "It's hard to get my mind around it."

"I've added up the checks," I said. "If we throw in the offers we've received, it still barely puts a dent in our debt. We still have phone calls to return, so we don't know exactly what those offers entail. But even if we keep the farm from foreclosure, we still have to earn a living off it. Where would we get the money to put in the crops, fix all the broken equipment, cover the taxes, keep the farm going in the long run?"

"I know. There's no money in cash crops right now, and the low price of eggs is what put us in this predicament in the first place."

"So keeping the farm isn't the root of the issue here. It's farm prices being so low that a farmer can't make a living at it anymore. It's scary to think, but what if the day comes when there are no more family farms? How sad would that be? All the farm wives I know are already working off the farm so they can make ends meet. Of course we love the farm and wanted to raise the kids here, but are we just prolonging the inevitable? And if we accept help and save our farm, how will we feel when our neighbors lose theirs?"

We both looked at the list on the table, the growing "con" column weighing heavy on our hearts.

"Even if some wealthy individual stepped in and took care of the outstanding debt and repairs, and helped set us up so we could earn a living off the land, it would still be a huge gamble," I continued. "It's like looking into a crystal ball and asking what the future holds for farmers. As much as we love this way of life, I'm worried. It's as if farmers have no voice. They just take whatever crumb is tossed their way."

The decision surfaced on its own, and it felt horrible. For a while we just sat, chins in the palms of our hands, elbows against the table.

"Thank goodness I have work welding down the road as well as my job with the state," Kenny said. Even with the salaries we earned at our jobs, we wouldn't have made it without the work we did on the side. Kenny was handy with all kinds of machinery, and I'd learned how to bake and decorate cakes to sell for extra income.

Our eyes touched across the table. Sadly, the decision had been made.

Through the window, I could see the bluffs I'd fallen in love with the first time I saw them. I never tired of gazing at them. Through each of the seasons, they were magical — draped in sparkling white snow, hazed in fog, green in spring, and a brilliance of gold, crimson, and chestnut in the fall. They were striking, like a moving picture I never wanted to end.

Where, I wondered, would we be a year from now?

I twirled the pen between my fingertips, searching for a way to express my appreciation for all the people who had reached out to help our family. Words usually flowed easily from my fingers, but there was nothing usual about this.

I tried to think what my response would be if I'd given a gift and the receiver sent it back. How would I feel if my check was returned with a letter saying, in essence, "This has been the hardest decision ever, but. . . "? I knew I would feel hurt. The last thing I wanted was to hurt anyone.

I finally set the pen to paper, simply letting my feelings flow out. After I finished the rough draft, I showed it to Kenny. He made a few tweaks, and then I wrote the letter in final form, made duplicates at the copy shop, and bought stamps. When I'd told Randy and Greg that I planned to return people's checks, they'd offered to have Farm Aid reimburse us for the costs of the mailing. Otherwise, with the hundreds of letters I had to send, we couldn't have afforded it.

After stamping and addressing the envelopes and tucking letters and checks inside, I left the scattered pile on the table, too tired to take on one more task. I would wait till the next day to stack the letters into boxes, take them to the post office, and send them on their way.

Sue Massey

To our many friends across the nation:

The outpouring of love and generosity has been overwhelming. You have offered words of support and continuous prayers which have touched and changed our lives as we enter our new beginning.

Kenny and I take pride in knowing that we have shared in the increased awareness of our nation's farm crisis. We have noticed the change in attitude locally and nationwide since Farm Aid. You, the American public, are upset to hear that farmers are losing their homes and land, and your letters reflect that fact. Like us, you question the government sending one hundred million dollars of ammunition and military aid to Nicaragua while doing nothing to help turn things around for farmers here at home. Together we will make a difference. We hope to attend the next Farm Aid concert and help out in any way possible. The Lutheran Social Services program is giving us the opportunity to stay involved as "peer-listeners" for those still struggling. We are channeling many offers of help (such as the offer to provide low-interest loans) through the World Development Farm Crisis Response Network for farmers in urgent need.

Despite so many generous offers, we have made the difficult decision to leave our farm. Our lives have been on hold for years, and the thought of continuing to fight leaves us weary. Even if we stayed, the problems would remain. Economically, neither Kenny nor I can afford to quit the jobs we've taken outside the farm. High interest rates, increasing taxes, low prices for farm products combined with high prices for the necessary supplies — all these factors create a vicious circle. Our farm home is in need of extensive repair and remodeling to fit our growing family of seven. Then there is always the time element with two parents working full-time and raising five young children.

Someday, if the farm economy turns around, we may look for another piece of property, because we will always be farmers, intimately tied to the land. But for now, we are concentrating on family and helping others still trying to survive.

Losing our land is like losing part of our family, but your letters and calls have brought hope, appreciation, and gratitude back into our lives. For those of you who sent personal contributions to our family, we are returning the money with the hope that perhaps you will donate it to Farm Aid to benefit other farm families who are hurting. We will remember your generosity and concern for our family always. We apologize for responding by form letter and want you to know that each letter and phone call was handled individually and left a distinct impression upon our minds and hearts.

With warmest regards,

Sue Massey

On January 28, 1986, I watched a disaster unfold: Just a moment after being launched skyward into an enormous sea of blue, the Space Shuttle Challenger broke apart, killing its seven crew members. Like the rest of America, I was filled with utter disbelief, horror, and compassion for the astronauts' families.

In less than five weeks, our own personal disaster would occur. On March 4, we would face the possible shattering of our family farm. Would our lives burst into a million pieces, drifting back to earth without form, too demolished to ever fit back together? The image haunted me.

I felt torn, never wanting to compare the loss of precious life to the loss of a home and a farm but fearing that our loss would feel catastrophic. True, it was a personal calamity, a small one in the scheme of things, but it was consuming our family with gathering force, primed to rocket us into the unknown — the loss of our past, present, and future in a rupturing span of seconds.

So many questions and decisions weighed on me that they made a parade through my head whenever I tried to fall asleep. The most immediate need was finding a new home. Once our farm was auctioned off, we would have only a day or so to leave our farmhouse, and I still had no idea where we would go.

I had checked with Realtors, looked through ads, even driven around the countryside by myself hoping to see a "For Sale" sign. I wanted to find a place in the same school district if at all possible so that we wouldn't have to dislodge the kids. All my decisions now were focused on trying to create as little disruption as possible for the children. It would be hard enough for them to leave the farm, the only life they'd ever known, without adding a new school full of unfamiliar faces on top of it. But finding a home in the same district was looking doubtful. I was becoming desperate.

Kenny had been telling everyone he knew about our predicament, and I figured that his vast network — colleagues, farmers, feed distributors, vendors, assorted friends and acquaintances — was the most likely route to finding the house we needed.

A call came in for Kenny while I was starting the dishwasher. Listening to his side of the conversation gave me a sense of hope.

"Who was it?" I asked as soon as he hung up.

"It was Mark. He said Steve's been transferred out of state, so his home's vacant. Sounds like he might be willing to rent it to us."

"And is it — ?"

"Yep, it's in the kids' school district."

"Wow, that's a prayer answered. Can we look at the house after the kids get home from school tomorrow?"

"Should be fine. He told me where the key was hidden and said to go take a look."

As we crawled into bed, my head was spinning with questions. What would the rental house look like? Would it be big enough for all seven of us? What would I do with my horse, Bojo, when we moved? What about all our belongings? How does a family vacate land that includes a farm, house, garage, numerous sheds, and other outbuildings all packed with years of accumulated stuff everywhere — 365 acres worth of three generations who have collected equipment, parts, pieces, and tools?

What about Kenny and me? Would our relationship heal with this transition? Would we feel like a family again? Would we be able to talk about all the things left unsaid for so long?

And something else rippled within me. If we moved off the farm, would I pack up the deep, dark secret I'd held so close inside for so many years, or would I leave her behind with the past? I wondered if the day would ever come when I could speak of her. For now, it felt impossible as we stood near the edge of this new precipice.

After picking the kids up from school, we drove to our potential new house. As soon as Kenny turned the key and unlatched the door, the kids ran inside and scattered in all directions, their voices echoing through the empty space. I heard "Wow!" and "This is so cool!" and felt a wave of relief. Maybe this would work out.

The house was lovely, much nicer than any home Kenny or I had ever lived in. It had a "great room" with a floor-to-ceiling stone fireplace, and lots of big windows. The house was built on the crest of a hill, with a large sprawling lawn, a few pines, and a beautiful view of the rolling hills below. It was dream-like.

I tried to envision living here. We would have to double up the kids. Corey and Maron were still small enough to share a bedroom, we could put Kelli and Dee together, and Naomi could sleep in her crib in our bedroom. It would definitely work.

There was even a deck out back, facing an open farm field, and a two-car garage, which I noticed Kenny eyeing. As we all climbed back into the van, a neighbor walked over and introduced himself. When we told him we might be renting the house, he welcomed us

Sue Massey

warmly and asked if we needed anything. Kenny mentioned we had a horse, and he said we could keep the horse in his adjacent pasture. I couldn't believe his kindness.

I heaved a huge sigh. We had a place to live.

But we still faced the unimaginable farm auction, just a few days away. I was going through the motions of preparing to leave our farm home forever, but in the back of my mind I refused to believe it would actually happen. It just didn't seem possible.

CHAPTER 11

Purgatory

The day began like any other day. Bacon crackled in the skillet. There was a diaper to change, a husband outside feeding a handful of cattle, a dishwasher to unload, tiny hands and faces to wash, a table to set, while our four girls played beside a Big Bird segment on *Sesame Street*. Corey was pulling on his fire-engine red boots, eager to see what his dad was up to outside.

The fog was dense and gray. It was March 4, 1986, the day set for the farm auction, a day I had dreaded for so long that I could barely remember what life had been like without a constant sense of foreboding.

I thought about the family pow-wow we'd held the night before. The seven of us had formed a circle around a white candle on a chipped saucer, the only light in the room.

"Let's take turns sharing memories," I'd suggested. "Here, I've cut up some blue and yellow paper, and each piece can symbolize a memory — blue for sad, yellow for happy. When you share a sad memory, you can drop a blue paper into the candle flame to burn away some of that sorrow. For happy memories, take a piece of yellow paper and set it in front of you. You can take those memories with you and keep them forever."

Sue Massey

As we reminisced, laughed, and cried for an hour, the candle flared and flickered, and stacks of yellow paper mounded up in front of us. Before we went to bed, I told everyone to tuck their pieces of yellow paper someplace special and bring them along when we moved to our new house.

There was no legal reason that Kenny and I had to be at the auction, but we'd decided to attend, and we asked the kids to come with us. We felt we needed to be together as a family for this milestone in our lives. It would be like a wake, a funeral, a final good-bye that would mark the end and also a new start.

"This may no longer be our home and our farm, but no one can take our memories," I'd said the night before. "We own our memories. They belong to each one of us. They give life to our souls." I remember Kenny nodding as he sat with Naomi in his cross-legged lap, his solemn face reflected in the soft candlelight.

Now, through the window in our laundry room, I caught a glimpse of Kenny walking hand-in-hand with Corey along the dirt field road that led to the back forty — the pine-covered parcel of Massey farmland that Kenny referred to as Purgatory because it was so far back, so thick, so dark that one could easily get lost and never find a way out.

Through the fog, their features were indistinct, but I could see Corey tilt his head to look up at Kenny. In that gesture was such innocence and trust that my heart ached.

As I pulled damp sheets from the washer, my eyes and thoughts were glued to Kenny and Corey, father and son taking their final walk on the farm. The farm that had been in the Massey family for three generations — and that we'd hoped to pass down to a fourth generation — was about to change hands.

We arrived in a daze. Even the kids were quiet, staring out the windows of our old van as we approached the Dodgeville Courthouse steps.

"Oh. My. God..." Kenny's words tailed off as he scanned the parking lot clogged with media, cameras, lights, and people as far as the eye could see.

For the past few days, the press had begun to call again, asking if we planned to go to the auction... and how were the kids holding up... and what if someone offers to buy it back for you... and what about the feed dealer... do you think he'll try to buy your farm to recover some of his debt from the unpaid feed bills... and how does this make you feel? And on and on, until my head was jammed so tight that I forgot the time.

Kenny shut the van off. Seat belts clicked. Van doors slid open.

A sick feeling came over me. Was this really going to happen? Was someone actually going to buy our farm? I had pushed the fear aside, certain this day would never come. But here we were, the worst day of our lives was about to unfold, and to make matters worse, there was an audience as widespread as the parking lot. For a moment, I closed my eyes, prayed we'd make it through.

I lifted Naomi, now eighteen months old, out of the car and onto my hip, tossed my purse over the other shoulder, turned around, and looked into the eyes of my mother, and my dad beside her.

"Oh, thank you for coming," I said. They reached to help us with the children. Police officers escorted all of us up the courthouse steps and into a conference room. I was so glad we were all together.

Kenny's parents hadn't come. Kenny's mom was teaching school as usual. His dad would be in his living room, his brother beside him, watching the auction unfold on TV.

How hard this must be for them, I thought, after working on the farm their entire married lives. Their decision to re-zone the land on which they built their house meant they wouldn't need to move, but they would have to watch someone else run the farm. I could only imagine how painful that daily reminder would be for them.

The sheriff began to explain how the process was going to take place and asked if we had any questions. If not, he said, it was almost

Sue Massey

ten o'clock, and we needed to proceed outside. The auction would take place on the courthouse steps.

We huddled in a corner to the left of the front steps. My mind was divided: part on our children, part on the auction, and part on Kenny. The sheriff began to shout for opening bids on the farm.

I heard the sound of the bidding as if from a faraway shore. One of the bidders, Raphael Peterson, was our feed supplier. Bett-Or Eggs owed him more than $60,000, and buying our farm was a way for him to recoup the debt. The only other bidder was the Farmers Saving Bank.

Then I heard "$45,000... going once... going twice... sold to Mr. Raphael Peterson."

I felt shell-shocked: 365 acres of rich farmland, a house, and outbuildings for $45,000. It was a shameful steal.

I leaned into Kenny's jacket collar and drew his scent in deep. But when I looked into his eyes for reassurance, all I saw was an enormous hurt beyond words. I had never seen such a look before, and it terrified me. It was as if his soul was gone.

I began to cry uncontrollably. From somewhere deep inside me, tears that I had held back for years, trying to be strong for Kenny and the kids, poured out.

Snap. The iconic photograph was taken at that instant — at the lowest point in our life. The moment of death.

I felt a hand brush my shoulder, heard some soothing words of comfort, and saw a clergyman I'd never met before. And cameras clicked and clicked and clicked. If only we could have dropped into a hidden tunnel, or been air-lifted off the face of the earth. I so wanted to disappear.

Someone shuffled us toward a row of microphones where reporters hurled questions. "Mrs. Massey, weren't you surprised when Willie Nelson's Farm Aid didn't save your farm? After all you did, the letter you wrote?"

When I looked up, there were strangers as far as I could see. When

I looked down, I saw the kids clinging to Kenny and me like a cluster of grapes to a vine. I leaned into the microphone.

"No," I said. "The problem is deeper, more widespread." Words spilled out, from where I wasn't sure. "Farmers aren't getting paid enough for what they grow. It costs more to put the crops in than what they get in return for their harvest. Farmers work so hard. They pour their heart and soul into growing food so we can all eat. How long can they work so hard for nothing in return?"

"Mr. Massey, what about suicide? Did you ever feel that bad?"

I heard the word "suicide," and the damp, chilly March air turned to ice within me.

"I've been so low," Kenny replied. "You know, you think you can't go on. But you gotta be there. You gotta think about your family." He choked back tears. "Your family needs you. . ."

His voice broke. The cameras kept rolling. I knew he had been despondent, but suicide? Not Kenny. He would never leave us like that.

I looked out over a sea of microphones and decided enough was enough. We pressed our way through the crowd and back to the van, cameras clicking all around us. The seven of us clung together as if on a raft plunging down the rapids. Our only task was to keep our heads above water, just enough so we could breathe.

Sue Massey

CHAPTER 12

Aftermath: Feral Cat

The drive home was silent, not a peep in the van. While the kids usually turned the back seat into a cacophony, they were now like five little mice hiding in their holes.

The farm auction had drained all of us. I imagined the kids were wondering what awaited us when we arrived home. I was asking myself the same thing. How strange it would be to return to a house and farm that were no longer ours.

I stared out the car window. The sky was still gray. I dreaded going home. It wasn't home anymore. I wanted to keep on driving, just disappear into the hills and valleys, camping in the van.

The side mirror reflected a wagon train of media dead on our trail. I could see Mom and Dad's truck two cars back. Thank goodness. I felt too weak to handle the barrage of media all over again.

Kenny pulled the van in front of the garage. Mom appeared out of nowhere. Fierce as a lioness, she firmly told the reporters and photographers, to give us some space and time. We trudged into the house, and Mom locked the door and closed the curtains. I collapsed onto the couch.

Mom went into the kitchen to make coffee and brought out crackers for the kids. Corey reached to turn on the TV.

"No, Corey, please leave it off. I've seen about enough for one day." I took the green toss pillow off the back of the couch and set it on my lap. Naomi crawled up, wrapped her little arms around my neck, and squeezed tight as she whispered, "I love you, Mommy." I kissed her ear and whispered my love back to her.

I could smell eggs boiling, and soon Mom passed a platter of egg salad sandwiches around.

I sat on the couch like a zombie. I knew I was breathing, but I felt lifeless.

Corey opened the toy box and pulled out some tractors. The kids began to chatter again, almost as if everything were back to normal.

The next morning, Kenny walked out to fetch the newspaper, which hung in the orange plastic bin beneath our rickety old mailbox. Carrying it into the kitchen, he set it on the table where I sat nursing a mug of coffee.

"Oh, my God, Sue, look." He spun the newspaper around for me to see.

Covering nearly the whole front page of the newspaper was a picture of our family, captured in that moment of shock, our souls shattered as we faced the death of our beloved farm.

The photograph reached the headlines of a nation and beyond. It became *the* photo, republished in newspapers around the world to symbolize the pain, anguish, and heartbreak of families losing their farms.

After the Farm Aid concert when the media had inundated us, hunted us down, and stripped us of privacy and serenity, I'd doubted that anything could be worse.

I was wrong.

This time the reaction was double, if not triple, what we'd endured after Farm Aid. It was utter chaos, bedlam on repeat.

Not only did the press hound us even more relentlessly, but we were in a far weaker state. The energy that had driven me during the

Sue Massey

first media blitz was gone, and I felt completely spent, ridden with grief, while faced once again with a mountain of media, phone calls, letters, and decisions. At times, I wasn't sure I could endure the whole ordeal again.

But there was no escape. Once again, we were forced to answer a constant roll of questions — the whys, the hows, the what nows — and face the accusations of poor management and poor choices. Even I wasn't completely clear on how we'd arrived at this point. I'd been so caught up in child rearing, my job, and making our marriage work that I'd had very little to do with the farm decisions. Besides, farming was like raising children: It didn't come with a manual. Even if it did, the weather would raise havoc with the pages. It seemed there was no way to make non-farmers understand.

One question that irritated me was: "Why did you take your children to the auction?" For this, I had an answer: because they were as much a part of the farm as Kenny and I were. They fought the battle alongside us. For years, they'd seen, heard, and felt it all: the arguing, the tears, the "There is no money." We needed to attend the farm funeral as a family, to say good-bye, cry together, hold one another, and know we would still be together on the other side of the farm death.

People questioned that decision of ours again and again. It was one thing I refused to feel guilty about. Others might feel differently; they hadn't been in our shoes. For Kenny and me, that personal decision was the right choice for our family. When I look at that iconic photo now, I see anguish, but I also see a family clinging to one another, bonded together, and it was that connection that gave us the strength to go on.

"Hello, Ms. Massey? Is this Sue Massey?"

"Yes," I said into the phone. It had been ringing nonstop.

"We've been trying to reach you for days. Ms. Terrill wishes to speak with you. Hold on just a second please."

Another line picked up. "Hello, Sue. I saw you and your family on TV, and I would like to help."

Naomi was yanking at my pant leg, wanting to be picked up. Corey was causing a stir in the other room. I tried to concentrate on what the woman was saying.

"Sue," she went on, "what I think your family needs is a home, a fresh start. What do homes in your area cost?"

My brain went dead. What did a home cost in our area? I didn't have a clue. Somehow "fifty thousand" spilled out of my mouth. I had no idea where it came from.

"Great. We'll stay in touch. When you're ready, I'll send the check. I'm happy that we'll be able to help."

Click. I tried to sort out what had just happened. I had no idea how to respond or feel toward such a generous gift. It sounded sincere. The thought of it made my head hurt, so I just picked up Naomi, walked into the kitchen, and found Kenny on our second line.

"Well, thank you, let me think about it," I heard him say. He hung up the phone, and before another call came in, he turned to me and said, "That was someone offering me a job in California."

"I just had a woman offer to buy us a home."

"This is crazy. In my wildest dreams, I couldn't visualize all these calls from people wanting to help."

The phone was ringing again. Kenny shook his head as he reached for the receiver.

I looked at the clock. It was only ten o'clock in the morning, and I was already worn out. I wished it were ten at night, and the kids were in bed, the phones silent. Who would have thought offers of jobs and a new house could leave a person so confused and numb, so wanting to be left alone, left to rest and figure things out?

I felt at a loss, not at all like myself. I couldn't put my finger on it. The pressure of answering questions and making one more decision exhausted me. A sense of intolerable stress was building inside me, like a teakettle about to shriek.

I'd kept myself going with the thought that I'd feel better after the auction was over. It would be a fresh beginning, the dawn after a storm, I'd told myself. Instead, I had a terrible feeling that the worst was yet to come.

Like a feral cat, I panicked and ran. I slithered beneath the bed, clawed my way under the cold, hard metal frame until I was sure I was safe. Hidden. Hidden from the outside world, the gripping talons of everyone needing something. Everyone wanting a piece of me. Questions. Decisions. Answers. With my breath a shallow whisper, I listened and watched in fear. Like a cat, I waited — waited for stillness to calm the storm I felt inside. I closed my eyes, the only sound a gentle wind whistling through the pine that stood in her cloak of green beside our bedroom window. I laid my head down against the thin Berber carpet, then peered out, checking to make certain that I was still alone, still safe.

I saw the world through the eyes of a cat: the feet of the dresser, the dusty old lamp base, the woven throw rug, the one Kenny's Gram had made, which now had a little worn patch from where Kenny set his weary feet at the end of each day.

I let the stillness fill me, the quiet lull my soul, and time lapped away. I disappeared into the silence. Like a broom, the silence swept away all feelings, worries, and pressures. Swept them into a heap of rubbish. I was left only to breathe.

For a fleeting moment, I wondered what life would be if my breathing ceased. To whom would it matter? Would I even be missed? Would this mess go away, be tossed out with the dust? Become yesterday's news? I was so tired of thinking, of feeling, of trying to decide which way to turn that, for an instant, death seemed the only possible way out. Or was it? I couldn't bear to leave Kenny and the kids, not now, not ever. But I was flooded with such tortuous grief that I didn't think I could go on. Maybe sleep? If I could push aside the tangled web of thoughts that filled my head, then maybe I could sleep, just hide and sleep beneath the bed.

Whispers startled me, and like the feral cat, my guard went up. The hallway steps creaked. I heard my name. Footsteps grew near, then stopped beside the bed. Shoes, black and shiny, a voice I thought I recognized.

Knees, then eyes upon me, then an outstretched hand.

"Sue, it's Pastor Henderson. I'm here to help you."

Our pastor's voice was filled with a soothing assurance.

"Come out, Sue. We'll take care of you. We won't let anything happen to you."

"Are they still here?" I asked.

"Who, Sue?"

"Everybody! All the reporters and photographers and people asking questions. Are they still down there? Because if they are, I'm not coming out!" I coiled into a ball, barely able to fit beneath the bed frame and floor.

I felt the warmth of his hand upon my shoulder. "No, Sue, no one's here except Kenny. He called me. He was concerned about you."

Concerned. The word landed on my heart.

"Please come out, Sue. Kenny has coffee. We'll sit and talk, get things sorted out."

Sorted out. I wondered if that was possible. But I uncurled myself, took the outstretched hand, and let him guide me out from under the bed and onto my feet.

My head bowed, my body rocking, I sipped the coffee, sitting cross-legged on the blue couch in our living room. I looked out the window that faced the road, filled with panic that someone might drive in, want the story, want a decision, want... want... want...

Kenny handed me my green vest. Over the years, it had become like a security blanket to me. Kenny had given it to me soon after we were married, chuckling and saying, "Early Christmas present. The rep tossed me a free DeKalb Corn vest when I placed the seed order for next year. I took one look at it and knew it had your name on it."

I'd worn the vest for so many years that the threads had turned pale and frayed. I didn't care how it looked. It was more than a vest to me. It was a symbol of home, a place to be myself and be with my family. It represented the stories, the seasons of my life: the births of our children, the harsh winters we made it through, our struggles and triumphs as a family. When I touched the soft, worn material, I was transported back to earlier, less complicated times.

I wrapped my vest around me and felt a whisper of peace, as if my mom had collected me into her arms.

We talked for a while, Kenny, our pastor, and me. I took long deep breaths, the way I'd learned to do in childbirth, to keep from being overwhelmed.

The feeling of irrational, unendurable terror began to recede. I didn't realize at the time that I'd had a panic attack. Instinctively, I'd done the right thing by focusing on my breathing. My racing heart fell back into its natural rhythm.

The kids were staying with my mom till the next day. "Let's get out of here, Sue," Kenny said. "How about going to a motel for a twenty-four-hour reprieve? Friends and family will handle the phone calls and media. We need to get away, clear our heads for a bit. Sound like a plan?"

I nodded gratefully.

The rest is a blur. I recall sinking into the comfort of the motel pool as if in a bowl of warm pudding. Kenny, a non-swimmer, sat on the edge, dangling his feet in the water.

A man with a thick Irish accent drew near and struck up a conversation with Kenny, so I lay back and floated away. The Irishman's voice carried across the water. I heard him ask Kenny where he was from and what he did for a living.

Kenny's voice was too soft for me to decipher, but I clearly heard what the Irishman said: "What? You owned a farm with fifteen thousand chickens? Why, in Ireland, if you owned that type of production, you'd have arrived!"

I swam in another direction, thinking: "owned," as in past tense. What, I wondered, does a farm family do without a farm? Every time I let the worry enter my head, my heart began to race, so I swam and swam and swam, focusing on each stroke of my arms and kick of my feet rather than the pending decisions left on the table.

A day later, we returned home. Awaiting us was a cake decorated with the words "Roses are red, violets are blue, the farmers are thankful to Kenny and Sue." I thought my heart would melt into the sweetness of the frosting.

Beside the cake lay a stack of pink slips. Not thinking, I picked them up and began to read: "Please call Mera at Channel 15 News." "Call WTMJ Radio in Milwaukee." "Call us collect, Dale at Channel 3." "Call *Country Music Magazine*." "We'd like you on our show tomorrow, Etna Channel 12, Chicago." "Call me ASAP; I can help you refinance!"

Our twenty-four-hour respite dissolved. I set the phone slips aside, wondering what to do next. All I knew for sure was that the kids would be home from school soon, and we needed to pack up all our things and move out of our house and off the farm.

With Naomi toddling after me, I began to take the pictures off the walls. Suddenly it felt a little less like home as I wrapped pieces of us in brown paper bags and set them in cardboard boxes.

By noon, I was sitting in the kitchen, the walls bare, the framed photos all packed, thinking how Mom, Dad, Kenny, and I had paneled, painted, stained, carpeted, and scrubbed to make this house our home. It was the only home our children had known. It was where they'd taken their first steps, learned to talk, smiled their first smiles.

I'd assured the kids that their toys would be the last things to be packed and I wouldn't seal them in boxes. No matter what, they would be able to find a favorite toy when they needed it.

Sue Massey

We had only two days to vacate the house. I couldn't imagine a more exhausting marathon of packing. It wasn't just a family of seven to relocate, it was a farm. And everything was important to Kenny — every wrench, every hammer, every board, every shovel — all the tools of a farmer's trade.

As I continued filling boxes, the place looked less and less like a home and more and more like just another house without a family.

Moving day arrived. Friends and family came with dishes of food and hands ready to help. With all the turmoil, the still-continuing stress of media calling and camping out in our yard, the children to tend to, and schedules to keep, I could hardly think. Thankfully, the women stepped in, telling the guys to "put that here" and "be careful with that," directing the arrival of truckload after truckload of boxes into our new rental house. There were so many familiar faces, so many to thank, that I didn't know how I would ever begin to repay them all.

I heard my mom's voice. "What's most important is the beds. Let's set them up so you have a place to sleep tonight."

I had few spare moments to remind myself that this was our very last day on our farm, in our home, on the beautiful land that was as much a part of us as the air we breathed. This had been our sanctuary since the day we married. It was all we'd ever dreamed of, and there was no new dream to take its place.

When the day ended, Kenny and I tucked our little ones into their beds. We tried to keep things as normal as possible, following our usual routine of reading bedtime stories to the kids and tucking them in. We turned a nightlight on in each of their rooms to help them get settled and told them that if they wanted to crawl in with each other, that was OK too.

As Kenny and I fell into our familiar bed, in a new bedroom, I was tired to the bone. Every muscle in every inch of my body ached. I knew Kenny had to be exhausted too.

A few cars went by, and their lights illumined the drawn blinds. A branch scraped on the side of an eavestrough, and I told myself I could trim it tomorrow. I thought of the excitement in Corey's voice when he asked if Kenny could build them a sandbox out back. I knew we would settle in, but I also knew that this was only temporary, a stepping stone in our odyssey as a family.

I looked toward the crib where Naomi was already sound asleep clutching her teddy bear beneath her bent arm. I looked at Kenny, lying beside me, staring blankly toward the ceiling. I was so tired, so sad, beyond knowing how to begin to solve the fix we were in. I closed my eyes and prayed: Please show me the way, for there must be a reason, a meaning behind all that we've been through.

The plane banked to the right, then the left, and out my window I saw "Hollywood" painted into the hillside, the white letters I'd seen on TV but never in person. A car met Kenny and me at the airport and took us to the ABC studio where we were to appear on the Gary Collins' "Hour Magazine" show.

Since the auction, Kenny and I had granted interviews to so many magazines, newspapers, radio shows, and TV stations that I'd lost count, but this was the first one so far from home. I liked "Hour Magazine" and its focus on what was happening in the world.

Being in the public eye was no longer as intimidating and overwhelming as it had once been. We kept agreeing to interviews in hopes that our story would help other people in turmoil. And the letters we received bore out the fact that we were providing encouragement to many who were suffering. As long as we could do that, I was willing to keep going, although I still felt shaken and sad about the huge hole of loss we'd endured just a few months earlier.

Inside the studio, there were stretches of long hallways and a bustle of introductions. Then I was seated in a makeup chair having powder, blush, and lipstick applied and my hair styled. In an adjacent

Sue Massey

chair, the same thing was happening to Kenny. It was all more intense and over-the-top than anything we'd experienced before.

A friendly assistant to the producer briefed Kenny and me on questions we would be asked during the live airing of the show. Then she passed us on to another woman, who led us briskly down yet another hallway. I tried to take in all the new sights and sounds — doors opening and closing, voices rising and falling, heels clicking up and down the halls, people hurrying purposefully in all directions.

When we reached the set, someone showed us where to sit while someone else fitted us with tiny microphones. The lights were blinding and hot. Black wires and cords snaked the floor in every direction as cameramen focused and zoomed in on our faces.

A light blinked "On Air," and Gary Collins greeted us with warmth. He made us feel as though we were having a leisurely conversation in our living room. I almost forgot we were on national TV before a live audience.

The questions were simple. We'd been asked them a hundred times before: What caused you to write the letter to Randy Owens and his band? Did you have any idea of the consequences? Why did you decide not to accept the money that poured in to save your farm? What's next for you?

That last one was a little harder to answer. We described the house we'd moved into and the work Kenny and I were doing to pay the bills. But as far as where we were headed and what was next for us, that was still a mystery.

During the commercial breaks, we chatted with Gary and his guest star, co-host for the day, Bonnie Franklin. The freckled, red-haired star of the hit TV series *One Day at a Time* kept us smiling with her effervescent personality.

I couldn't believe how quickly the time flew. Before I knew it, the "Off Air" sign flashed red, and the interview ended. We walked off the set and were thanked profusely. Someone escorted us to a taxi outside the studio, its rear door open and waiting for us to get in.

The studio was paying for the whole trip, including a night at a hotel in downtown Hollywood. As we settled into the most luxurious room I'd ever laid eyes on, I told Kenny I couldn't wait to shower, wash the layer of makeup off my face, and slip into something appropriate for exploring the streets of Hollywood. Little did I know what would be appropriate for the streets of Hollywood.

We had one day to sightsee before our plane flew out the following day. After I showered and dressed, I called Mom to check on how the kids were doing and to tell her that the interview went well; it wasn't as scary as I'd thought it would be. She had watched it on TV and said we looked very natural.

We rode the elevator down. As we walked across the huge lobby, I felt completely out of place, underdressed, too country. The women around me were wearing sparkling jewels, stiletto heels, and glamorous furs. Their bodies dripped with gold and diamonds. The carpeting was so plush that I felt each footstep sink an inch or two into the nap.

Once outside, Kenny and I stood for a moment surveying the downtown scene. Then our eyes met. Without uttering a word, our glances at each other said, "We're not in Wisconsin anymore." Cars and taxis hurtled by, honking nonstop. The storefronts screamed "out-of-your-league." We decided to hop on a city bus to tour the streets of Hollywood.

Finally, exhausted, we flagged a taxi back to our hotel and dove into our sea-sized jumbo-king bed for a nap. Kenny was lightly snoring within minutes as I buried my head into a feather pillow so plush I couldn't see out the sides.

The next day, as our plane took off and I watched the Hollywood sign grow smaller and smaller through the pane of my window, I sighed with relief. I could hardly wait to get home, to see the kids, to step back into my world.

Sue Massey

It was July 3, 1986, and Willie Nelson had sent us plane tickets and arranged for a hotel so our family could attend Farm Aid II in Austin, Texas. We would be appearing onstage with headliners that included the Beach Boys, Bob Dylan, Julio Iglesias, Waylon Jennings, George Jones, and Bon Jovi. The kids were so excited to be part of it, and their enthusiasm spilled over and into me.

We boarded the plane — first me with twenty-one-month-old Naomi in my arms, then Kelli, then Dee holding Maron's hand, and finally Kenny grasping Corey's hand in his. This was the first time the kids had flown in an airplane, and they were mesmerized, checking out everything.

As we settled into our seats, I checked my purse for Xanax, my little crutch in case I needed something to lean on. During the farm foreclosure ordeal, my doctor had introduced me to Xanax to alleviate the panic attacks I now had at unpredictable moments.

During some of those early panic attacks, before I understood what was happening, I thought I was dying. I could hear the blood swishing through my veins. Fear erupted like a volcano inside me, sputtering and boiling. An animal-like instinct filled me with an urge to run and hide, the way I'd hidden myself under my bed like a wild creature during that first panic attack. It was horrifying.

In the months since then, Xanax had become my friend — the only friend, it seemed, that I could count on in a bewildering new world. If I felt a panic attack coming on, I couldn't get the tiny peach pill in my mouth fast enough to melt, to dissolve beneath my tongue like bliss, as a soothing tranquility melted over me.

"Hang on, kids. Here we go," I chirped as they all squealed with excitement, necks outstretched toward the windows. Kenny smiled and winked at me.

"Honey, I'm so glad your parents had the time to run up north to the Girl Scout camp to pick up Kelli and Dee for us," I told Kenny.

Kelli smiled. "Mom, the camp director gave Dee and me permission to wash our clothes in the counselors' laundry room, since they knew we were repacking our camp bags to step directly onto a plane."

I pictured the two of them, only ten and eleven, doing their own laundry, as if they were in college.

"That's great, Kelli," I said. "I'm sorry you had to cut your time at camp a little short."

"Are you kidding? This trip is so worth it."

My searching hands found the pill bottle in my purse where I'd tucked it. I would be fine, I reassured myself as the plane turned onto the runway.

The Farm Aid concert at Manor Downs Raceway Park ran from 7:00 a.m. to 1:00 a.m. the next morning. I knew our little entourage of seven would survive for only a few hours in the Texas heat with seventy thousand concert-goers shoulder to shoulder in one big overflowing party.

Willie Nelson met us soon after we arrived at the park, and he was as down-to-earth in person as he was on TV. We were told where to wait for our introduction, near the huge stage. Around our necks hung backstage passes, making it easy for the security guards to recognize us as they escorted our little tribe through oceans of bystanders.

The smell of beer, pot, and cigarettes filled the air. TV cameras and lights were everywhere. Guitars were being tuned, bands were tearing down and setting up. There was so much activity that I don't think the kids knew where to look first.

After calling us to the stage, Willie Nelson introduced us, and a roar came from the audience. The seven of us stood in front of the vast sea of cheering, stomping concert-goers, doing our best to smile. Willie shook our hands and told the audience about my letter and how it had helped draw attention to the problems of family farmers during the first Farm Aid concert the year before.

Soon we were escorted off stage and swallowed into the crowd. Strollers weren't allowed in the park during the concert, so I'd been carrying Naomi while constantly counting the kids' heads to be sure no one had wandered off.

Suddenly I felt faint. I stopped in my tracks and set Naomi down.

"Sue, what's wrong? You OK?"

The sky began to swirl. The next thing I knew, I was in a medic tent on a stretcher staring at the canvas ceiling, being treated for heat stroke. I had been so busy watching over the kids and taking in the concert, I'd forgotten to drink much water.

It was four in the afternoon when we arrived back at our hotel room. The kids were doing well, considering it was way past their nap times. Kenny and I had decided to watch the rest of the concert on TV and order pizza in our room when the kids woke up from their naps.

As my head sank into the pillow, I pulled the sides up like a giant ear muff and tied my fingertips together at my nose. All I could think was that I wanted to disappear into the feather softness and not come out for days. Hibernate. I was drained beyond the point of a nap to repair me.

At the time, I thought I would feel better once I was out of this strange environment and back on my own turf. I had no idea that shortly after we returned home, my whole world would come crashing down.

1. And Naomi completes our family of seven. 2. Sunrise on Pelican Lake.
3. Cabin Mantra. 4. Row the boat: together in the Northwoods. 5. Our rental
ranch in rural Barneveld. 6. Five pumpkins in a patch.

Sue Massey

7. Our dream spot to build a home on the Massey farm. 8. Blanchardville Lutheran Church, Blanchardville, WI. 9. Author, Ben Logan. *The Land Remembers*. 10. The big maple that graced our front yard. 11. Lost in the meadow. 12. Kenny (center) on the Massey farm with his cousins and sisters.

Letter from the *Heart*

13. Backstage with country band Alabama (Randy Owen).
14. Farm Aid II — backstage with Willie Nelson.

Sue Massey

15. Guests on Hour Magazine with Gary Collins and Bonnie Franklin.

16. Kenny and Bonnie Franklin on Hour Magazine, 1986.

17. Mom and Dad.

18. White Birch — searching for the sunlight.

PART III
CAUGHT IN THE WAVE

Limitless and immortal, the waters are
the beginning and end of all things on earth.
~ Heinrich Zimmer

CHAPTER 13

Quicksand

"Sue, I could see this coming."

I glanced up at Mom.

I was on her couch, hugging my knees into my chest, rocking back and forth, trying to release the strangling fear I felt inside. I was smothered by worry that I could never climb out of this tight ravine, lodged between mountains of responsibility. Their towering peaks blocked even a glimmer of hope, a ray of sunlight from reaching me. The sun, my warm friend that always before had soothed my fears, seemed lost to me.

"What do you mean?" I mumbled, looking up at her towering frame standing over me.

"Every time I saw you, you kept getting thinner and thinner, running here and there, you never stopped. I thought, 'That girl's headed toward a train wreck.'"

I had been at my vet clinic job when reporters started calling me, and I'd felt a panic attack coming on. I had fled to Mom's house, hoping for solace. Instead, she seemed almost irritated with me. I could tell that she thought it was past time for me to set my grief aside and move on. Moving on had always been my strong suit. And I had tried

— oh, how I had tried. The problem was that I had no control over this weight pressing down on me. I didn't understand it, and that made it even more menacing. In desperation, I'd turned to my mom. Now I wished with all my heart that I hadn't come. I felt more criticized than understood.

"Why didn't you say something?" I asked, staring at the floor. The clumpy design in the taupe carpet made me think of all the mounds of obligations in my life — the constant peaks I had to scale and the deep, dark valleys that I had to claw my way out of. As I tried to climb out, the rocks on the mountainside would loosen, push me back, and smash me beneath their weight. My body and mind could take no more. I was crushed. I didn't have the strength to figure my way out.

"Sue, you have to get a grip, snap out of this. You have a family to think of."

All I heard was "snap out of this," and my eyes moved across the floor to Mom's shoes — the worn shoes she laced her feet into every day and took off only late at night when her work day ended. I felt her words pierce my heart and then realized her reaction came from a place of unknowing. She had never stood in my shoes and felt helpless, as I did. I felt shame at disappointing my mom when I'd tried so hard not to let anyone down, especially her.

I looked up into her face and tears tumbled out with the words, "I wish I could snap out of it." What I wanted was to run upstairs to my childhood bedroom and dive in under my grandmother's quilt, to be young and safe again, to pretend none of this had happened.

I never wanted to die. Despite the depth of my torment, I knew I had too much to live for, too many responsibilities left on the table. What kind of a mother would I be if I deserted our kids when they needed me most? But like the unrelenting draw of a love affair, every day I dreamed of the moment I could get my fix, lay my head down on the pillow, take two Xanax and not feel or think, drift aimlessly like a cloud in the sky.

I couldn't wait to place the pills on my tongue and feel them dissolve instantly into me, a gentle soothing wave to relax me. I would float, an all-encompassing bliss taking me away.

One day, I looked at the clock and saw that I had an hour until nap time. One whole hour, and the hands on the clock were moving with infinite slowness. When the kids were napping, that was my time. My time to feel nothing for two hours. All I wanted was silence to settle the tangled web in my mind, my arms and legs puddles with nowhere to go, not a care or a feeling, just me, free from responsibility. How could I wait another minute, much less an entire hour?

No, I didn't want to die. All I wanted was to sleep. And when I woke, I would be OK. All I needed was this time alone, a time just to be.

Time disappeared. Days, maybe a week passed. I moved through the motions of being a mom. Then one morning, I opened my eyes and knew at once that something was seriously wrong.

I could hear the kids playing down the hallway. *Sesame Street* was on the TV in the background. I didn't want to move, wasn't sure I could if I wanted to. I just wanted to lie there and stare at the wood grain in the paneling that lined the walls in our rented home. I didn't understand why I felt so sad, so immobile. A few weeks earlier, Willie Nelson had flown our family to Farm Aid II. We'd had a spectacular time. Why did I feel so miserable?

Trance-like, I lay there. I knew what awaited me at the end of the hallway: mountains of responsibility. And today I just couldn't find the energy to deal with any of it. I had never felt like this before.

Tiny footsteps drew near. "Mom, you OK?" Kelli asked. She knew I was always up by the crack of dawn, but not today.

"Yeah, I'm OK, just a little tired today. You guys doing OK?" It was almost too much effort to lift my head off the pillow, let alone find words to speak.

Kelli peeked around the corner of the bed so that she could see my face and confirm for herself that I was OK. "We're good," she said. "We had cereal for breakfast. Corey is out in the sandbox, and Dad is working on his truck in the garage." Since losing the farm, Kenny had buried his heartache in the overhaul of a small pickup truck.

"Thank you, sweetheart. I'll be out in a bit. I just need to rest a little longer."

Her footsteps disappeared down the hallway. A short while later, I heard the front door open and close. Then heavier footsteps. I recognized the sound of Kenny's footsteps from hearing him come down the hospital corridors when our babies were born. With my eyes closed, I knew Kenny's footsteps. I imagined that Kelli had told him I was still in bed and something must be wrong so he'd come to investigate.

The mattress creaked as he sat on the edge of our bed. He pulled the covers away from my face. "Sue, what's up? You never sleep in. Are you sick?"

I turned to look at him. "I wish I knew. My spirits are so low I don't have a clue what to do. Believe me, there is no 'snap-out-of-it.' I have never felt like this. I want to cry, but I'm afraid if I started, I wouldn't be able to stop. Part of me wants to fall asleep and not wake up for weeks."

"Should I call your mom?"

"No. Remember when I was on the verge of a panic attack and Mom told me to 'get it together, snap out of it'? If I don't know why I feel this way, how can I expect anyone else to understand? It feels so foreign to me. God, help me, I don't know what to do. I honestly don't."

"We need to take you to see a doctor." He stood and called down the hallway. "Kids, get dressed. Load the van. We're going into Madison. Mom isn't feeling well."

Kenny took me by the hand, and I stepped out of bed and pulled on sweatpants and a hoodie. Inside the swirling darkness of my mind, sorrow had grown like a cancer, its spider-like tentacles reaching every cell in my body, even penetrating my bones. Everything was bleak and colorless. Each of my footsteps, once barely touching the earth, was now an effort, each foot heavy as concrete.

A sad face stared back at me in the car mirror while little voices chattered behind me. Kenny parked the van, and the seven of us shuffled into St. Mary's Hospital, where each of our babies had been born. Above me there was a sign that read "Psychiatric Unit."

"Right this way," a nurse told us, and we were seated in a private room that smelled sterile and clean. "The doctor will be in shortly. I just need to ask you a few questions, if that's OK."

I nodded, completely confused, wondering why we were here.

"Sue, are you feeling suicidal at all?" asked the nurse, charting on a clipboard.

The question felt like a thud against the side of my head. Ten little eyes were upon me as I shook my head from side to side.

"No, no," I said. I struggled to explain. "I woke up this morning, and it felt as though all the life had been drained out of me. My spirits were so low that all I could think to do was cry, and for what, I don't know. I tried to think of things to do to pick up my spirits, but my head was in a fog. I could tell it wasn't just an off day."

The nurse leaned forward, looked into my eyes, and said, "Sue, I know you feel lost and confused right now, but that's why you're here. We're going to help you through this, and you'll come out a stronger person. I've seen it happen time and time again."

"Mommy's not staying here, is she, Daddy?" asked Dee, all eyes with blond tendrils of curls framing her little face.

The nurse responded, "Mommy needs to stay with us for a few days and get strong so she can come home and be able to take care of all of you. We'll take very good care of her here. Would you like to see her room?"

We walked down the hall and into a locked unit, patients in gowns, robes, and slippers. An uncontrollable fear swept over me. I grabbed the nurse's arm. "I think I'm having a panic attack. Can you help me? Please!"

The nurse put her arm around me. "The doctor's on his way. He'll give you something, honey."

I shut my eyes, trying to will away the terror. When the nurse led

Sue Massey

me into a hospital room, I wanted to crawl under the bed, but knew the kid's eyes were on me, and that would scare them more. How I hated to see the fear in their eyes. How badly I wanted to be the mom who always made everything all right. But I wasn't that person anymore. I was helpless against these overwhelming feelings.

My doctor appeared and placed a Diazepam in my hand. I recognized the little green pill that he'd recently prescribed in place of the Xanax I'd been taking. It seemed to work a little better in calming my panic attacks. To me, it was a godsend — a miracle that sedated the rippling, out-of-control anxiety within me.

The nurse handed me a glass of water, and within minutes, I felt my racing heart settle, my breath return, and the anguish slowly subside.

A village within a village — a dark village. A village of shadows and smells, none of which I recognized: something strong, acerbic. The street dimly lit, short and narrow, lined with latched doors on both sides.

A pair of spooky eyes gaped at me through the barred window in the door to my room, then disappeared. My head throbbed and echoed with each beat of my heart.

Where the hell am I? I wondered, and then a bottomless despair filled me, and I felt the longing to fall asleep, to a place beyond wondering or caring. I closed my eyes and, blessedly, I slept.

I awoke to a blinding streak of sunlight that split through a crease between the heavy gray drapes that hung floor to ceiling in a room I didn't remember entering, in a bed I didn't recognize.

I felt a warm hand on the back of my shoulder, then a soft voice in my ear.

"Good morning, Sue. I'm Violet, I'm the nurse who'll be taking care of you." Her voice was soft, laced with reassurance. "You can call me Vi. Everyone does," and I heard water running from a faucet in a nearby sink.

I didn't move. I let the memory of May violets blanket my mind like the purple wildflower field that sprawled across the hillside of my childhood farm, back where life was simple, life was beautiful. I lay between the stiff sheets trying to freeze myself in a time when happiness surrounded me. But one by one, the thoughts and the reality crept in, refusing to let me forget. My head surged with questions: Who, what, when, where, and why was I even here?

Vi wrapped me in a robe and tied the cotton sash at my waist. "Slip on these booties, Sue," she said. "Your husband will be bringing your own robe and slippers sometime today."

I noticed my familiar black hoodie draped over a chair. I reached for it, pulled it on over my head, like a safety blanket; it even smelled like home.

"There's a routine in here. You'll get used to it. We all take our meals together in the central dining area."

Immediately, I felt tense and guarded. "What if I want to eat alone in my room? I don't feel like eating with a bunch of strangers. In fact, I don't feel like being with anyone." The words spilled out, surprising even me.

"Sorry, Sue. It's hospital rules. It's like that for a reason, you know. Patients suffering from depression tend to drift toward isolation, which is never a good thing. You'll discover in group therapy, everyone's here for a reason, and this is a safe place to heal."

As I followed Vi down the hall, I was preoccupied with the meal rule. Were they going to make me eat stuff I didn't want to eat? It made me anxious just thinking about it.

We entered a room labeled "Group Therapy." Blue booties, white robe, my black hoodie, hands buried in my pockets, eyes on the floor, I stepped carefully in the middle of each tile, avoiding the cracks. "What the hell is group therapy?" I asked myself.

Inside was a circle of faces, all ages, all strangers. Never had I felt so defenseless, so helpless, so not wanting to be here. I took a seat in the corner and pulled the hood of my sweatshirt up over my head to disappear, pretend, if only to myself, that I wasn't there. I was invisible.

Sue Massey

A woman who introduced herself as Bea, a certified psychologist, had far more dark curly hair than fit her petite body. She began to speak in a soft, gentle tone, encouraging us to say our first name and briefly why we were here. I pulled my hood forward until my face was almost completely hidden, just my eyes peeking out.

"Jimmy, why don't you begin, and then we'll go around in a circle. For those of you who are new, welcome. For those who know the routine, please help support and encourage one another. What's said in group therapy is confidential and won't leave this room. We all respect confidence, as it's important to talk about our feelings so we understand ourselves better.

"It can feel awkward at first because you may not be used to expressing emotions. It's often through dialogue that you'll learn to name a feeling. As you do, you'll begin to feel lighter, as the weight is lifted off your heart. You'll release a heaviness you felt without knowing the source." Holding her clipboard in her lap, she smiled and turned ever so slightly toward Jimmy.

"I'm Jimmy, been here two weeks, lost my job, became homeless. I'm trying to get back on my feet," and he looked toward the girl to his right.

"I'm Ann, parents got divorced, can't stand my new stepdad. I hate the way he treats my mom, and she's like blind, ignores it. He's a total asshole. My final cry for help was when I slit my wrists and landed in here." Her lip was pierced, both arms tattooed, hair jet black, large, pain-filled brown eyes.

"Mary," the next woman in the circle introduced herself. "We been trying to have a baby for five years. Got pregnant three times, miscarried, tried again and again until it finally sent me here — to this looney bin."

"This is Sue. She arrived late yesterday," Bea said, and all eyes turned to me. God, how I wanted to disappear. I reached for a worn throw pillow resting on the nearby couch, cradled it in my lap, for comfort or courage, I wasn't sure. Though fully clothed, I felt naked, vulnerable, on the edge of staring down at each ghastly monster that lived inside me. When my guard was down, they'd crept in and taken up residency.

Some words stumbled out. "I, um, um, am just really sad, really confused. I have a supportive family so I don't understand why I feel this way. I do know that I need help because yesterday I lay in bed not wanting to get up, wishing silently that I would fall asleep and never wake up."

"We're so glad you're here with us, Sue. Here is where you'll get the help you need. I know it seems like a mountain to climb, but you have the strength to do it." Bea jotted notes on her clipboard. I could hear the tip of the pen as it crawled across her notepad.

"I don't know. I hope I can find my way out, 'cause it feels like I've hit the bottom of a ravine where every time I grasp for a rock to climb out it slices my hand and I fall back, paralyzed by the pain, the sorrow."

"You said you have a supportive family?" Bea encouraged.

"I do." I nodded.

"That's a great starting point. As you work on your demons, try to focus on the bright lights in your life, your children, your husband."

"We lost our family farm, it was foreclosed after a drought, feed bills escalated, it was in the national media, something we had no experience with," I said. "It was like an avalanche fell on us, covered us up. Now we're trying to figure out what to do. We have five young kids."

"You have five kids?" A teen's voice popped up. "That would be enough to freak anyone out."

"I guess. I just have a lot to think about, to figure out. If I'm not emotionally happy and healthy, how can I be a good mom?"

A frail, white-haired woman spoke up in the corner. "I'm almost eighty, lost my husband after sixty years of marriage. Talk about lost. Some days, all I want to do is sleep and forget."

I began to lift my head and push back my hoodie. Something about the raw, unadorned sincerity with which each person spoke drew me slowly out of myself.

Sue Massey

A young woman sitting across the room from me, a natural beauty with dark eyes and tangled black hair, was the next to speak. "My husband was in a bad car accident, lost his leg, and while I can cope with that, it's him. He's just not the same man I married. I'm so tired of trying to convince him that I still love him. I married him for who he was inside, not what he does or looks like, but he doesn't believe that. I'm at the end of my rope. Don't know what else to do. He's the one who's given up on life, and while I feel bad for him, I'm caught in the mess as well. Unable to move on with my life. It's like a boat anchor tied around my neck, every day is such a struggle."

"Boy, can I relate." A voice emerged from within me. "I think that's the worst — wanting to move forward and feeling stuck, whether it's lack of money or just bad luck that keeps us from fulfilling our dreams." I held my pillow and rocked, back and forth, back and forth, trying to ease the tumult inside me. Thoughts of the past were leaking into my head, and I tried desperately to block them out. I didn't want to go there. I wanted those memories to just go away.

Bea said, "Much of what we're working through is loss and grief, and there's no easy way around it. To arrive on the other side, we have to work our way through, and that's why we're all here, to listen and help each other." Bea paused, looked up at the clock on the wall. "Well, our time's about up for today. I'll see you all here again tomorrow morning at ten. In the meantime, here's your assignment. Take a notepad on your way out; they're on the table beside the door. Make a list of all the issues you're dealing with. Tomorrow, we'll work on a technique where you envision a hallway with lots of doors. You'll learn to put each issue inside a separate closet and shut the door. Then you'll pick the most pressing one, open that door, and deal with that one issue. One by one as you resolve each issue, you'll feel confidence grow and strength replace those closet spaces. Learning to let go of what you can't control is such a freeing feeling. Just remember to be patient with yourself."

On my way out, I grabbed the daily calendar of required events: physical work-out in room 201, lunch in the group dining hall, outside courtyard free time, a nap, one-on-one with the psychiatrist, craft hour in room 206, dinner at 6:00 p.m. in the group dining hall, free time, TV in the group room or family visits in patient rooms. I was the one usually keeping the calendar, organizing the day for seven of us; now someone else had taken on the task, and all I had to do was follow the beat within the village. Parts of the calendar, the dictated regimen, reminded me of a hard-core boot camp. The word "no" or "I'll sit this one out" were unacceptable. On another level, parts of it reminded me of a nursing home: craft time, naps, activities at prearranged times. I wasn't sure if I felt like a child or an elder being told what to do, but one thing was certain: I was broken, and I knew I needed help. There was no doubt in my mind about that.

By the end of the week, I was exhausted. My parents had been called in for a family therapy session to discuss my childhood. It was mortifying. It had been the toughest, most grueling series of emotional exercises I'd ever imagined.

Our little village within a village had grown close as we listened, talked, shared, and cried together. As I packed my bag the night before I was to check out, worry seeped in. Although I missed the kids, I didn't miss all the demands that would pile on me the minute I walked through the door. I'd grown safe and secure in this village, a village of survivors fighting for their lives. This had in part become my family; the thread of emotional pain connected us, yet we each had to fight our way back to recovery on our own.

I sat on the edge of the hospital bed, dressed and ready to go home. I looked at the clock on the wall. Kenny and the kids would be here in less than half an hour. My eyes landed on the cross — the crucifix that hung on every wall in St. Mary's Hospital, identical to the one I'd fixed my eyes on during the endless hours of laboring the births of our five children. I couldn't believe this was me, the love-for-life Sue I'd always known, sitting immobile, my feet dangling uselessly off

Sue Massey

the bed. Even though I'd lost weight and was thinner than I'd been in years, my body felt leaden.

Time disappeared in the hospital. So much had happened, a whole lifetime it seemed, and yet it felt like I'd arrived here yesterday, my spirit shattered in a million pieces. I'd learned that through therapy and antidepressants, piece by piece, day by day, I could do what seemed impossible — glue the splintered fragments back together. The result seemed miraculous but very fragile.

The blinds were closed so that only a sliver of sunlight sliced the gray mood in the room. I wondered how I'd arrived at this broken point in my life. I remembered the doctor telling me that it wasn't unusual for someone who has been under extreme stress for years to reach a breaking point as I had. It was common for a collapse to come after the precipitating events were over. I'd been running on adrenaline during Farm Aid I, the media blitz, the auction, the move from the farm, the second media storm, and then Farm Aid II, trying to carry on and be strong for the family. It was only when things settled down and I relaxed my vigilance that I crashed into a wall.

My head was a tangled mess, a yarn ball of snarled circles, all ending in one question: Now what?

A nurse popped her head in the door, "Sue, today's the day. You get to go home and see your family." She bustled in and whisked open the blinds. My dark sullen room was filled with blinding sunbeams.

"Just think, tonight you'll get to sleep in your own bed." She filled my water glass at the sink, handed it to me, and headed toward the door. Then she paused, looking back to ask, "Honey, aren't you excited about going home?"

"Yes and no." I was apprehensive about leaving this tiny universe and stepping back into a world of boundless responsibilities. But at least I didn't have to return home to an alcoholic wife-beating husband, a sexually abusive stepfather, or any of the other tragic realities I'd heard others speak of here. I thought of all we'd gone through together — the deep conversations, the anguish, the swearing, the anger, the tears, the wanting out, the longing for death. I wondered what would happen to Jimmy, to Ann, to all the others, and to me.

I felt blessed to have five healthy children and a loving husband, who were reason enough to make me want to dig out from the darkness. I fiercely missed Kenny and the kids. Still, I wasn't sure I was strong enough to go home.

"Sue, it's normal to feel scared about leaving the hospital," the nurse said. "But you have such a lovely supportive family, I know you'll do great. Go to your therapy appointments, and keep up on your meds. I'll be back in ten minutes with your discharge papers, and we'll talk more then." Her voice sounded matter-of-fact, reassuring, and a comfort.

I looked out the window. It was late fall, and the trees stood like black skeletons, leafless. Even the oak had dropped her leaves. I was mesmerized by a lone aspen leaf that hung on a branch near my hospital window. That was how I felt — clinging to life by a fingertip.

The door flew open, and the kids and Kenny burst through. The little ones clung to me as tightly and desperately as that aspen leaf gripped the bare branch. I hugged them back with all my might.

As we drove home, I watched in silence out the car window. I could feel Kenny's concerned eyes upon me. The kids laughed and chatted behind me in the van.

As soon as we pulled into the driveway of our country rental home, the kids clambered out. Like little spiders, they disappeared in all directions.

Kenny pulled my small suitcase back to the bedroom, just as he had after each of our children was born. I could still recall the feeling of holding a new baby in my arms. My arms seemed heavier now, even though they were empty.

He tossed the suitcase onto the bed, unzipped it, turned, and hugged me. "If you need me, I'll be in the garage," he said. Somehow

Sue Massey

he knew that's just what I needed — to be alone for now but to know he was nearby.

Supper, reading books, and a bedtime prayer while tucking the kids into bed unfolded like second nature. I can do this, I thought.

But by the next morning, that feeling of confidence, shaky as it had been, was completely gone. My eyes opened when I heard the sounds of the family getting ready for the day, but I quickly closed them again. I didn't want to move. It was safe beneath the covers, and I dreaded coming out.

I'm not sure how much time passed, but the sun was higher when I opened my eyes again. I felt the weight of Kenny's body as he sat down on the bed where I lay encapsulated in my cocoon.

"Sue, I just called your doctor. He said this is very normal. It's a shock to come home after all you've been through. He said you need to force yourself to get up and into the shower, get dressed, and he guarantees you'll begin to feel better, more able to grasp the day. I've called your mom and she's coming to get the kids for the day. She'll bring them back this evening."

He leaned over, kissed my cheek, and whispered, "You can do it, Sue, I know you can. I'll start the shower for you and get the kids ready for your mom." His footsteps disappeared down the long paneled hallway, and soon I heard the shower running.

I began to uncoil from my fetal position, relieved I only had to take a shower and look after myself for today. I dragged myself out of bed and down the hall.

Under the hot shower, I felt pieces of the overwhelming sadness trickle down the drain with the water. The rising steam seemed to clear the fog inside my head. I grabbed a towel and dried off inside the shower slowly, carefully, preparing myself to leave the misty warmth and step out into the cold world.

I held the check in my hand. "Pay to the order of Sue Massey for twelve hundred dollars from *Family Circle*," it read.

Soon after I'd emerged from the hospital, still shaky but function-al again, an editor from *Family Circle* magazine had called and asked if I would share the story of our farm loss with the magazine. "We pay a dollar a word, and we'd like a 1,200-word story from you, if you're interested. We feel your story would be perfect for our readers," she said.

I couldn't envision being paid for a story I'd written. "I'm extreme-ly grateful for the offer, but I haven't really had professional writing classes," I said hesitantly. "I just sort of write from my heart." I re-called the letter I'd written to thank Randy Owens and his band. I couldn't remember thinking about the words before my pen formed them. It was as if they had appeared by magic.

"And that's exactly what we're looking for," she said.

I tried to imagine 1,200 words. One full typewritten page was usu-ally 500 words. So it would be three pages. That seemed doable.

"OK," I said, trying not to sound too dubious.

"You'll do great!" she said. "I'll help you."

I had written down some of my feelings during the whole ordeal, so I put them in a more manageable form and sent them off to her. She replied with enthusiasm. "You have a nice down-to-earth, homey way of expressing yourself that we want to capture in the story," she said. "I'd just like you to make a few additions and clarifications."

A month of rewrites and phone discussions ensued. I found I en-joyed the process, and it gave a new purpose to each day.

It was during this time that Kenny's dad, Orval Massey, showed me a newspaper clipping about a writing class being held on the Uni-versity of Wisconsin-Richland Center campus. The class was taught by Ben Logan, who had recently gained national attention with his best-selling book about farm life, *The Land Remembers.*

"Sounds like this is right up your alley," Orval said. "I'd be honored to drive you if you want to go. Anyone who can write a letter like the one you wrote, a letter that captivates the whole world, oughta delve into writing more thoroughly."

How could I turn down such an offer, especially when my mother enthusiastically offered to pay the class fees? While I was fully capable of driving myself, Orval seemed thrilled to take me, and we had some nice talks on the sixty-minute commute. While I was in class, Orval went to the university library and read.

I was thankful. I think he was looking for a way to help me dig my way out of the depression, and I appreciated it. I was trying very hard to summon the enthusiasm I'd always had for life, but the world still seemed pale to me, without its usual vividness.

And Orval was very wise. Nothing could have resurrected my spirit as much as the writing course did. I could lose myself in my assignments, and I discovered that writing was a channel that helped release the grief locked inside.

I'd never considered writing as a way to earn a living. All I'd ever heard was the phrase "starving artist," along with the fact that a person needed a *real* job to earn a living. But when I received the check in the mail, it gave me a different perspective. When I considered all the time I'd put into writing and rewriting the article, I hadn't earned much per hour for my work. But it had given me a huge amount of satisfaction.

Ben Logan was a wonderful teacher. He was full of stories that made indelible points, like the one about the writer who kept a rotten apple in a nearby wastebasket when he wrote. The smell reminded him to think of all five senses as he described something. I started keeping a crabapple on my desk to serve that same purpose.

I discovered that writing wasn't the mystery I'd thought it to be. I still had those moments when words emerged from an unknown place deep within me, but I also saw how I could polish those words until they gleamed.

The morning after the check arrived, while Naomi was napping, the other kids were off at school, and Kenny was at work, the doorbell rang. I opened it to a man holding a bouquet of flowers.

This was another new experience. The only time I'd ever received flowers was when Kenny brought me a single rose after the births of each of our babies. Fresh flowers were and would always be an incredible luxury to me.

I buried my nose in the arrangement of white daisies, tulips, lilacs, hydrangeas, and daffodils, letting the fragrance fill me and their colors lift my spirits, reminding me spring was beginning to burst outdoors.

I opened the handwritten card: "Hope Springs Eternal! JoAnne, your editor friend from *Family Circle*." My eyes blurred with tears. This was one of the most touching moments in my life. I wanted to just stand with my face in the flowers, absorbing all the meaning, thought, and feeling that went into such kindness. I hoped someday I could afford to return the touching gesture that represented an appreciation and understanding beyond words.

When you live in the country, not far from the highway, you can hear almost every car drive by. I was serving Naomi a small plate of lunch at the little kids' table when I heard a vehicle approach. I looked out the window and saw the rural mail carrier's car pause at our mailbox and then pull back out onto the highway.

"When you're finished with your lunch, we'll walk to get the mail," I said as I wiped a rag across the kitchen counter.

"Bojo? Sugar lumps?" Naomi suggested, her eyes beaming up at me.

"OK," I agreed with a smile. "As soon as you're done eating."

"I'm done!" she exclaimed, managing to clean her plate in mere seconds.

Reaching into the cupboard, I grabbed a handful of sugar lumps and stuffed them into the pocket of my green vest. I bent to wipe applesauce off Naomi's face, and we were out the door. Hand in hand, we walked across the lawn toward the neighbor's pasture where he had so graciously agreed to let us keep my horse. Bojo spotted us, whinnied, and galloped toward us. He tossed his head side to side, full of spunk and energy even at age sixteen.

At the fence, I knelt in the grass. "Here, honey, remember how I taught you to hold it?" I placed the white cube of sugar into the flat open palm of Naomi's hand, and she reached through the fence. Bojo lowered his gigantic head, opened his soft furry muzzle, and the cube disappeared, leaving only a crunching sound behind. Naomi squealed with excitement, rubbed her hands together gleefully, and asked for more.

It had become our after-lunch routine before nap time: a short walk, some fresh air in the warm sunshine, a little attention for Bojo. Then we walked down the driveway to get the mail. These days, it was usually bills, nothing very exciting.

The gravel crunched beneath our tennis shoes. Every few steps, Naomi stopped, picked up a favorite stone, and tossed it ahead of us. When I opened the mailbox, there were two magazines. One was *Farm and Ranch*, which Kenny adored. As the winner of their Forty-Hour-Week Contest, I received a free lifetime subscription.

I was shuffling through the junk flyers and bills when my eyes fell upon the *Family Circle* magazine. Oh my God, I whispered to myself, this must be the issue with our story in it.

I pulled off the clear plastic sleeve. There it was on the cover in full color — the photo of our family on the courthouse steps as our farm was auctioned off. I opened the magazine and saw my article and the words "By Sue Massey."

My head seesawed between elation and disbelief. I wondered how the final story would come off, given the endless phone conversations I'd had with the *Family Circle* editor as we worked to capture the essence of my story while holding true to the magazine's style.

I clutched the mail against my chest, grabbed Naomi by the hand, and said, "Come on, let's race. Winner gets a box of animal crackers."

While she munched her crackers, I flipped to page 13, and there it was: my byline and my words, slightly shifted, but very close to my voice. Pictures of the kids and the farm, the land we'd loved and lost, were strewn along the outer edges of the pages.

I sat down and read the article as if I were someone who didn't know the story, trying to imagine that person's reaction. Then I closed the magazine and stared again at the cover, suffused with a new feeling, perhaps one of a new beginning.

In November of 1986, eight months after moving into the rental house, I turned thirty. Atop my lingering depression, I felt another layer of sorrow. I'd never lamented a birthday before, but there was something about the age of thirty. We had five healthy children, and of course our family was large enough. But most of my life so far had been consumed with the excitement of having babies, and I felt a bit lost to think that era was now over. I would have to turn my energy and focus elsewhere.

The kids and Kenny were waiting for me to unwrap my birthday gifts. I opened the small package first. It was a Cross pen, slender and sleek. I was still taking the campus writing class with Ben Logan, and this was Kenny's way of telling me he supported me 100 percent. As I turned the silver pen over in my hand, I could sense that it was the nicest pen I'd ever held. It fit my hand perfectly.

The kids couldn't wait, coaxing me to open the big present. When I pulled off the wrapping paper, I was struck dumb with amazement. It was an electric, correctable typewriter — state-of-the-art in the eighties.

I took those gifts to heart and began a period of writing that opened a well inside me. I would wake at 3:00 a.m. when everyone was asleep, the house dark and still, and let the emotions flow through my fingertips. Only while writing was I able to release the hovering grief, the loneliness, the relentless worry. The brief respite was far more valuable than sleep to me. I could always catch a nap with Naomi in the early afternoon before the kids came home from school.

Sue Massey

One warm evening in April, the whole family crowded into the car, and we drove a mile down the road to a hidden, private lake. It belonged to our neighbor, who had told us to visit as often as we liked. Kenny and I sat by the water's edge watching the kids play.

I had always loved the water, and it was beautiful by the lake. A few calves grazed nearby. A fish jumped and splashed back into the water, and the kids squealed. If I had been myself, I would have relished the scene, but as hard as I tried, a sadness beyond my control settled into me. When I looked into the water, I saw only misery looking back at me. I was so disappointed in myself. The kids were having so much fun, and all I could think was to go home and pull the covers over my head. Disappear like the little turtle who poked his head up for an instant and then melted soundlessly into the mud at the water's edge.

Dusk closed in, and we drove back to the rental house. As I maneuvered myself out of the car and turned to pick up Naomi, I saw Kenny standing stock-still, gazing toward our neighbor's farm with a wistful, lost look on his face. My eyes crossed the landscape and I noticed the neighbor plowing the nearby field. It was spring. Every farmer yearned to be in the field when spring arrived. The thought of Kenny's heartache made me feel even worse.

The days were long and dark as I worked with my psychiatrist to recover from my depression. Every week we talked things through, and then he adjusted my prescription. We experimented with many different meds. None made me feel much better, and some made me feel much worse. Those that took my creative highs away made me feel only half alive. I wondered if I would ever feel like myself again.

One late afternoon, I was home alone with Naomi, and we had just laid our heads down for a nap together when I began to hallucinate.

I was terrified, yet I couldn't move. When I was finally able to break out of the trance, I ran to the phone and called my doctor. He told me that hallucinations were sometimes a side effect of a drug he'd prescribed, and he told me to stop taking it immediately.

I was a bit leery whenever my doctor suggested a new med. I worried about the possible side effects, like the hallucinations, horrible nightmares, and blankets of fog in my head. Still, together we established a plan that worked for me. I was desperate to reclaim my self.

Inch by inch, I moved forward. Each day was an uphill climb, sometimes one step ahead, then two backwards as I labored to patch myself together. It was an exhausting, emotionally grueling trek from the bottom of a cavernous pit.

Over the years, through intermittent phases of therapy, I discovered everyone is uniquely wired. Some people can handle more stress, more challenges in life, while some are overwhelmed by the smallest shifts in their day. I had made a fateful decision when I was seven and my kitten was crushed to death. Holding her in my arms, deluged by emotions too vast for me to handle, I'd decided that if I didn't have control over something, I would simply move on. I wouldn't dwell on it. I taught myself to roll with it, like when we were kids and tucked our arms tightly against our sides to tumble down the hill. That way, we wouldn't hurt ourselves.

But the depression that landed me in the hospital was completely different. There was no way to move past it and leave it behind. Stomping on it, yelling at it, telling it to go away — none of that worked.

Day after day, I struggled to pull myself out of the quagmire. I noticed I would have five bad days, then one good day in which I lost myself in the playful delight of our children, thinking and hoping that this would last, that I had recovered. Then, day seven would arrive and sorrow would fill me again, paralyzing me as if my feet were balls of lead.

Sue Massey

I would stand in the kitchen, immobilized, unable to think of a single thing to cook for supper. The pleasure I once took in putting together healthy, tantalizing meals for my family was gone. I wondered if I would ever take joy in it again.

I kept going to therapy, knowing it was crucial to my recovery. But after an hour with my psychologist, I would be exhausted and more confused than ever. When I got home, I would collapse on the couch and lie there replaying the conversation, trying to make sense of it. I would read pamphlets on how to recover from depression, but I'd already tried all the suggestions. It was as if I had a bad virus that had to run its course. I could not will it away.

Then I would have a good day, when things seemed clearer and I felt hopeful again, then four bad days.

Writing provided an outlet for the toxic emotions stuck inside me. I discovered there were words for how I felt, and when I wrote and then reread them, it was as if the burden of pain was released.

One day, I stood at the window where I could see Kenny puttering on his truck overhaul and Kelli shooting hoops. The hollow bouncing, bouncing, bouncing of her basketball penetrated the wall of desolation, and I realized: Oh, my goodness, Kelli looks so grown up. I'd been so miserable, so in a fog, working so hard to recover that I hadn't noticed how much the kids were growing. In just a few years, Kelli would be a teenager.

A few days later, Kenny came home from his university job and mentioned that a UW rental house had become available and that we qualified to rent it. The rent would be taken out of Kenny's paycheck each month. We decided to take the plunge.

During the summer of 1989, we packed up and moved to a house on the edge of Madison. The oldest home in the area, it had a fenced-in yard, three bedrooms upstairs, a tiny bathroom downstairs, original hardwood floors, and plenty of room. It was poorly designed with a bad traffic flow, but I wasn't going to complain. The rental rate fit our budget, and it was our ticket into Madison. Kenny was working in the farm labor division of University Research Farms, which was directly across the road from our new home. Our new location simplified his life immensely, cut out hours of commuting for him, and gave him more family time.

It was a leap for all of us. Kelli went from a class of fifty kids to a middle school of seven hundred. I enrolled the next three children in an elementary school in a country-like setting. Knowing the three of them would have one another to lean on helped me feel less guilty about uprooting them.

Naomi wasn't yet in school, so she and I had our own daily schedule. Eventually, I would get a job, but for now I was working on getting well. Our days fell into a routine with walks, library hour, lunch, and nap time. Soon the older kids would be home from school and Kenny in from work, and then there would be supper to fix, homework to tackle, laundry to do, toys to pick up, and finally bedtime. And so the circle continued.

The routine helped me stay focused, though there were still days now and then when crawling under the covers looked more than inviting. But, with five kids and a husband who was working much of the time, that was simply not an option.

I continued to go to therapy appointments twice a month and took an antidepressant daily. Good days began to outnumber bad days. I would feel sad only once or twice a month, and my old zest for life started to trickle back. When I realized that I could experience a full recovery from depression, I was so elated and relieved, so happy to know that one day I would feel like my old self again.

"What's in the box?"

The five kids were on the floor at my parents' home ready to open their Christmas presents. Everything was the image of holiday perfection: the house, the decorations, the dinner table complete with Mom's handmade place tags, the gifts all wrapped with shiny bows and tucked neatly beneath a freshly cut balsam. Mom was meticulous

Sue Massey

in everything she did, right down to spending the exact amount of money, to the penny, on each one of us.

"This present has all our names on it. Can we open it now?" Corey pleaded.

All five kids had fingers grasping a seam of the wrapping paper, ready to tear, looking my way for the OK. When I smiled and nodded, paper flew in all directions like confetti falling from the sky. There was nothing like five little kids to make the holidays fun.

As soon as the print on the cardboard box was exposed through the wrapping paper, Kelli squealed, "Look, it's a red wagon, a Flyer!" Flyer was the top brand for kids' wagons, and while our family wasn't usually brand-conscious, this was one trademark we vehicle-loving farmers knew.

Corey, who loved anything with wheels, went wild, pulling Kenny from his chair to cut the box open with his pocket knife. The kids wrestled the wagon from the box, and we all ooh'ed and ah'ed over it. It was gleaming, cherry-red, and beautiful.

Within my deep gratitude toward my parents for this wonderful gift was a soaring sense of liberation. I could now pull the kids anywhere and everywhere, and the older ones could pull and run alongside the wagon, too, and I would know exactly where they were: in or near the wagon. I was always counting heads and holding hands. This magical gift would set me free.

Oh, the places we did go with that red wagon. I pulled the kids in it nearly every day. When the four older kids were in school, Naomi and I had our own routine with the wagon. I would pull her up and down the roads that looped around the research plots. The harder I pulled, the faster my heart would beat. With every step, I heard my doctor's voice telling me that I would need a vigorous physical outlet for the rest of my life. Exercise was a vital part of becoming mentally healthy.

When the sky was blue and the sun warm, I loved our daily walks with the wagon. When the ferocious wind blew, cutting through us like a knife, it wasn't as much fun, but we didn't let the cold stop us. We'd bundle up and follow our usual routine. I was determined to mend the pieces of my splintered self.

We used the wagon for everything: filled it with fresh-cut grass in the spring and leaves in the fall. The manual task was good for me both physically and emotionally, warming me inside and out.

We walked in snow and rain. When it rained, we wore raincoats and rubber boots and played in the puddles together. Naomi and I grew close as I pulled her behind me in the wagon and, little by little, worked to reclaim my emotional life. The red wagon was built to ride the wind, and she did.

It came with all the force of an unexpected blow. I had gone to my appointment as usual, believing it would transpire as it always had before.

By now, my psychiatrist's office had become all too familiar: the tweed couch, the box of Kleenex, his framed college degrees, the five-inch-thick research manuals lining his bookshelf. I knew every inch of it.

That particular morning, I handed him a wooden dove with an olive branch in its beak and the word "Peace" that I'd hand-painted for him. A tiny gift, a small token of the journey he'd taken with me toward recovery.

He thanked me for the gift and asked how I was doing.

"Better," I said. "I'm feeling more hopeful than I have in a long time."

It had been a long road. Now, four years after my hospitalization for depression, my therapy sessions had grown farther and farther apart. Through trial and error and a huge dose of patience, we'd found the perfect match in an antidepressant that worked for me, and I was well on the way to a full recovery.

Sue Massey

"You're doing great," the doctor said. "Let's see you in a year. I'm going to discontinue the Diazepam and we'll gradually reduce the antidepressant you're taking." His eyes moved between me and his notepad.

My feeling of peace and well-being dissolved. "Wait, what did you say about the Diazepam? Discontinue it?"

I hoped I had misheard him.

"Yes," he said. "I feel you no longer need it."

I couldn't believe his words. It was as if a branch had fallen from a tree, ripped off by a powerful gust of wind, and landed on my head. How could I convince him that I still needed the tiny pill that I viewed as my savior?

"But what if I have a panic attack? And how will I get to sleep at night?"

"Sue, Diazepam is a controlled substance, very addictive. It's time for you to go without it. You'll be fine. If anything comes up, feel free to call me. " He swiveled his chair to face his desk.

Fear flooded me. I thought longingly about the orange bottle beside my bed. Only three pills were left. Then what?

⌒⌒⌒

I turned off the car engine and sat, immobile. I was still there when Kenny's car pulled up beside mine.

"Hey, kid." He hadn't called me that since our dating days.

I burst into tears.

"Oh, my God, what's wrong, Sue?" He leaned into my open car window.

"I just saw my doctor. He won't refill my Diazepam. Kenny, every night after the kids are in bed, I look forward to my Diazepam. It's the reprieve in my day. It's the only way I know to turn myself off."

"I'm sorry, Sue." He opened my car door and reached for my hand to help me out. "Sue, maybe it's a good thing. I mean, I know it feels awful right now, but you're strong, you can do this. The kids and I will help you. We'll stand with you every step of the way."

Together we walked into the house.

"Why's Mommy been crying?" Corey blurted out. Hearing him, the rest of the kids came running, all eyes on me.

"Mommy saw her doctor today, and he took away some pills that he says she no longer needs. It's not easy to break a habit, so we're all going to help her adjust to life without those pills," Kenny told the kids.

"Mom, Dee and I can make grilled cheese sandwiches for supper if you want to lie down for a while," Kelli offered.

"Kelli, mac and cheese, too?" Naomi pleaded.

"Thanks, guys. I think I'll take you up on that and go to my room for a bit."

As I climbed the narrow stairway, my feet felt encased in wet cement. I dragged myself onto the quilted surface of our bed, the patchwork of faded lavender and mint green, tied by my grandmother's hands. I could hear Kenny and the kids downstairs, and yet I felt utterly alone.

I looked yearningly toward the bottle of Diazepam on my bedstand, the wonder pill that quieted my panic attacks and let my brain, with its constant flow of energy and ideas, take a break, rest for a while. When I put those pills into my mouth, I felt the bliss of numbness, as if a tiny baby spider crawled down each of my limbs, curled into a slumbering ball, and left me feeling nothing. I was always wound so tight, the numbness was like a blanket, a comfort, a high of relief I craved every day.

I propped my pillow up, reached for the bottle, and unscrewed the lid. Tipping the bottle back and forth, my hands shaking, I watched the three pills roll around inside.

I was scared to death. How would I cope when night fell? How would I lull the cauldron of feelings that bubbled inside me? What would I do without the little pill I had grown to count on? She had become my best friend, the friend who soothed me, got me through the days and nights, hushed my disheveled nerves.

I wanted the numb feeling she gave me so badly I could hardly breathe.

Somewhere inside, I'd known I was hooked but had pushed the fact away. And like any addict, when I thought about living without my drug, panic overtook me.

I didn't know how I could go on. But I had no choice. I had to try.

Kenny and the kids helped me through it. The first few days were excruciating, but with each day that passed, I thought less and less about the crutch. I remembered the things that had sustained me before I fell into the disabling depression. I kept myself busy and dived into things I loved to do, playing with the kids, taking long walks, and letting nature soothe me.

The doctor had encouraged me to find physical outlets for my energy, and I chose ones that were fun for me: dancing, biking, swimming laps at the local pool. I was especially drawn to activities, like riding my horse or my bike, that gave me a chance to feel the wind in my face. My childhood friend, the wind, became my friend again, much more trustworthy than the one in the orange vial.

A V of honking geese glided through the azure sky. It was one of the last warm days before winter. Every fall, though I loved each of our four Midwestern seasons, I felt a hollow note of melancholy, not wanting the carefree days of summer to pass — the sandals, the shorts, eating outdoors, and tending the garden.

Soon we would reach for our bulky winter coats, the thick goosedown gear that hung in the back corner of our closet. I knew I would miss my friend the wind caressing my face and tousling my hair. For in winter, she turned bitter and left my fingertips white and numb.

I lay on a blanket, looking skyward as their convoy moved south, honking, flapping. Their V pattern reminded me of our family: By flying together, each goose provided extra lift and reduced air resistance for the one flying behind it. Studies proved that this arrangement allowed them to fly farther with 70 percent less energy spent.

When a goose dropped out of formation, it quickly returned to take advantage of the boost that came from flying together. I thought of the days that turned into months and then into years when I was so depressed that it was only through the lifting power of my family and friends that I pulled through the darkness.

And the most amazing fact was that the geese rotated leadership. When the front-flying goose had expended most of its energy, it dropped to the rear, where resistance was lightest, and another goose moved to the leadership position.

If a goose became ill or hurt and fell behind, two fellow geese dropped out of the configuration to assist. They instinctively helped one another. Their honking was the way they kept in touch so that they shifted position and advanced seamlessly.

It was our family's instinct that kept us in a V design. We faced so many unknowns: Illness could strike at any time, setbacks were continual. The rotation of position gave everyone the chance to lead as we continued toward our destination.

Like the V of Canadian geese, marriage was a constant team effort. It was critical to communicate needs and feelings in a safe environment, free of judgment and criticism, anchored in respect, appreciation, and trust. Like the geese, when we fell back, took a rest, and let ourselves be lifted by the flight wind, we renewed our spirits. It was a delicate, constant flight.

Horrifying as my depression had been, it taught me how crucial it was for marriage partners to communicate. Even before we were married, I knew that Kenny and his family held their feelings close. I had always been like an open book, while Kenny was much more reserved. As I kept trying to move toward a more open relationship, Kenny seemed resistant. Miscommunication and tension still hovered between us.

When I returned from my one-week inpatient stay in the psych ward, I told Kenny what the doctors had made clear to me. My breakdown came because of all the untold feelings, the unnamed grief. It wasn't losing the farm that had derailed me; it was the silence surrounding it. It was the overflow of dark emotions with no place to put them. I was like the goose that tried to fly in isolation. It was the surest way to death.

I tried several times to open up a conversation with Kenny, but he remained at a distance. At first, just getting through each day was so hard for me that I let things slide, too tired to fight. But as I began to feel better, I resolved to find a path to communication with him, a way to lighten both our burdens.

Finally, after waiting till the time seemed right, I told him, "Kenny, something isn't working here. We need to talk more. We have to discuss how we're feeling."

"We're fine. Just a busy stretch. We'll get through it."

"No, Kenny, it's more fundamental than that. I bet a couple sessions with a marriage counselor will put us back on track."

"I'm not going to a marriage counselor. Our personal business is our business."

I knew that this was a defining moment, too important to let go. If I didn't take a stand, I was certain I couldn't survive in this marriage, not the way it was now, not the way I was suffocating under the mountains of silence

"Marriage counseling is confidential; no one will ever know what we talk about there. Sometimes a third set of eyes can shed new light on an issue we hadn't even noticed. We're so busy working and caring for the kids, it's like we've forgotten to appreciate what each of us does to keep this ball rolling."

"I'm not going." He reached for his hat and headed toward the door.

He didn't hear a word I said, I thought. I should have known. Whenever conflict threatened, his habitual response was to escape.

I was going to have to do something I never thought I'd do.

I pulled my suitcase down from the closet shelf, stuffing clothes, makeup, and shoes inside. I zipped it shut, grabbed my purse, and called my brother on the phone.

"Hey, Bruce, it's Sue. Say, Kenny and I are having some major differences. I want to get marriage counseling, and he won't hear of it. I hate to ask, but could I crash at your place for a week or so? That'll give him time to realize I'm not willing to go on like this… The kids'll be fine. I'll talk to them… See you in a few."

I rolled my suitcase into the living room, where the kids were reading and watching *Sesame Street*.

"Where ya going, Mom?" Ten eyes fused on me, on my suitcase.

I sat on the edge of the couch. "Come here for a minute." I gestured to the five of them. They huddled instantly at my feet and on my lap.

"I'm going to stay with your Uncle Bruce for a few days. Dad and I have had a disagreement. It has nothing to do with you kids and everything to do with how out of balance our lives have become. Here's the phone number at Bruce's house, and you know my work number. Call me anytime. I'll miss you like crazy, I love you to pieces. I know we can get through this. My hope is that Dad will realize I'm serious about getting our marriage on track with a bit of counseling. As much as I don't want to leave, I can't think of any other way to get through to him."

"What about us?"

"Kelli will be in charge, and if you don't listen to what she says, I want her to call me immediately."

They all looked at Kelli. She looked solemn, up for the task.

"I promise this is only temporary. I have to believe this will only strengthen us, our marriage, and our family." I kissed and hugged each one and wheeled my suitcase out.

Sue Massey

Thankfully, in a matter of days, Kenny called and asked me to come home. He said our marriage was worth fighting for and agreed to go to counseling with me.

We walked into the first session with ruffled feathers, angry and frustrated, and walked out heavy in thought. Expressing our feelings was difficult for us both, but listening, talking, and sorting through all our issues with a professional, objective ear, I'm convinced, saved our marriage, just as my own personal therapy saved me.

Hard as those first sessions with the marriage counselor were, it got easier. We learned valuable, concrete steps that we applied to our daily life.

After a series of sessions, we were back on track. The experience was so positive that we knew we would return if we felt derailed again. It wasn't unusual for everything to work smoothly for a while till financial strain, family demands, and our wildly different personalities acted like a downdraft that sent us backward again. Weary and drained, our initial reaction would be one of avoidance. Then one of us would remind the other how to get back into sync with the tips we'd learned.

Once we opened up about our feelings, we realized how misguided perceptions can be. Talking opened us up to becoming a team, lifting off in the same direction, once again fitting together like pieces of a puzzle: a beautiful puzzle titled Kenny and Sue.

CHAPTER 14

Cocoon

I was cleaning a shelf in our closet when a twelve-foot, lime-green remnant tumbled down on my head. Where it came from, I had no idea. I was about to toss it aside to donate to Goodwill when suddenly the vision of a caterpillar came into my mind.

The green of the material reminded me of the caterpillars I used to find in the farm pastures I explored as a child. I loved to lie on the ground and watch them inch their way up and down the leaves, munching mouthful after mouthful of the decadent green.

One day when I was eight, I decided to bring a caterpillar home so I could watch it turn into a butterfly. I captured several and put them in a shoebox that I'd lined with grass.

I can still see the look on my mom's face when she returned from a conference with my teacher several days later. She told me the teacher had opened my desk to show her the shoebox with the caterpillars inside. Mom was taken aback, yet not terribly surprised.

I told her that whenever I was bored I would peek inside the shoebox to see if my caterpillars had begun to spin their cocoons. It was like an experiment.

Mom handed me the box. "The teacher wants you to keep it at home and not in your desk at school," she told me.

I took the box, grateful that the teacher hadn't thrown it out, ran upstairs, and tucked it safely under my bed.

Every day, I would drop milkweed leaves and droplets of water inside the box for the squirming, munching caterpillars. One day when I opened the box, the wiggling had stopped. Tucked on one side of the grassy bed were cocoons with the caterpillars woven tightly inside.

From then on, I watched my caterpillars almost constantly, using a magnifying glass to see if anything was happening inside the cocoons. It seemed like forever before, finally, I noticed that the cocoons' color was changing and the outlines of wings were beginning to appear.

And like magic, one day I found my first damp-winged butterfly stretching its new legs, trying to pull itself free from the cocoon. I lay on my tummy, elbows bent, chin in the palms of my hands, completely captivated by the miracle happening before my eyes.

First one leg, then two, then one wing, then another until the butterfly was free. It nibbled on a milkweed leaf as it unfolded into a beautiful orange and black monarch butterfly.

I ran downstairs clutching my box to show my mom. She looked astonished.

"Sue, you did it! How beautiful! What are you going to do with the butterfly now?"

"Release it into the sky," I told her. That had been my plan all along. The big blue sky was where it would be free to fly.

Now, sitting on the closet floor, I smiled as I remembered the jubilation I felt watching my butterfly lift off into the blue. Then I looked back at the fabric on the wood floor in front of me. It was lime green, exactly like a luna moth caterpillar. (My monarch butterfly had come from a yellow-and-black-striped caterpillar, which eats mostly milkweed, but I often saw luna moth caterpillars eating leaves from walnut trees, and their bright-green color was impossible to forget.)

Halloween was a week away, and I'd been waiting for an idea for the kids' costumes to hit me. Suddenly it did.

I cut holes in the green fabric — holes for each child's head and arms to poke through. The kids would be a giant, twelve-foot long caterpillar. I bought five pairs of matching black tights and five headbands that wobbled like the antennas of a caterpillar.

That's all there was to it. Through the years, I'd learned: Keep it simple. No masks or makeup. If they tripped and cried, their face paint would streak and ruin their costumes.

This was the part of being a mother that I had most looked forward to when I was a kid imagining having my own family. I relished chances to make things special for my kids in ways that cost nothing but a bit of time, creativity, and resourcefulness, the way my mom had done for my siblings and me.

A week later, as the sun was beginning to drop, we parked the van in front of my brother's home. The five kids jumped out, and Kenny and I pulled the caterpillar costume over their heads and popped their headbands on.

Off they went to knock on the front door. Each child had a pumpkin for candy in one hand while the other hand held on to the sibling in front. I could hear them practicing their lines: "Trick or treat, Uncle Bruce." Their ten legs in black tights looked adorable crossing the lawn in birth order: Kelli, Dee, Corey, Maron, and Naomi.

Within minutes, I realized I hadn't thought about the different lengths of the children's strides. The older kids were bumping into each other, while the little ones could barely keep up. It looked hilarious and endearing at the same time. Kenny and I turned away, bursting with laughter, afraid they might hear. This was a serious team effort, and they were making a determined attempt to walk in unison until they reached the door for the ultimate treat, candy.

The front door opened, and I heard my brother say, "Wow! I've never seen a five-headed caterpillar before. You guys deserve a treat."

Kenny and I waved at Bruce and stifled our laughter again as the kids tried to turn without tripping over the sibling in front of them.

Sue Massey

When they reached the van, we slipped the green fabric off and buckled their seatbelts as they checked out their treat buckets.

Sitting in the front passenger seat, I turned and looked back at five happy trick or treaters, unwrapping caramels and candy bars and stuffing them into their mouths. "You did great!" and they beamed as we drove toward Blanchardville and Hollandale to trick or treat both sets of grandparents.

As we hit the country roads, I thought what a typical Halloween night in Wisconsin it was, windy and drizzling, with a few wet, glistening leaves stuck to the windshield. The leaves were orange and sheer, their dark central veins eminent. They reminded me of the wet wings of my monarch butterfly — the wings that gave it the ability to fly. As I smiled at my five little ones, I knew one day they too would fly away. Until then, I would nurture and watch over them carefully, as I had done with my little caterpillars.

Knowing that Naomi would start kindergarten in the fall, giving me more time for myself, I began searching for a part-time, low-stress position. I was hired at the corporate office of TDS (Telephone and Data Systems) Computing Services, a large information technology company headquartered in Madison and Chicago. I immediately loved the job — working as a receptionist — and interacting with the people.

A year into the position, my manager, Pam, came into my office and handed me a piece of paper. "That's the job description for the communications editor position that just opened up," she said. "I think you would be a perfect match for it. I'll give you a good recommendation."

My mouth dropped as I glanced at the description. "Wow, thanks for suggesting it," I said, "but I haven't had any formal training in editing, and I'm not exactly a technical person."

"Don't worry about that," she said. "TDS will educate you in everything you need to know."

It was one of the best "yes" decisions I made in my life. I was a little intimidated when I started as editor, but Pam was right. It was a perfect position for someone who was open to learning and growing.

The main focus of the job was putting together a company newsletter. As I interviewed employees and wrote pieces about them, I found I had a knack for it.

The back page of each newsletter was designated "After Hours" and focused on an employee's favorite hobby outside of their work day. To get a feel for each pastime, I would shadow the person: I found myself turkey hunting in a blind at 4:00 a.m., fly fishing on a remote river, training police dogs, flying around the track in a race car, and looping through the air in a small plane. This part of my job was a thrill for me.

I also enjoyed putting articles together with pictures. I learned desktop publishing and had fun experimenting with graphics to make the newsletter visually interesting. I could disappear into graphic designing the way I had with my box of crayons as a little girl.

Sue Massey

CHAPTER 15

Gambel's Quail

Their feathered heads pointed forward into the tangled brush. With their topknot feathers and forward-tilting plumes, their flight was explosive and powerful. I found these plump, baseball-sized birds with short, broad wings totally endearing. They darted beneath the desert shrubs in little family clutches, always on the move. I loved the little comma-like plumes on top of their heads, always pointing forward. In life and when writing, I love a comma. It gives me a moment to pause, to think, to arrange the words in my head with the feelings in my heart before pressing ahead like the brave little Gambel's quail that instinctively presses into the unknown underbrush.

Every morning, from my bedroom window, the dawn light catches a special piece of rusty garden art, the outline of a sun with a Gambel's quail inside. It is framed by a delicate tangle of emerald ivy. When the ivy vines get unruly, I tame them, trimming them with my favorite hand pruner so that I can see the sun and quail again.

I remember the moment I first set eyes on the piece of art. I was attending a seminar called "Dialogue in the Desert" on a remote ranch near Phoenix. During my stay, I saw the hand-cut metal piece hanging in the outdoor area of an art gallery, the warm Southwest sun beaming down. I knew it would be the perfect memento of my trip. It would remind me of what a landmark this was for me.

It was my first business trip as communications editor for TDS. As I drove through the desert in my rental car, I fell in love with the Southwest. The starkness of the desert seemed to make the color of a flower even more striking than usual. The saguaro cactuses stood like soldiers, heads and arms reaching out as they watched over the flatland below.

Off in the distance, a beautiful row of white-capped mountains framed the horizon, and gratitude filled my heart. Here I was, just a country girl, flying to and from Phoenix, renting a car on my own to attend a communications seminar, all a business expense.

Each day at the seminar, as well as at TDS, was a learning experience. I was like the little roadrunner on the desert floor, scooting here and there to catch whatever droplets of water I could to quench my thirst to learn.

I knew that in five days I would be driving back to the Phoenix airport, overwhelmed with thankfulness to have been given this opportunity, and like the Gambel's quail, my comma plume would be tilted forward, pressing into the unknown, trusting the instincts within.

In addition to his state job, Kenny had been mowing lawns for extra income. Word-of-mouth referrals began pouring in, and we realized we could turn his side jobs into a full-time business.

Then he was offered a sizeable contract, maintaining the lawn for a large homeowners' association. He was dying to take on the challenge, but it was too much to do while keeping his full-time job. We had to make a tough decision: Should we take a risk and start our own landscaping business with this contract as the seed? Or should we turn down the contract and keep going as we had been?

Although Kenny was never one to complain, he'd become less and less happy working for the state, where he was told what to do with nowhere to plug in his ideas or his vast amount of farm experi-

Sue Massey

ence. He never adjusted to the bureaucracy, and it pained him to be forced to quit working for scheduled breaks and lunch hour. A farmer through and through, all he knew was to work until the job was done.

After much reflection, we decided to take the leap and start a small business. We would call it Masseys Landscaping. We were both thrilled that we would have something to call our own, something we could build together.

Every choice reverberates, of course. The consequences aren't always apparent at first and may even take generations to disclose themselves. This time, however, the fallout was immediate and harsh. Our rental house, which was just beginning to seem like home, was university-owned, and only university employees could live there. The inexpensive rent we were paying was one of the biggest perks of Kenny's job. If he quit his job, we would have to move.

House-hunting became our main focus, and we were able to find a modest rental home in the area. But just after Kenny turned in his resignation, we received word that the rental had been sold. We were now homeless again.

I was reminded of flowers yanked from the soil just as they'd started to bloom. Once again, worry became my daily companion as I tried to find us a place to live. With each day that passed I felt more and more desperate.

I did what I had done the last time we'd had our home plucked away from us. I told everyone I knew about our predicament and asked Kenny to do the same.

It was my mom who came to the rescue this time. She called to tell me she'd seen a sign just up the road from us: "Home for Sale by Owner."

After Sunday dinner, the kids, Kenny, and I jumped in the van to go take a look. When I saw the yellow ranch house, my heart sank. I knew we would never fit into the teeny place.

As we walked inside, I went to the kitchen window and couldn't believe my eyes.

"Kenny, look!" I called.

He came to stand beside me. We were looking out past a huge back yard to a sprawling farm field.

It was planted in corn.

We looked at each other, smiles spreading across our faces.

Mom had told us she would loan us money for a down payment if we found a house we wanted to buy. While the house was small, we knew we could make it work, and someday perhaps we could save our money and delve into home remodeling projects. We put an offer in at once and leapt for joy when it was accepted.

We finally owned a piece of land again.

Meanwhile, both TDS and I were growing. During my years there, I'd soaked up everything around me. In a way it felt as if I'd earned a college degree.

At the time, TDS offered each employee ten days of free education a year, and I took full advantage of that wonderful perk. I was able to acquire a hands-on education, which was exactly how I enjoyed learning. I was flown to seminars and encouraged to join a professional organization, where I learned even more from leaders in the communications field. I adsorbed the wisdom of those who inspired me.

I cherished the time I'd spent at TDS, but I felt ready for a new challenge. The newsletter I was overseeing would soon be moving from a paper publication to a digital version, which didn't excite me as much. As TDS developed its phone, high-speed Internet, and TV services, the technical environment expanded, and I spent most of my time on the computer and less time working with people and collaborating on creative projects. Kenny and I were both accustomed to being on our own in the out-of-doors, working hard for something that was ours, not someone else's, something that belonged to us.

The plan was for me to help Kenny as much as I could with our new landscaping business while keeping my position at TDS so that we had health insurance and I could keep absorbing business knowledge. I plunged into the marketing of Masseys Landscaping and helped to design a logo incorporating symbols of each of the four seasons and the line "Into the Earth." The idea of the two of us bury-

Sue Massey

ing our hands in the earth again to earn a living felt like another step toward going home.

"Naomi, you and I are on a mission today. This is a job that takes two, and you will be my helper."

She beamed at the idea of being given a big-girl responsibility.

"OK, here we go." I grabbed some boxes of flyers promoting Masseys Landscaping. I'd created them on the used computer and desktop publishing software I'd bought from TDS.

"Where are we going?" Naomi asked as we walked to the car. That was her infamous question.

"You'll see." Within minutes we pulled into a new neighborhood: Streets were being built, sod being laid in newly occupied homes, trees installed, sidewalks poured. A bustle of opportunity everywhere, I thought.

"Where are we?" Naomi asked.

I pulled to the curb to explain my idea. "This is the perfect place to introduce our landscaping business. It's a brand new subdivision. They'll need someone to mow their lawns and clear their snow, and that could be us."

Naomi rolled down her window and looked out. "Where do we put the flyers?"

"Well, it's illegal to put them in the mailbox, and we can't afford postage," I explained, "so we'll stuff them in the newspaper boxes or behind the flag of the mailbox. Don't worry, I'll show you."

Two newspaper boxes later, I said, "You're an absolute pro at this, Naomi. You're doing great. I'm so excited to think someone might read our flyer and sign up for our services." I pulled the car as close as I could to the next newspaper box, and Naomi leaned out the window and shoved a flyer in.

"What do we do with the houses being built that don't have newspaper boxes?"

"No worries, we'll come back in a week or two and catch the new homeowners. What I like about this concept is: These are new clients who need our services; it's not like we're taking work away from someone else. I've always felt that there's enough work out here for everyone, and this little marketing strategy is ours. Yours and mine, Naomi!"

"Hey, Mom, look." She pointed toward a couple getting out of their car and walking into their new home. "Where's their newspaper box?"

"See the bucket attached to that post? That's their temporary box. Watch this." I pulled over, parked, jumped out, slid a flyer under their windshield wiper, and hopped back into the car. Two driveways later, I tucked a flyer under the two-by-fours by a door with "Sold" taped to the glass.

"Wow, how cool is that?" Naomi's eyes sparkled with shared enthusiasm.

"I know. Don't you just love this? Sometimes I get so enthused about marketing, your dad has to reign me in and remind me we have to be able to provide the work. Marketing excites me, Naomi. I think it's because of the possibilities, the hope that something will evolve as a result of our efforts."

As I swung out of the neighborhood, I thought about how, as kids, my siblings and I sold sweet corn at the end of our farm driveway, each of us assuming roles geared to our personalities. Bruce always calculated how much we would earn if we sold all the corn we'd picked. Sandy liked to package the ears neatly in bags, ready to sell. And I bounced around like a cheerleader waving a sign at each car that drove by, a sign I'd created that read, "Baker's Dozen for $1.00!"

I glanced at the clock on the dash. "Look, that only took us an hour. We did great. I couldn't have done it without your help. Thanks, Naomi!"

"It was fun. I can't wait to do it again with you."

"We deserve a treat. How about a bran muffin at our favorite place?"

"*Yes!*"

We clicked the tips of our pinky fingers in mid-air between our car seats. "Mission accomplished. Now we just have to wait for the phone to ring to see if our marketing plan was a success."

"I bet there will be messages on the machine as soon as we get home." Her smile was so wide her dimples appeared.

~ ⌣ ⌣ ⌢

We had created a monster.

"Sue, no more flyers. We have more work than we can handle." Kenny spoke from beside his dresser as he filled his pockets with the usual trinkets for his day: loose change, billfold, pocket knife, cell phone. He was staring at the notepad, filled with names and callback numbers, that sat beside the phone.

Once I started marketing, it was such a thrill that I never wanted to stop. It was like a game: If we stuffed fifty flyers into the newspaper boxes in a new subdivision, how many calls would come in? Kenny was right; I needed to be reined in.

As our business grew, so did our house and garden. We began remodeling the tiny house, adding bedrooms, a larger bathroom, and big windows to create a feeling of being outside. The backyard gardens became a place I could take clients to show them a variety of plantings and stimulate ideas for their own landscape projects. It was also a sanctuary where I could restore my spirit. There were pockets of color: the blue corner; the orange lane; the country patch where roots ran deep; red, yellow, and chartreuse ribbons of color. Some years there was a theme to the annual border of color, and sometimes whatever was left over from client projects got planted in our yard. Sometimes nursery stock, tossed out as junk by clients, found a home in our garden, where it flourished.

Then there was the treehouse that Kenny built with some Mennonite friends in the fork of the backyard poplar. Complete with a double bed, reading lamp, a couple of old chairs, and a handful of my oil paintings, with a suspension bridge connecting it to our second-floor deck, it was everyone's favorite spot to sip lemonade, view the gardens below, and savor the sunsets.

In a sheltered corner beneath the treehouse, a small coop housed my flock of hens. Every morning they would burst out, excited to greet the day. Though winters were often cold and harsh, the hens seemed happy and hardy. I could see them from the kitchen window strutting around on top of the snow. They gave movement and life to the gardens and always brought a smile to my face.

The aspen tree stood bare like an undressed torso, her cloak of golden leaves in a crumpled pile at her feet. Her pale, olive-colored trunk and reaching arms seemed to shiver in the chilly air, but there was nothing she could do except endure.

I stood beside the aspen, snapping a picture of our five nearly grown kids with Pikes Peak in the background. My feelings were mixed. I loved being on this family vacation in the Rocky Mountains, but from this moment forward our family would forever be changed.

It was the fall of 1994. Kelli, our oldest, would start college in another week, and this trip marked the end of our family of seven as we knew it. A landscaping client had loaned us their motor home for the road trip, and another client begged us to stay in their Breckenridge condo. Kenny had always gone above and beyond for everyone, and this was their way of thanking him — thanking all of us, really, for as he helped so many, the rest of us pitched in, picking up the slack on the home front.

When we arrived at the condo, we piled our bags inside, took a few moments to admire the gorgeous home, and then went in search of a stable. We'd asked each of the kids to pick one thing they wanted to do on the trip, and Naomi had decided on horseback riding.

We found a ranch that leased horses to us for the afternoon, and we all had a wonderful time cantering through the mountains — all except Maron, who decided horseback riding wasn't her thing. That evening as we ate dinner in the condo's large kitchen, the kids couldn't stop laughing at how Maron's horse kept trying to wipe her off his back by rubbing against tree trunks. He could sense Maron's gentle spirit and took full advantage of it. Maron laughed just as hard as everyone else. "At least I tried," she said.

The next morning, it was Corey's turn to pick what he wanted to do. His choice was to ride the gondola up the mountain. It was glorious on the mountaintop. We hiked a mountain pass and discovered fields of wildflowers that stretched for miles. As multicolored as my mother's thread box, the flowers were like a flowing carpet as far as the eye could see.

I smiled at the way each child's choice of activity reflected an intrinsic passion, each one completely different. Dee decided she wanted to visit an art museum. Kelli wanted to browse in a sports shop and buy some athletic gear. Maron loved geology and digging for things, so we found a place to pan for gold. Kenny and I didn't care what we did. The joy was in being together and watching the kids' glowing faces.

I'd first laid eyes on the Rockies on our honeymoon trip in 1974, and their steep, cliff-lined sides covered with evergreens, aspens, and bluff outcroppings, soaring up to glistening white peaks, had captured my heart. Taken by their beauty, young and carefree with no clue what lay before us, Kenny and I had vowed to return to Pikes Peak for our tenth anniversary. And we did. We made that 1984 trip under the most modest of means, both of car and pocketbook, and while there, I discovered I was with baby again, number five.

At the time I never dreamt that ten years later we would return for a third trip to the mountains, only this time embarking on a new kind of journey, one of letting go. During our twenty-hour road trip home, I had plenty of time to think about my feelings and how life would be as Kelli went off to college. As quickly as they came into our family, all five would be leaving the nest. And like the aspen standing naked in the autumn wind, I too had no choice but to endure. New incantations, those of surrender — all is as it's meant to be; this too shall pass; let it go; let it be — joined the mantras I carried inside to help me withstand whatever life brought my way.

We waved good-bye. Tears blurred my eyes, and an empty ache filled my heart as we piled into the van and headed back toward Wisconsin.

Our family of seven was now six, and a year from now, it would be Dee's turn to leave the nest. She'd already grown restless, ready to follow Kelli to college.

The University of Minnesota seemed forever away. The van was quiet. We were each lost in thought, remembering what a huge part of our life Kelli had been, recalling her head bent eagerly over the sports page each morning, the echo of her bouncing basketball, her bedroom wall papered with inspirational clippings that spoke to her, a bedroom now vacant, only the familiar scent of her and a few remnants left behind.

Five long hours later, we arrived home and, like a family of fledglings, flew in different directions, I to Kelli's bedroom, where I buried my head into her pillow and let our eighteen years together swirl through my head. I had planned to spend more time with Kelli. Instead, she became like a second mom to the younger kids as daily struggles consumed my days. Somewhere in the tangled pile of life, I hoped the adversities had given her an inner strength that would carry her through her own trials and triumphs in life.

"Mom! Where's Mom?" Corey banged into the room. "What's for supper? We're starving. I'm really hungry for that creamed chipped beef you put over toast, Ma. Can you make that?"

"Yes, I'll be there in a minute," I replied.

On the merry-go-round of life, there was precious little time for grief. There were now four kids, a husband, a business, and a living to earn. As I walked out the door of Kelli's bedroom, I read the snippet she'd left taped on her dresser mirror: Push On.

And push on we did.

Sue Massey

I was visiting Kenny's dad as he recovered from a fall when I surprised myself by pouring my heart out. I told him I was at my wits' end with Corey, who was now a teenager. He was on medicine for his ADHD but still acted impulsively from time to time, not connecting consequence with action. Recently he and a friend had gotten in trouble with the police.

Sitting on the chair next to Orval's bed, I broke down and told him I didn't know what to do. I had never had any involvement with the law, and I felt completely helpless, utterly ashamed, horrified, and fearful that Corey would end up with a criminal record due to his impetuosity.

Having a special-needs child can be overwhelming, painful, and exhausting. Corey's records were three inches thick. They had outgrown the flat folder and spread into an accordion file. His life was a series of endless hills to climb: therapy sessions, anger management appointments, speech therapy, school meetings, testing, tutoring, problems at school, attempts to find the right combination of medicines, constant headaches, and stomach issues.

If we'd had the financial means, we would have placed him in a private school. Instead, I had to fight to enroll him in a special-education curriculum. At first, I was told that he tested too high in some areas to be eligible for special-ed. But I knew he was drowning in regular public-school classes. After writing a number of letters and meeting innumerable times with school officials, I was able to get him into special-ed.

Somewhere along the way, it occurred to me that I might have ADHD myself. I'd always had problems in school, finding it hard to sit still, to focus enough to read a book, to listen to lectures without feeling restless — tendencies I'd seen in my father as well.

At one of Corey's appointments, I asked the doctor about it. She tested me and said that I had some ADHD tendencies but that my strengths overcame the weaknesses and she wouldn't diagnose me as ADHD. However, I could relate to Corey's struggles. How often I'd told Corey that he was very special, gifted in many ways, wired in a unique way. Just as I'd always focused on Corey's strengths, I tried to do the same with myself. I realized that my hyperactivity had given me the energy to accomplish a great deal that I couldn't have done otherwise. There were blessings as well as drawbacks to being, in my mother's words, "high strung." I tried to focus on the benefits.

At the time, ADHD wasn't well known or understood by most people, so I didn't speak of Corey's ADHD very often. I kept the diagnosis close to myself. But as Corey grew into the world, I realized that it took a community to raise a child, and I began to open up. As I slowly found my voice to speak of it, I began to shed the skin of embarrassment, the feeling that I, or we, had done something wrong.

Orval shook his head from side to side and clicked his tongue as he listened to my fears about Corey. He helped me talk through the problems and possible solutions. As I kissed Orval good-bye, I was amazed at how much better I felt. For the first time, I had an inkling of the freedom that might lie in unburdening myself to someone other than Kenny. Marriage counseling had helped Kenny and me talk more openly about our feelings, and my psychologist's room was another place where I had learned to express my emotions. Now the possibility of talking frankly outside of those two safe relationships crept into my thoughts.

Yet, in the shadows of my mind, a dark secret still lurked every minute of every day. I tried to make sense of it, but I couldn't. So I stuffed it away, hoping one day I would come to terms with it. For now I was too engrossed in the needs of others to take time to plumb the depths of my own.

The years of starting Masseys Landscaping and watching it flourish were exhilarating. But at the same time, some of those years were the most agonizing of my life.

Sue Massey

A year after Kelli left, Dee joined her big sister at the University of Minnesota. As the two oldest, Kelli and Dee had understood the challenges we faced in the wake of losing the farm and must have sensed that one more straw would break our family, so they seemed to put their teen rebellion on hold until they both went off to college. When they did rebel and break the family ties to find their own voices, they did it by distancing themselves from us. They withdrew from our family completely. In a way, I understood. There were so many needs in our family that they must have found it hard to draw close without pitching in to help rather than concentrating on becoming adult women themselves.

Even as I did my best to make sense of it, I missed them terribly. It was as if they were MIA and had fallen off the face of the earth, into a place I couldn't reach.

Back when Kenny had been working long hours, the two older girls had helped me manage the family, becoming almost like my best friends. When I lost touch with them, an awful gap opened up, one of grief and loss that I knew wouldn't heal till they returned to the fold.

The hardest part was going to bed at night and wondering if they were OK, if they were safe. I prayed. I spent sleepless nights wondering what I'd done wrong to cause this separation. When I felt exhausted in thought, I told myself, this too shall pass, forced myself to let go, and fell into a deep sleep that I secretly hoped would last for a week.

I vented my pain to only a few close friends and a wonderful therapist, who taught me that sometimes we try to rationalize irrational circumstances. I discovered support groups for people with estranged family members and realized that such estrangement was more common than one would think. Like mental illness, people tend to shy away from talking about it.

The five of us who remained pulled together, drawing strength from our shared hurt and becoming a strong unit. Together, we vowed that if the girls returned, we would welcome them with open arms, no questions asked, and if they ever wanted to talk about it, we would listen; otherwise we would simply move forward.

With Kelli and Dee on their own in the world, our family of five evolved. I got to know Corey, Maron, and Naomi in a whole new way. Household chores shifted, and they helped one another with homework and daily needs. The craziness of our still-hectic schedules left us little free time to dwell on the crack, the break in our family.

People told us that if we had a strong family, Kelli and Dee would eventually return, and that's exactly what happened. After working hard to find their voices in the world, they did come back. As we rebuilt our relationship, I was determined to grow from the experience, working to improve my communication skills. I learned that, as a mother of adult children, I couldn't fix everything in their lives, but I could listen, openly and without judgment. I could relax my grip and simply listen.

Sue Massey

CHAPTER 16

Yellow Finch

Whenever I see a yellow finch, I pause. It's Easter Sunday, and we're gathered for a family dinner at Mom and Dad's. We're seated around the kitchen table, passing bowls and platters heaped with ham, mashed potatoes, gravy, vegetables, salads, rolls...

"Mom, stop, there isn't any room left on the table," I protest. She stands in her kitchen, passing the platters out like a mini assembly line, all the while critiquing, how this could have been... or that was too... and I won't make that again...

The chatter around the table is of what's new in high school... Is the garden up? Does Dad like his new mower? How's art class? Can I get this recipe for the salad? How's work? Did you taste this fabulous tomato dish? I look over at Kenny, and there are no words to describe the contented pleasure his face reflects.

"Hey, look!" I point.

The clanging forks and conversation fall silent as everyone looks toward the bird feeder outside the window. "Mom, six, seven. Wow, I see at least seven finches. That's amazing." All eyes shift outward.

"Ma and I been watching 'em all spring," Dad says. "Those little fellas can really eat." He reaches for a second scoop of mashed potatoes.

"I've never seen so many yellow finches in one spot." I'm mesmerized.

"Sandy, did you get green beans?" My dad reaches across the table. "These are straight from Ma's garden last year. I think she canned some thirty or so jars." Pride spreads across Dad's face as he passes Sandy a bowl heaped with green beans.

Half my brain is on the conversation around the table, the other half on the finches as they playfully hang upside down, flutter, and spar with one another outside. Just beyond the hayfield, now green with alfalfa, are the outcropping of rocks we played on as kids.

"Do you ever miss milking, Dad?" I glance toward the head of the table, Dad's spot.

"Nope. Night and morning for over forty years, that was enough for me. Ma and I are busy with other things now. Town and church activities keep us more than busy. Lately, Ma's doctors' appointments been taking us into Madison every week. Isn't that UW Hospital somethin'? Man, that place is huge. It took a while, but we finally got it figured out." He looks toward Mom. "Ma, sit down. Come eat."

She pulls her chair out to sit, and everyone passes the food in her direction.

"How've you been feeling, Mom?" I ask.

"I get tired easy, so I do a little, then rest, do a little, then rest." She places a piece of cheddar cheese on the side of her plate.

"Do a little? Look at this meal. What you call 'little,' some would barely get done in a day."

The clock on the wall chimes, and I look up. It's 12:30. My parents may have retired off the farm, but their lives still run by the clock. Sunday dinner is always at 12:00 sharp.

I look at the finches, their color as brilliant as the sun, and wonder what next year will bring. Mom was diagnosed with multiple myeloma six years ago, and they told her she might have seven years to live. She has done the chemo-radiation thing, lost her hair, then seemed to recover her strength. Today, she looks like the picture of health.

How can she possibly have a terminal illness? I can't lose my mom to cancer when I'm only forty-three and we have so much yet to do together.

If she doesn't make it another year, then what? What will we do next Easter, and what about Maron's graduation from high school, one year from now? When Maron was a baby, Mom helped with her every day so that I could continue to work at the vet clinic. She would bring Maron by the clinic so that I could nurse, then take her back to the farm. Mom and Dad came to everything: Sunday School programs, ball games, dance recitals, swim meets, concerts, baptisms, Boy Scout and Girl Scout events, confirmations, birthdays, graduations, holidays, picnics. We celebrated everything together, and with five kids, there was always something going on.

I look out the window toward the horizon that once was mine. I wonder if my childhood patch of wildflowers is still there, just beyond the crest of the hill.

Those flowers marked my childhood, just as the yellow finch will mark this moment in time: a moment when all is right in my world. We are together, sharing a meal, talking of life, reminiscing the old days.

Inside the pages of my mind, I am little and running through the buttercups and violets, picking handfuls for my mom. Later she'll place them in a vase in the middle of our table for everyone to see. And when we gather around for supper, I'll look at my bouquet and remember my walk down the dirt path, up and over the hill and onto my favorite rock, its surface warmed by the sun's rays. I can feel the rock beneath me, the delicate stems I hold carefully in my small fist, the breeze so fresh and clean it carries my thoughts away. For a moment, I'm lost in a world rich in simplicity until I remember I need to give the flowers to my mom before they wilt, and I leap off the rock, running as fast as I can toward home.

I slipped on the silver ring.

Sitting on the edge of my parents' double bed, part of a blond bedroom set they'd had their entire married life, I thought of the hundreds of times I twisted that ring on Mom's finger when I sat beside her in the church pew counting the minutes until the sermon was over and I was free to run outside.

I had tried to imagine this day. I knew the cancer would eventually take Mom's life, but I had no idea how deep the hurt would burrow. Like a little prairie dog, the grief would pop its head out suddenly and unexpectedly. I was having a terrible time getting a handle on it.

Just a week ago, I'd gone to visit her. She was sitting with the newspaper in her lap, her persistent cough making it nearly impossible to have a conversation. Our eyes were glued on a TV screen with no idea what we were watching. Then, from someplace deep inside me, I felt a yearning: a yearning to sit one last time on my mom's lap. I looked at her and asked.

"Sit on my lap?" She set her paper to the side, still coughing. "I guess so."

I crawled up onto her lap, all forty-three years of me. I wrapped my arms around her warm neck, placed my ear against her chest, and listened to the faint beat of her heart.

I knew this would be the last time I would ever sit on my mom's lap, the lap where I always felt loved and safe. This was the last time I could smell her sweet scent, kiss her soft cheek, and run my fingers through her thick hair. The hum of her sewing machine had been quiet for the past week, so I knew the end was near. For as long as she possibly could, I knew my mom would manage her daily chores. She loved her chores.

I thought of the hundred spools of thread in every imaginable color in Mom's thread box and wondered where they would go. I thought of the little scrap of paper I'd saved from the last time she sewed on a button for me, her familiar handwritten note — "button" — that reminded her of what needed to be mended. Whenever I opened my jewelry case, I saw "button" and sometimes when I was faced with a

Sue Massey

tough day, I touched that little note and heard her whisper, "Sue, you can do it." Every day, I glanced at my little portrait of Mom standing in her flower garden. She was smiling, in her bed of blooms. A scarf on her bare head, she was smiling even though beneath her sweatshirt she was wearing a bandage and brace from surgery. She was smiling.

She shifted beneath me. Her cough deepened. If only I could stay here with her forever. The only comfort I could muster was knowing that someday very soon she would no longer cough. She would be in a place without pain. When we met in that place, I would crawl up onto her lap and feel her warmth and love for me. I would burrow my face into her soft, plush skin and savor the moment, for it would be just me, and my mom, and her lap.

"Sue, take the ring if you want." My sister's voice came to me. "I might as well take most of these clothes to Goodwill."

I glanced back down at Mom's ring. Two simple silver bands held five birthstones: one for each of us. Two red garnets for my mom's and brother's January birthdays, a purple gem for my sister's February birthday, topaz for me in November, and moonstone for Dad's birthday in June. As I touched each stone, I recalled how Mom made each of us feel so special on our birthdays, baking our favorite cake and carrying it to the table as she sang "Happy Birthday."

In November, despite her weakened condition, she had baked a final birthday cake for me: angel food with lemon filling and light, fluffy seven-minute frosting. With every bite, I felt bittersweet sorrow sweep over me. I wanted to eat the cake, but there was a lump in the back of my throat that prevented me from swallowing.

Standing in the face of death, I found that everything mattered: the sound of her voice, her scent, her soft skin, her gentle, tireless ways. I could not imagine life without her. What would life be for Dad, married forty-seven years? I imagined his pain to be like the loss of a limb.

"I'm going to the kitchen to help Dad write thank-you notes," Sandy said. "Come join us when you're ready."

"OK," I said, still gazing down at the silver ring. Right now, I just needed to sit on their bed and remember their voices with each other, Mom at her sewing machine, Dad at his workbench. Despite the peaks and valleys, I thought they would say they had a good life.

The doorbell rang. I opened it to a man holding a beautiful crimson poinsettia, nearly the size of a small Christmas tree.

Awestruck, certain it had been delivered to the wrong house, I read the card: "We were so sorry to hear about the loss of your mom. Love, G & M." I felt tears well up at the thoughtfulness of these dear friends and clients. I carried the plant to a corner table in the kitchen, and thought, "This will be our Christmas tree this year. We'll place the gifts beneath it and clip a star onto the top branch: our first Christmas without Mom."

That was a December of record snowfall for southern Wisconsin. Masseys Landscaping was among the businesses that plowed the one hundred inches of snow that fell that winter. By March, Kenny looked exhausted, and we were headed into the busiest months of the landscaping season — the time when everyone wants everything yesterday, and there are never enough hands to do all the work.

Somewhere in the mix, a companion appeared in my dad's life. Dad seemed vulnerable, grieving the loss of the love of his life and relieved to let the new woman take over. The following April, the home my mom and dad had built on a corner of their farm was up for sale, and Dad was moving to Waunakee with his new companion.

I saw the look of hurt on our children's faces when they arrived at the estate sale and saw their childhood memories set in piles tagged with masking tape. Naomi picked up her favorite Bunko game while Maron fingered the skillet Grandma had used to make them crepes for Sunday breakfast. Their eyes met, they dissolved into tears, hugged, and left as if fleeing a crime scene.

I tried to catch them, to comfort them, but I was too late. My heart ached for them. Wasn't one farm sale enough for a family to endure?

Sue Massey

The estate auctioneer turned to me and said, "Hi, Sue, sorry about the loss of your mom." He looked toward the tables, the remains of what was left of our childhood. "This can't be easy, either. I'm sorry."

"Thanks," I said. "It all seems to be happening so fast. We haven't had time to grieve or gather ourselves."

"I can tell you one thing."

"What's that?"

"Your dad won't ever need to make another decision in his life. His new woman is going to handle everything for him."

"True." I nodded as I watched Dad's companion take control of everything at the estate sale, telling everyone what to do where and when.

The blond bedroom set, sold. The pony knickknack that Naomi used to talk to for hours on end when she was little and played at my parents' house. Mom's china, the special set she brought out only for special occasions. Sold.

I picked up a necklace, one of Mom's favorites. The tag read twenty-five cents. I could see the necklace shimmer above the open collar of her blue cotton dress. It looked so nice on her. I set it back on the table. All around me were crowds of people sorting through pieces of our lives strewn out on tables, taped with a value of a quarter or fifty cents. I knew this was not for me.

I turned away, searching for my dad. He was over six feet tall and always wore a farm hat. I spotted him.

"Hey, Dad, I think I'm going to head out."

"Already?"

I nodded, "I love you, Dad. Good luck with the estate sale. Call if you need anything." He hugged and kissed me as he always did, and I hoped that would never change.

I drove through town, past the vet clinic where I once worked, past my grandparents' home, the school, the park, the pool, the post office where Mom had worked, the grocery store, the library, up and over the Pecatonica Bridge. I detoured down a side street past the cemetery. Although I didn't stop, I knew Mom's grave was there.

The lilacs were beginning to bud as the grass turned a light green. Tractors were in the fields. Patches of bright yellow daffodils swayed as if celebrating their release from the snow-covered land. I felt the wind in my face, smelled the fresh clean country air, followed the familiar curving road past the turn-off sign that read "Star Valley Road" where our farm used to be, and aimed the car for Madison and home. I felt the warm tears streak my face, then blow off out the window.

A special aunt, one of my mom's four sisters, handed me a round Tupperware container. "I saved this for you, Suzie. I thought you might like to keep it."

Puzzled, I wondered why my aunt had gone out of her way to give me the old, slightly yellowing container. Nevertheless, I thanked her, took the dish home, and popped it in the cupboard.

The next morning, when I reached for the coffee creamer, my eyes landed on the dish. I snapped open the lid and like a jar of butterflies released from captivity, the memories lifted and flittered and filled me with warmth.

When I was growing up, the Tupperware bowl, filled with sweet brown sugar, graced our kitchen table. For every meal, three times a day, seven days a week, it sat like a quiet bystander as conversations passed back and forth between our family.

The stories that sugar dish could tell. It heard of joy and heartache, challenges and triumphs, daily happenings and plans, silliness and celebration. How my brother Bruce hated the fat on his meat and always sliced it off and slid it over onto Mom's plate. Sandy's love for fresh green beans, Dad's mashed potatoes and gravy. Me thinking about the new kittens I'd discovered in the hay mow that morning. The talk of the day.

As the little butterfly memories escaped from the jar, I felt them. Some of their wings were as soft as a fluttering eyelash, and some landed square on my heart and stayed for a moment.

Every day, I opened the cupboard, and like a mirror into my child-

Sue Massey

hood, I saw the world in which I grew. I understood now why my aunt thought I would like to have the sugar dish, nothing fancy, just plain and simple, and as with each of us, the treasure lay within.

As my fingers flicked through the cards in my recipe file, the sight of Mom's handwriting made me pause, and I could hear her voice telling me exactly how to fold in the flour, how to do this and how to do that. Each recipe brought to life the moment we came together as a family and shared a meal.

Whenever I wanted to feel close to my mom, I flipped the lid on my recipe file and saw her handwriting and signature: Ma Johnson. Mom cooked from her heart.

Assembling ingredients for Mom's sugar cookie recipe, I recalled sitting at her kitchen counter when I was ten years old, dunking a cookie into a cold glass of creamy milk, fresh from our farm bulk cooler. In front of me, I had a rubber mat, a mound of pecan nuts, and a small hammer. It was my job to tap open the smooth, chestnut-colored pecan shells and expose the perfect nutmeat tucked inside. I knew Mom's plan. I'd see these royal beauties show up in a pecan pie, her gooey pecan cinnamon rolls, or as the sweet nutty center of a sugar cookie.

As I tapped, the nuts would shatter, pieces would fly, and I'd scramble across the floor to retrieve them. I was on my tummy on the cool linoleum floor, reaching between the stove and cupboard for an escaped pecan when I looked up at mom on her stepstool. She was a large-framed woman, five-ten, and she looked like a giant towering over me as I asked, "Mom, do you ever take a nap? You're always working." I crawled back onto my chair and reached for my sugar cookie. The pecan that had been pressed into the cookie's center dropped into my glass and sank to the bottom.

"No. No time for naps. Too much to do." She smiled, stepping off the stool to set a stack of china on the table. There was a steady calm about my mom. She worked methodically, task after task, until her day ended in bed beside my father reading the daily paper. The newspaper arrived every morning but was never opened until my parents crawled into their double bed together. Reading seemed to be a luxury, a treat earned after a hard day's work, like the pecan or cherry on top of a banana split.

"Are you going to wash those? They look clean," I said, using my spoon to fish the pecan from the bottom of my milk glass.

"I always do spring and fall house cleaning, you know that, Sue. Everything comes out of the closets and cupboards and gets washed and put back neatly." Mom walked to the sink to wash the first stack of china she'd taken from the cupboard.

"Will I do that when I get big and have a house?" The task looked daunting and boring. Plus, the dishes looked clean before she even started washing them. I couldn't imagine myself doing it.

"You will if you want a nice clean home." She smiled at me over her shoulder as she submerged each plate, single file, into the sudsy water, then into the clear warm rinse water, then into the tray to air dry. She handed me a white, neatly folded dish towel. "If you're really careful, you can help me dry the china."

Great, I thought. Would I like to help wash and dry already clean dishes or go outside and bed the calf pen, sweep the barn, or feed the pigs? I knew my answer. "I think Dad needs my help outside, Mom."

"Imagine that. Sue, you're such a tomboy," Mom said as she placed a clanging handful of silverware in the upright bin of the drying tray.

"Mom, you're washing clean dishes and wiping down walls, closets, and shelves that are already clean. I'm not sure I want to do that. I don't like cleaning all that much. I want to be outside. I like to see results. Like when I feed the animals, they're so happy and content. When I bed the calf pen, the calves frolic around and kick up their heels in joy."

"I feel happy when the house is clean." Mom carried the stack of freshly washed dishes back to the table, grabbed her wash bucket, and wiped out the inside shelf where she planned to set the clean dishes.

Sue Massey

"Hmm." I tapped a pecan with the head of my small metal hammer, and it split in half, exposing a perfectly formed nutmeat that looked like a baby in a crib. I gathered my pile of nutmeats and examined them closely. From a distance they might all look alike, but up close some had folds where others didn't. *Perhaps it's the same way with people*, I thought. *We're each unique, and I just may not have the cleaning wrinkle ingrained in me.*

Years later, when I found myself married, I followed my mother's example and, twice a year, took everything out of every cupboard and washed it. I didn't think about what I was doing; I just knew this is what a good housewife did.

This lasted until my third child was born and I decided I'd much rather spend my precious free time with my kids than washing already clean objects and spaces, and I gave myself permission to stop. It wasn't an easy transition. I had to convince myself it was OK. The letting go of expectations continued to be hard for me, but whenever I managed to do so, I discovered a lightness that made my heart sing.

CHAPTER 17
Foreboding

By now, our landscaping business had tripled in size. Kenny could no longer manage it all and asked me to join him full-time in our business. I'd been handling the marketing newsletters, phone, and invoicing — once again stretching myself between what seemed like two full-time jobs. It would feel like luxury to give up my TDS job and concentrate on Masseys Landscaping. I continued to enjoy my TDS co-workers, but my heart was outside with Kenny, working on the land, helping him grow our business.

When I explained the situation to my manager, she was kind enough to offer me a three-month leave of absence. I was so grateful, because it gave me the opportunity to try out the arrangement before taking the final plunge. If our business didn't make enough money for us to live on, I could return to TDS.

Being in the landscaping business with Kenny was heaven. We worked well together, and we were both doing what we loved. I remember driving out of Madison toward a new country subdivision, the window down on my maroon Silverado pickup, which was tightly packed with flowers to plant for a client, the wind tossing my hair into tangles, and feeling completely immersed in freedom.

I had been to Chicago for TDS business meetings but never for pleasure. It was December, 2008, and our landscaping business was nearing the twenty-year mark. After decades of struggling financially and watching every penny, Kenny and I finally had some money to spare. We decided to treat the kids — all adults now — to a two-night stay in downtown Chicago as part of their Christmas gift.

Kenny and I settled in our hotel room while the kids unpacked in their rooms down the hall. We were sitting on our bed relaxing when the five kids appeared at the door. They were heading out to explore Michigan Avenue on their own. I opened my wallet and handed them each a neatly folded one-hundred-dollar bill.

"You're kidding, Mom... Dad. Really?" They were as elated as two-year-olds on Christmas morning.

"Merry Christmas, guys! If you're going to discover Michigan Avenue, you need a little money in your pocket."

Half an hour later, Kenny and I struck out on our own. The kids had agreed to meet us back at the hotel to dress for dinner in two hours. As we wandered down Michigan Avenue, I turned to Kenny. "You know what my two favorite parts of this weekend are?"

"No, what?"

"I love the thousands and thousands of twinkling lights. But even better is seeing the looks on the kids' faces when they experience something for the first time. Do you see how much they appreciate this opportunity?"

"They can barely handle it."

"I know. It's rare for any of us to splurge like this. But if things keep going the way they are, we'll have many more chances to explore the world."

"I hope so, Sue. I hope so." We hugged each other tight.

After an hour of window shopping and sampling the best caramel corn on Michigan Avenue, Kenny and I walked back to our room. Lounging on the bed, we split a small travel-size bottle of Merlot. An hour later, right on time, the gang burst through the door with bags and packages galore and excited voices: "Wait till you see this." "I've always wanted one of these." "I saw things I've never seen before." "That was amazing," "Look at this!" "How great is that?"

Their enthusiasm made my weekend. "Cool!" I said, admiring their purchases. "Now we have to dress for a seven o'clock dinner reservation. Can we make it? A friend suggested we dine at Lawry's Steak House, so here we go. It's close enough to walk to. See you in the hotel lobby in thirty minutes." With packages in hand, the kids tumbled out the doorway.

The three days and two nights flew by. The ride home was a non-stop stream of reminiscing: "My favorite was eating brunch at the top of the John Hancock building." "I know! The view was unbelievable, and the food was great, too." "I loved the Shedd Aquarium." "I'm so glad we got such good photos of Chicago's skyline." "Shopping on Michigan Avenue was the best." "I felt like I was in another world when they draped our napkins onto our lap and offered to cut our meat." "How about the assistant in the bathroom who handed us a towel to dry our hands?" "The whole trip was an experience we will never forget." "Thanks, Mom and Dad!"

A week after we returned from Chicago, the TV news was on in the kitchen as Kenny and I set the table for dinner. I had just grilled salmon, drizzled it with Hollandaise sauce, sliced bread warm from the oven, and placed a tiny candle on the table between our plates.

I was listening to the news with half an ear as I leaned down to ignite the flame. Then I stopped dead as the newscaster's words penetrated. He'd been discussing the failure of financial institutions such as Lehman Brothers. The result had been a collapse of inflated housing values, and people could face losing their homes.

"Experts are predicting that this could be the beginning of a major economic recession or even a depression as bad as the one in the 1930s," he said.

Sue Massey

I stood stock-still, trying to digest the words. Kenny, who had been listening intently to the newscaster, turned to me, and our eyes met.

"What do you think this means for our business?" I asked.

As usual, Kenny paused for a moment, deep in thought, before he answered. "I don't know," he said slowly. "Our clients are primarily high-end, financially independent, and into the stock market, careful with investments. Let's just hope things turn around fast. If it's a long recession, the whole country could be in trouble, not just us."

"Well, it won't help to worry," I said. But a fear I hadn't felt in years sent a shiver down my spine.

1. There were days I wished I were little again: Sue, Sandy, and Bruce.

2. Our Madison university rental home, 1989.

3. Red Flyer wagon, Naomi and I.

4. Massey cousins.

Sue Massey

5. Searching for the color in my world.

6. Five Masseys move from small rural schools to big city schools.

7. Finding purpose: Corey on our first commercial lawn mower.

8. I discovered cake decorating as a way to earn extra income. Dee's wedding cake was a new, creative challenge for me.

9. Finding refuge at
Women's Week Camp.

10. One-by-one they
leave the nest.

11. Our forever home, 1992.

12. A field of smiling
sunflower faces.

Sue Massey

13. Kenny's beloved John Deere 4020.

14. Born to run equipment (Corey).

15. Reflection: a fall reprieve at Kenny's mom's cabin in northern Wisconsin.

PART IV
HEALING THROUGH THE EARTH

Earth laughs in flowers.

~ Ralph Waldo Emerson

CHAPTER 18

Lifting Up, Falling Back

When Kenny and I started our landscaping business, it was just the two of us — along with ten-year-old Corey, who helped by mowing lawns after school and on weekends. As if we were farming, we worked long days, often through the weekends. Our farm pride, work ethic, and dedication transferred into our new small business.

As our business and reputation grew, we began to hire people to work with us. Eventually, we were able to employ one of the best professional landscape architects in the region. Together, we brainstormed ideas and designs for large and small-scale projects, and Jerry, our architect, meticulously drafted them into works of art. Every project Jerry strategically estimated came in with a profit. We felt we had a dream team. Our personalities and strengths complemented each other. It was a magical time.

When I accepted the fact that we wouldn't be raising the kids on a farm, I threw myself into a new vision: creating landscape designs, beautifying the earth. I'd always loved to garden, and suddenly I found myself obsessed with designing outdoor flower containers for each of our four seasons. To me, the containers seemed like a canvas in which I could paint a living picture with foliage and blooms in endless textures and colors. We had our flowers locally grown, loved to experiment with new trends, and often created our own styles.

We were establishing a name for ourselves as creators of unique gardens. One client hired us to change out and design the seasonal color four times a year at each of his hotels — one of my favorite projects. He wanted his guests to have a "sense of arrival" when they drove up to the entrance of his hotels. I was over-the-top excited when Maron and I flew in his corporate jet to preview outdoor flower container styles and positions at new hotel locations.

The kids were now grown and stepping onto their own paths in life, which thrilled me. They'd become very self-sufficient. The girls, all married now, had paid most of their wedding costs and taken out student loans for college.

As the business flourished, I needed help with the flower orders and design work, so our daughter Maron became my sidekick. Before long, Naomi, our youngest, stepped in and took over the office, which freed me to spend more time meeting with clients, creating land-scape designs and flower containers. Working as a close-knit family team felt in many ways like running a family farm.

Naomi was a techno-wizard. Her obsessive-compulsive tenden-cies were a perfect match with the detailed lists and office tasks. She loved organizing files, keeping the books, and making sure every-thing was shipshape.

Maron had an artistic flair and was my creative partner in design-ing landscapes and containers for our clients. She also worked in the office with Naomi. As the two youngest, Maron and Naomi had a special bond and worked seamlessly together.

As for Corey, working outdoors beside his dad was exactly where he needed to be. Because of his learning disorder and ADHD chal-lenges, Corey learned by watching and doing. And, fortuitously, the way Kenny taught best was not by lecturing but by showing. He only had to show Corey once how to operate any machine, and Corey was off and running.

With each success, Corey's confidence grew. As he helped Kenny in the day-to-day business, he grew to enjoy people and learned to handle problems that came up in the field. Watching the two of them work side by side was like watching a well-oiled engine spin. No words were needed; each of them knew what the other was to do. Through the business, Corey had opportunities to try new things, even oversee the lawn mowing crew. Some were a fit, and some were not. All that mattered was the trying, and he was always willing to try.

Corey was a testament to my belief that people with physical or emotional challenges can be highly successful if they align themselves with supportive, encouraging companions, friends, and co-workers. He was meticulous with every task he took on: weeding a flower bed, pruning a tree, looking for typos in the newsletter I sent bi-annually to our clients. No one was more adept than Corey when it came to operating snow plows, lawnmowers, and especially the skid-steer, the small, handy machine with a large bucket in front that we used to dig and move dirt, rocks, and bushes. He could run the skid-steer as if it were an extension of his hands.

His biggest challenge was learning to pace himself. If the wood splitter broke, he would plunge in and split the entire load of wood by hand, not stopping once till he was finished. He was like Kenny in always making do, working until the job was finished.

Kelli and Dee were still forging their own paths for themselves, Dee by pursuing her degree in art and Kelli as a registered nurse. Although they weren't part of the family business, the office was in our home when they were growing up, and they knew all too well about taking client phone messages and rolling with the daily workload of managing a small business. Though they had their own lives now, they were once again an integral part of the family. I'd always said that when they were ready to rejoin the fold, we would greet them with open arms, and we did.

Maron, Naomi, and I used the lower level of our house as an office, strategy room, and brainstorming space, while you were most likely to find Corey and Kenny at the big shed that held our landscaping and snow removal equipment, which we leased nearby — or, more likely, out in the field, working with the crews.

Maron's husband, Seth, also worked in our business. It was a joy to watch him grow into his role as brick crew manager at Masseys Landscaping. He, Maron, and I often went on road-trip flower runs together, and grew close as we worked elbow to elbow.

For me, the best part of my job was presenting our combined ideas on paper to the client along with pictures and presentations on my iPad. I especially remember the day that Maron and I visited a new client who reminded me of my mother. Like Mom, she had a soft voice and a gentle, straightforward, easy-going way about her. She pointed to a bare patch in her yard and asked if I had any ideas what to do with it. Maron stood dutifully with a pen and clipboard in hand taking down notes as I looked at the modest surroundings and asked if she had a budget in mind. She said about $2,000.

With that, my mind lifted into the clouds, and two visions appeared to me. "I can think of two possibilities," I said. "One is to remove the weeds and rotting garden timbers and reseed the lawn back into grass. Then add a row of dogwood along the chain-link fence to provide backyard screening and color throughout the year. In the winter, the bare stems of red dogwood will stand like a holiday bouquet against the snow.

"That option would be the least expensive," I continued. "My second idea is to clear this area and create a mini English garden with rows of boxwood and crushed granite for the walkways. In the middle of the garden we'll plant a rainbow of perennials, like lavender, and some herbs, like flowering chives for cooking. It will be colorful, beautiful to view from your kitchen window, and easy to tend. It will even provide you with cuttings to clip and put in a vase on your kitchen table or bedroom vanity."

I wasn't sure where these ideas came from. It was as if I had been transported to another world where my vision was so sharp that I could see every detail of a garden that was meant to be. When I stopped speaking, it felt as though I'd been hovering above the earth and suddenly landed back on my feet.

My eyes met Maron's. She looked as if she were five again, captivated by one of my stories.

Then I looked into our client's face. She snapped her fingers, her eyes sparkling. "Option two," she said. "That's exactly what I'd like."

I asked her a few more questions while Maron jotted notes. Then Maron and I headed back to the truck.

"I can't believe what just happened," Maron said as we drove toward our next landscape appointment. "She loved your ideas so much that she gave you a snap of her fingers!"

"I know. That was a near out-of-body experience. What a thrill. I love sharing my ideas so much that sometimes I can't believe I get paid for it. When she snapped her fingers, that was frosting on the cake."

Memories like that one kept me going through the hard times. Though we never had much excess money, for several years we had enough so that I no longer stayed awake at night worrying about paying our bills. The business grew exponentially until it grossed $1.5 million a year. It was both a daily challenge and a thrill. I grew into many hats: marketer, designer, estimator, sales manager, partner, accountant, mediator, mentor, supervisor of work crews, a Jill of all trades.

As the business blossomed, we leased a wonderful piece of land, a high-profile parcel with a shed where we stored our landscaping and snow-removal vehicles and equipment, as well as space where our crews could meet, punch in and out, and pick up orders. As our business continued to flourish, we added a rented trailer, which we perched beside the shed. The next step took us into a ranch-style rental house on the property.

Just as in farm life, there were good years and not so good years. We always did well enough in the good times to get us through the bad — at least till we were hit by a triple whammy.

Sue Massey

First came a winter with no snow, which meant no snow plowing income. Our cushion of emergency funds disappeared.

Then, came a summer with no rain, which meant a drop in lawn mowing and maintenance income, and we slipped further behind.

And the final blow: The economy sank into a recession — the worst in fifty years.

We kept on, stretching our money and time as we could, hoping the economy would improve. But it didn't.

With the recession, out-of-work people began to mow lawns and shovel snow for half the price we charged. There was no way a business like ours, with all the overhead and personnel expenses, could compete with a one-person operation that often didn't claim income tax.

We moved out of the leased office space on the land and back into the lower level of our home. We had to cut expenses, especially fixed expenses, drastically if we were to survive.

But even with our cost-slashing, we kept losing ground. We consulted with a financial advisor, and he delivered the news we'd been trying to deny: The business numbers were upside down. The expenses, debt-loan payments, taxes, and overhead exceeded the income.

I began to shy away from the shop, the space where we stored equipment and where employees punched in and out for work. A few mornings a week, I would greet each of them while I gathered my pruning tools, used my iPad to show them pictures of their completed projects, and told them how much we appreciated their efforts. I'd hand each of them a ten-dollar bill for lunch-a-month (a way to express our gratitude and encourage them to eat together). But I never stayed long. My enthusiasm had waned. I couldn't stop thinking about our finances. Every time we thought we could pay some bills, the IRS pulled money from our account for past-due taxes. As hard as we tried, we couldn't catch up. Just the thought of going to the shop made me sad. Everyone was so devoted, they all deserved raises, but our hands were tied.

Like all farmers and landscapers, we were optimistic by nature, understanding the ebb and flow of things, willing to persevere through life's storms. We were certain the economy would improve. But months turned into years, and the recession only deepened.

Kenny, Maron, Naomi, Corey, and I all started looking for second jobs. We were already spread thin, but we had to find ways to pick up extra money. Kenny began using his welding skills to create beautiful metal sculptures. Maron was growing a name for herself as she delved deeper into painting and sold work at art shows. Naomi worked part time at University Hospital and started selling the stylish line of Thirty One bags. Corey split and delivered firewood.

Looking for a part-time job that would offset the high cost of our health insurance, I emailed my first TDS manager. Though she was surprised to hear I was looking for work outside our landscape business, she hired me on the spot to take over my old receptionist position, now vacated by a gal on maternity leave.

I could hardly believe it. Finally something good had tipped my way.

Indeed, when I thought of all the people who were suffering as a result of the recession, our troubles didn't seem so bad. We didn't always have much food, but we did have enough to eat. While others were losing their homes, we still had our house. After being away from our family for years, Kelli and Dee had returned, while other families were mourning the loss of children they would never see again. I knew that an intact family was the most important thing in the world. I wasn't sure what lay ahead for us, but one thing I knew: Nothing was as important as the bond we shared, and we wouldn't let anything tear us apart.

CHAPTER 19

Kernels of Love

A t least once a week, no matter how busy I was, I had always made time to visit my old friend Bo. I would pull to the side of the road, walk to the fence line, whistle, and call his name. His ears would perk up and he would come running, then nibble at my pockets till he found the sugar lumps buried inside.

I had known his time on earth was coming to an end, but it was still hard to let go of someone who had been with me for so long, ever since I was fifteen. He and I had grown up together. Over the span of his life, he'd been moved from my farm to Kenny's, then to a neighbor's field. After we moved to Madison, he'd been taken in by my parents, a cousin, and finally a dear friend, where we put him to pasture to live out his final days. By then, his coat was dull, his eyes tired, his frame drooping, but he still seemed happy as he stood on the sunny knoll, his tail swishing flies away, his eyes almost closed.

He was thirty-two years old when he died. In all those years, he had never been sick. With each turn in my life, I'd had less time for Bojo, but my love for him had never waned. Despite the years he'd endured, my vision of him hadn't shifted. I always saw him in his glowing prime. He was my guy, along with Kenny, my dream come true. I still envisioned him as the prancing, whinnying, galloping steed he once was, back when we were both young, riding with the thrill of the wind through our chestnut manes.

~~~~

On August 5, she turned eleven. We celebrated.

I set Sophie's plate in front of her and sang "Happy Birthday." Her fluffy tail wagged, and she seemed to enjoy every crumbled morsel of browned ground beef on her plate.

A mix of shitzu and bichon frise, with fur as soft as a duckling's down, Sophie was the perfect match for Kenny and me. Sometimes she made us laugh and raised our spirits. At other times, she was quiet, just there for us. When I had a tough day, I would lie on our bed, and she would crawl up and smother me in her warmth and love. I would bury my face in her black, white, and caramel colored fur, stroke her silky, silvery ears, and feel my stress dissolve.

We'd found Sophie during what I thought of as the boom years of our little business. We were finally earning enough money to put some into savings and spend some on wants as well as needs. Our last child was leaving the nest, and I felt a longing for a puppy to cuddle.

One day, in the middle of a home remodeling project, I thought: What better time to housebreak a puppy than when the old carpets have been removed? When a friend told me about a litter of "teddy-bear" puppies and said there were two left, Kenny and I drove there the next day. The minute I saw Sophie, I felt a connection so strong that it was as if I were a mother meeting her newborn for the first time.

I thought how lucky it was that we'd had those years of good cash flow. If the economy had been as bad as it was now, we never would have taken the plunge and introduced a new puppy into our household, knowing the expense of having a dog.

Over the years, we'd taken Sophie to two expensive surgeries for torn ACLs (anterior cruciate ligaments). "What do people who love

Sue Massey

their pets and can't afford their medical expenses do?" I had said to Kenny. "It breaks my heart to think about it." And now we were in that spot ourselves — tapped out, totally without credit, not to mention the luxury of cash.

Thank goodness we'd found Sophie before the economy crashed. If we hadn't had her to comfort us and make us smile, how would we have gotten through these hard years?

My near constant companion, Sophie was the Massey business mascot, and our clients adored seeing her. She would ride shotgun in her Jeep car seat when I went on client calls and ride between Maron and me when we hit the road to plant flowers for clients. She watched me fill commercial flower pots, tug tarps of debris, talk to clients, prune, run errands, stop by worksites, make callbacks: She was my little co-pilot, game to go everywhere.

I decided that she was meant to be shared, so Sophie and I trained to become a certified pet therapy team. She was made for the job; she had good manners, loved people, and had a vast reservoir of real-world experience, since I had taken her everywhere since she was a puppy. We made a perfect team.

Sophie and I began volunteering every other week at St. Mary's Hospital, where all five kids had been born. It felt so good to give back to the hospital in gratitude for all the care they gave us over the years.

I could tell Sophie enjoyed our volunteer visits as much as I did. Although she was always worn out after an hour at her job, she would come running, tail wagging, the next time she saw me take out her green service vest. She loved the special attention she got when she wore her vest, and it gave her a new purpose.

I soon came to understand why they called what we were doing "therapy." Right before my eyes, I would see patients' whole outlook improve. Just seeing Sophie soothed their pain, anxiety, and loneliness, even before they touched and caressed her. A visit with Sophie was healing, calming, and one of the best medicines a person could ask for.

I had learned this firsthand: Touching the animals on the farm and then my household pets had often been the only thing that consoled me. I could attest to the therapeutic impact of Sophie's steady warmth, undivided devotion, nonjudgmental acceptance, and soft-as-silk ears. Sophie's gift was in being herself: attentive, accepting, and open to being touched.

He sleeps between my legs.

When I was little and lost my favorite black-and-white kitten to an awful accident, I wondered if I would ever have a special kitten like that again.

I do. His name is Jack the Cat. Three years ago, Kenny and I took a drive to pick out a ragdoll kitten. Ragdolls are cats bred to have the friendly, cuddly temperament of a lap dog.

The woman selling the kittens brought them, one by one, from her basement for us to meet. I kept glancing at Kenny, and I could tell that we hadn't yet met our forever kitten. After the eighth kitten, I began to wonder what we were missing. Then, the woman came upstairs with a slate-gray-and-white kitten with markings similar to the little black-and-white kitten of my childhood. She placed him in my lap, and he licked my chin with a tiny meow. I looked at Kenny, and he nodded. We had found our kitten.

Jack the Cat is a very special guy. He rides in the Jeep, welcomes guests into our home, stalks small chippies outdoors, sits on Kenny's morning newspaper insisting on being scratched, and naps in warm piles of laundry. He is full of spunk and is the entertainment at the beginning and end of our day.

Sophie liked being an only child, and Jack sometimes plays a little too rough with his claws, and she snaps and scolds him. But most of the time, she tolerates him.

At night, when we crawl into our nest, Jack jumps up onto the comforter, curls into a doughnut between my buried legs, and falls asleep.

Sue Massey

As kids growing up on the farm, we were told the animals belonged outside. Now that I'm a big kid, I can't imagine our home without our pets living inside with us.

～ ↄ ⌣ ↄ

The morning mist hung like a delicate white veil over the cornfield beyond our back yard. The tassels poked skyward like the fingertips of children wanting to be picked up, to be carried.

There were times when I would have liked to be carried. But I couldn't. With both parents gone, it was my turn to clear a path.

My father died last week. Perhaps that was why I was feeling a moment of wanting to be carried. I wrote a piece for his funeral and surprised myself when I was able to stand at the front of the church and read it. I had felt that when Mom died, I lost my dad, too, and grieved for them both, for Dad was never the same.

Just before the funeral, the usher carried in the oil painting of our farm that I'd painted when I was in high school. As he placed the four-by-two-and-a-half-foot painting beside Dad's casket, a trickle of corn kernels fell out onto the floor. I was amazed that something so simple could spark so many memories inside me. The corn. The ribbons of cornfields that wrapped the rolling Wisconsin countryside. The corn I watched my dad plant each spring. The corn rows I played between as a child. The sweet memories that a single kernel of corn evoked in me. Like a kernel of popcorn, it burst open and filled my heart with feelings of warmth and a yearning for home.

I smiled as I realized the source of the kernels on the church floor. I'd given the painting to my parents, and when Mom died, Dad gave it back to me. I hung it in the treehouse in our back yard. A squirrel must have stored corn in the back of the painting for winter meals. The simple thought touched me, made me grin. A comfort swept over me, knowing Mom was there to take Dad's hand and together they would journey home.

In my heart, I was at peace, I was home.

Dear Dad,

Today is a day about reminiscing, remembering the wonder-filled moments of having you as my dad. Throughout my life, you were always there. You taught me values: integrity, honesty, loyalty, a country work ethic, and above all, to keep the faith. You were there when I was born, took my first steps, started school, was confirmed, then graduated, married, and gave birth to five children, all of whom have your blue eyes. When we lost our farm, you were there. You stood beside us like a rock. You and Mom were always quick to lend a helping hand.

Dad, when I was little, you were my hero. If Mom ever wondered where I was, she'd look you up, and I'd be two steps behind you. You chose a wonderful path in life when you married Mom and raised us on the family farm.

I fondly remember the time we three kids were given pet bunnies, and you loaded us in your pickup and we were off on a mission. We needed a cage for our bunnies, and you were going to build one. I remember kicking around a junkyard until you came upon an old metal frame. You handed the junk dealer a couple bucks and loaded it in the truck. Honestly, I didn't know how you would transform that piece of junk into three separate rabbit cages, but that's what you did.

I saw you grab your saw, your drill, your hammer, and transform that old piece of scrap metal into the most beautiful rabbit hutch I'd ever seen. You even cut windows in the dividers and covered them with mesh so the rabbits could see each other inside their separate cages. It was beyond anything I could have dreamed of for a rabbit hutch.

Sue Massey

Dad, you were never an easy "sell" to new ideas, and I thank you for that, because it forced me to develop the art of persuasion at quite a young age. A steady stream of ideas ran through my head, and I was constantly trying to sell you on one idea or another. It took me fifteen years to convince you that I was old enough for a horse. You always worried that one of us kids would get hurt on one. Almost daily, I colored a picture of a horse from my coloring book, tore it out, and left it on your supper plate with the words, "Please, Dad, can I have one?" When I turned fifteen, we put racks on the back of the pickup and drove to a neighboring farm where there was a colt for sale. I could barely contain my excitement. We parked, I jumped out and ran to the fence, and there he was, my dream. A shabby roan colt, covered in burrs, and untamed, he stood in a heap of overgrown weeds. But inside my mind's eye, I saw my dream come true, and he was beautiful. As we drove home, I couldn't take my eyes off him in the back of our pickup truck. You puffed on your pipe as the song "Mr. Bojangles" played on the radio, and I said, "That'll be his name, Mr. Bojangles." You built him a stall and hung hooks for his halter, pail, and gear, and I was the happiest girl on the face of the earth.

You kept our farm, barn, and sheds immaculate when we were growing up. Time was precious, and it was not to be wasted looking for something. Perhaps that's why you so loved your bibbed overalls. There were so many pockets on those bibs, to a kid they were like a treasure chest waiting to be discovered. When you pushed back your chair from the supper table, that was my cue. I would crawl onto your lap, play with all the pockets on your bibs, and trace the chain that dangled out of your watch pocket. I could feel the faint tick-tick-tick coming from inside.

Your voice was deep and full and rattled inside your chest as you talked with Mom about plans for tomorrow. With each breath you took, my head would raise and lower, raise and lower, my ear pressed against the soft fabric of your worn flannel shirt. Your wide shoulders, huge work-calloused hands with skin permanently tanned from working hours on end in the sun spelled security to me. I loved the way you smelled, a hint of tractor grease, fresh mowed hay, dairy barn, tobacco, and fresh air.

Five minutes was never enough time on your lap. As I felt your work boots drop to the floor and your chair push back, you'd say, "Well, Suzie, it's that time again, time to milk those ol' bossies." I'd wrap my arms around your neck, squeeze on tight, just one last time. You'd kiss Mom on the cheek, thank her for the good supper, reach for your hat on the hook, slip into your two-buckle rubbers, and head out down the worn path toward the barn, and I would follow behind in your foot-steps.

During summer break from school, I loved tagging along to the feed mill with you. You'd have the back of the truck filled with corn and oats to take to the mill for grinding. You would shave, change into a clean striped pair of bibbed overalls, and toss on a splash of aftershave. While the grain was being ground and mixed and poured into gunny sacks, you'd take me into the office and buy me a strawberry soda pop in an icy-cold glass bottle. I would sit on an old wooden chair while you wrote a check to the feed mill. The ladies behind the desk would tease you, and you'd tease them back. Then you'd reach in your pocket and hand me a wintergreen Life Saver, and together we'd head out the door and into the dust and hum of the feed mill.

Once, on the ride home, I remember telling you, "Dad, you always know what to say to people. Sometimes, I can't think

Sue Massey

of anything to say, and sometimes I get so excited the words just tumble out and sound stupid."

You grinned at me from ear to ear and said, "Suzie, you can always talk about the weather." And you were right. Even today, I can hear your reassuring voice in the back of my mind, and over the years, I have even discovered the solace in stillness.

I am grateful for all the gifts you passed on to us: your love of life, your strong will, your abundance of love and devotion to family, and of course, your love for dancing. Everyone knew you worked hard and played hard. You were the fun in every party. It was you who taught me to hop polka in the barn during milking chores. Whenever I hear a big-band song, I can see you pointing at Mom, motioning for her to join you on the dance floor, your feet already in motion. There was something about the beat of a song that you couldn't resist. Your fun-loving streak was contagious.

Like the time when Sandy and I were little and we crawled down the dark hallway to tape-record you snoring at night. In the morning, the two of us were giggling at the breakfast table, and you asked us what was so funny. We set the tape recorder on the table, hit the "on" button, and watched the expression on your face.

"Why, that's not me," you exclaimed.

"Dad, yes, it is. That's just how loud you snore at night. We tape-recorded you because we knew you wouldn't believe us."

"Let me listen again. . . (pause) Why, that's your mother."

I love you, Dad.

Every morning when my eyes opened I had the most beautiful view. It was of my childhood farm: the big white farmhouse with wrap-around porch. The porch where we gathered in summer — my grandparents, parents, siblings, and I — to sip root beer floats, talk about the day, and watch the cars drive by below on Highway 78. The porch where I used to set up little farms using tinker toys and plastic farm animals. The porch where my mom swept and swept and swept the leaves and dust that always collected in the corners, driven by the constant wind.

There was the window above the porch where I would sit at the desk working on my dreaded homework. With the window open, I could hear the sound of the milking pump drifting in, yearning to be out there helping Dad with the chores. I loved learning, just hated homework. It cut into my time outside.

There was the big red barn, flanked by two concrete block silos, the hay mow where most of the kittens were born, the huge maple where I would swing for hours, a prime seat for watching all the daily happenings unfold. There, too, were the paths that lay like the arms of an octopus, outstretched in all directions. Some led to school, some to the fields, some to the pasture land, some through the woods, some to the outcropping of rocks we played on as kids. It was all there, my entire childhood. It lay before me in every stroke I painted when I was seventeen.

Seventeen was many, many moons ago. The painting, after being displayed at Dad's funeral, came home with me. Unable to choose a spot to hang it, I set it on a small white shelf in our bedroom, against the barley-colored wall. The ceiling light shed an iridescent glow like the sun at dawn within our bedroom. At the end of a long day, I could now melt between the sheets and stare at my childhood, all captured in a painting ten feet from my eyes. Every evening as I collected my thoughts from the day, I could reflect upon my childhood. I knew every inch of that farm: the view from every hill, every valley, the dips in the lawn, the apple tree that produced the most apples, the sounds, sights, smells, tastes, the feelings — they were all there alive within

Sue Massey

me. I knew how the landscape looked during every season and all types of weather.

"I hope you leave the painting there," Maron said, poking her head into the bedroom.

"I think I will," I said, gazing at the oil strokes I painted so many years ago. When a section had stumped me, my art teacher would take my seat and show me how to capture the mid-day shadows just right.

~~~

Fall was closing in. The wind twirled clusters of leaves into corners everywhere. The grass was stiff beneath a thin, white blanket of frost.

The days were shorter now. It was pitch-black at five in the morning when I opened the door to let Sophie out and watch her tiny ghostlike figure disappear into the predawn darkness. The air smelled fresh and clean, almost like farm country, and soon the hum of the neighbor's corn dryer from across Mineral Point Road would begin.

I had seen Kenny's eyes on the neighbor's new, gigantic combine, and I knew what was in his heart. He would be in the cab of that combine in five seconds, as fast as he could run across the field, if given half a chance.

I wasn't surprised when he called me later that day. "Sue, it's me. I just wanted to let you know I might be over at the neighbor's for a bit after work tonight. They're harvesting the soybean field. Gonna check out their new combine."

I was elated. He had felt so down about finances lately that he usually came home and curled up in a corner of our bedroom, got lost in his reading. I thought he must be feeling better to want to cross the highway, walk into the neighbor's field, and step back into a dream that once was his.

As I drove home from work, a cloud of soybean dust blew across Mineral Point Road, and I could see the combine in the distance. I hoped Kenny was inside it. I walked through the door, and there sat Sophie and Jack waiting to welcome me home. I dropped my bags and sat for a minute soaking in their soft licks. I heard Kenny's truck pull up, the old Ram with 450,000 miles on it. The back door opened and closed.

"Hey, I thought you'd be combining," I said.

Kenny hung his hat on the hook above the laundry-room door and came dragging in. For the first time, I thought he was looking old. "I thought so too," he said. "Then the lawn mowing crew pulled into the shop and a mower had gone down. I had to fix it so it'll be ready to roll in the morning." He sat down with a sigh.

"Your mechanic couldn't fix it?"

"That would put him into overtime, and we can't afford it."

I took my glasses off, rubbed my eyes. "Is this ever going to end? Honey, I think we're due for a lucky break to come our way."

"You would think." He unlaced his work boots.

"I'm sorry, Kenny. I know you were looking forward to driving the combine. Don't let it go. Try again one day. You know they'll be harvesting those corn and soybean fields for weeks."

"I suppose." He walked to the counter and opened his morning paper, still folded like a log.

Moonlight was beginning to stream across the front lawn. I opened the door. "Looks like a full moon tonight, Kenny." The night sky was aglow. The stillness of our quiet cul-de-sac was broken only by the hum of the neighbor's corn dryer — a constant reminder of the unexpected path our lives had taken. A path we had taken as a family. A path we were trying to make the most of.

CHAPTER 20

Orgasm: In the Mood

The big-band CD music filled the Jeep, and I was in the arms of my dad as he twirled me around on the floor. Dancing with my dad was such a joy. I felt as light as a feather, skimming along, barely touching the smooth surface beneath my feet. Not a thought in my mind, only the ease of the beat. If only I could have one more dance, just one more dance in the arms of my dad, I thought as the music vibrated through the steering wheel of the sunflower-yellow Jeep.

The music touched my soul and demanded that I tap and sing. I wanted to pull the Jeep over and break into a dance on the lawn beneath a tree. I didn't care what anyone thought, I was so happy, so "In the Mood."

I remembered how, as a young woman, I watched couples on the dance floor. Some glided to a rhythm all their own. I decided then that if a man is a good dancer, he must be a good lover, for he knew when to dip, when to sway, when to firmly guide. I could have made love to Kenny during the entire CD, knowing full well I would completely exhaust him. I was a handful, always was, always would be.

"I miss dancing!" I told Kenny later that day as we munched nachos, sitting at the little green bistro table on our deck. "Us dancing. I'm so tired of the day-to-day grind we've fallen into. I wish we could somehow find balance so we'd have energy left for each other at the end of our workday. We pour too much of ourselves into the business."

"I agree, Sue." He shifted slightly and shook his head. "But whatcha gonna do?"

That was Kenny, always willing to accept whatever came his way — the opposite of me, always wanting to fix it, make it better, make it fun.

"If we could get out from under this financial cloud, can you imagine all the energy we'd have to focus on good efforts rather than on constant worry? When I think about it, my mind races with ideas. Kenny, it's like pretending we had a windfall, and what could I do? I could buy that little farm over the hill from us and create art studios and a Village for the Arts and a deli named Sophie's Plate where we'd serve family recipes we've collected over the years. When I think of being debt-free, I'm filled with so many ideas, I can barely handle it!"

"I've noticed." Kenny had been sitting calmly as I flew to the moon and back to earth. He's my rock. He's my reality check when my dreams fill a blue sky. He is the problem solver, the genius as to how to make something work, how to make a dream become reality. He doesn't squash my enthusiasm; instead we share in the dance of life, I in his arms, and he in mine. He is my lover, my equal, my partner in life. A simple look, no words, just a shared song between two hearts, a beat that says it all, we're "In the Mood."

I reached for the thin black case that lay in its spot, the clear, upright makeup organizer that rested above the cubby in my closet. I flipped the lid open and saw my blue-green eyes reflected in the mirror above a square of sparkling pink blush with specks of gold embedded. My skin was tan from working outdoors, but I wanted rosy cheeks. A couple sweeps of the brush, and *voilà*! Like magic, my face had color, matching the sparkle I felt inside. I was good to go, ready to take on the world.

The blush had been named "Orgasm" by the NARS brand. As I set the case back into its cubby, I thought how the word "orgasm" could, on its own, make me blush. I thought of all the wild times Kenny and I had shared. I was usually the instigator, and he was always happy to follow: open to new ideas, new techniques, new places, new... new... different. He rarely turned me down. It was usually a timing factor in our hectic lives. The sly way we managed to connect brought a smile to my face. With Kenny, part of the thrill was in the "shock" factor. Like, let's try this, here's what this is for, touch here, do this, do that, a caress as soft as a feather, grab the liquid silk, and on and on.

I much preferred the natural blush, the afterglow Kenny put into my cheeks after making love. I desperately missed our closeness. The intimate moments: the cuddling, the holding close, the giggles, the whispers, the silk and lace and leather, the inside jokes between just the two of us, the funny little toys that only he and I knew about, the box hidden high on the closet shelf. I missed collapsing into each other's arms, breathless, lost in sheer ecstasy.

Lately, he was bone-tired. Drained. His caring, helpful nature had taken a toll, left him exhausted after saying "yes" to so many requests throughout his long workdays.

The thought of sex hung in the back of my mind amidst the colors, the feelings, the hopes, desires, and dreams. Sex was like creating art, ageless — the ultimate feeling in the world, and it didn't cost a dime. When we were young and broke, no money for entertainment, we went to bed, played happily, like a couple of kids beneath the sheets.

Shy by nature, Kenny was always patient, respectful, waiting for me to shoot him an arrow from my heart. The secret message we'd agreed on was that whenever he was in the mood, he was to spritz on his earthy cologne. I knew what that meant, and the game was on. The scent ignited a spark inside me, which became a flame that needed to burst, to explode and release the glow in my cheeks.

For today, I swirled on the blush with a couple strokes of the brush, but tomorrow, or the next day, maybe next week, after Kenny had a few days off work, a few days out from under the cloud of worry, maybe the spark would reignite, and we would hold each other, two hearts beating in unison, in the afterglow of orgasm.

Sue Massey

CHAPTER 21

The Magic Thread

The phone was ringing as I dove through the door. I answered a breathless "hello" while wiping garden dirt from my hands.

"Mom, it's Dee. I'm calling with some good news. Jacek and I are going to have a baby."

My thoughts shot through the air. I wished I could share a hug, a happy dance with her, but we were states apart. She had moved to Florida to work on her master's after receiving her undergrad degree in fine arts from the Milwaukee Institute of Art and Design. That's where she met Jacek. Just four months earlier, they'd had an intimate wedding in our backyard garden before the two of them headed back to Florida.

I'd imagined this day would arrive, when one of our adult children would call with news of a baby. I loved children, but I wasn't sure I'd recovered from the daily demands of raising our own five children on a shoestring.

When Dee told me that my first grandchild was on the way, my first thought was: Dear God, may their life be filled with happiness, minus the never-ending struggles we faced when our kids were little.

My mind darted back to the years when Kelli and Dee separated themselves from the family. The distance was deep and painful. There was never a day I didn't think of them and wonder how they were doing. Knowing they were very independent, could fend for themselves, and possibly had each other for support were my only consolations.

I had a feeling they, and we, would come through it stronger than before, and we did. I was so happy we were a family of seven again, plus spouses, and soon to meet the newest little member of the Massey family.

There was no question how I felt. "Oh, Dee," I said, "I'm so happy, I can barely stand it!"

I was fortunate enough to be at the births of all four of my grand-kids, three boys and a girl. First came Adam, Dee and Jacek's son, in 2007. Three years later, Maron and Seth's son, Troy, was born. Then, two years after that came Naomi and Dannon's daughter, Savannah. And just one month later, Maron and Seth's second son, Klay, came along. Each of the four births was different, just as each of the babies was a one-of-a-kind marvel.

As the time for our first grandchild's birth grew near, the miles between Wisconsin and Florida seemed achingly long. Kelli felt the same way. She and Dee, as the two oldest kids, were deeply connected. Kelli and her husband, Shawn, both working as registered nurses in California, came up with a plan. They rented a townhouse so that our entire family could be in Florida for the delivery. Kelli, with her special training in labor and delivery, assisted with the birth, while Kenny and I waited right outside the room. Being there for Adam's first moments on earth was something we would never forget.

Recently I talked with Maron about the birth of her two boys. She had asked if I was ever scared, and I replied, "Remember when you were in the hospital about to have a C-section with Troy? I was scared then. I knew what you were in for, and I knew I had to be strong for both of us. That was really hard."

"Yeah, I was terrified. They were about to cut and lift the baby out of me. I was a wreck."

Sue Massey

"When they wheeled you into surgery, you should have seen Seth, dressed in his blue sterile scrubs, ready to meet his first-born son. As he passed through the waiting room he said, 'Game on,' and ten minutes later, we heard the baby cry, and Seth brought him out to meet us. Of all the special family moments in life, that has to be right near the top for me."

"Then we brought him home, and two days later, he started to cry with colic, and it's been three years, and he's still sensitive and demanding."

"I think Troy is very bright and emotionally astute; he picks up on the energy in a room."

"Can you believe Klay and he are brothers?"

"They couldn't be more different in temperament, could they? Klay is Mr. Chill, our happy-go-lucky little guy, who never misses a meal."

"The two of them make quite the pair," she said, laughing. "I'm so glad you were there for both their births."

"I wouldn't have missed such special moments for the world," I said. "I feel an incredible bond with all my grandkids. Something unique happens when you see them take their first breaths."

Our only granddaughter, Savannah Sue, was born five weeks before Klay. We wept — Dannon, Maron and me — as we gathered around Naomi and celebrated Savannah's arrival. It had been a long, strenuous labor.

With the birth of each of my grandbabies, I was awestruck. The little ones dubbed us SuSu and Poppie. The magical miracle of birth will forever be a sparkling light in my life.

It was three days after a fun Halloween of watching the little neighborhood monsters and skeletons, including our own grandchildren, parade door to door. I was determined not to let the "strapped for money" reality stand in the way of enjoying these family milestones.

"It's Sunday, let's do something fun," I said to Kenny. "How much cash do you have in your wallet?"

He and I pooled our money and had ten dollars between us. "We can take Pearl and Sophie to Bagels Forever, grab bagel sandwiches for under eight bucks, and have a picnic," I said. "This warm weather isn't going to last."

Pearl was what we'd named the Harley I'd won, to my astonishment, in a raffle — Pearl because she was as beautiful, dazzling, and unexpected as a jewel in an oyster shell. After buying the lottery ticket, I'd put it out of my mind, and I was flabbergasted when I won.

The 650-pound glowing chrome machine had sexy written all over her. Pearl had become our Sunday ride.

"All set, babe," I told Kenny as I climbed on back with Sophie on my lap. As he swung on, he looked eighteen again — all boy, all tousled hair, all fun.

I leaned over, pulled up his shades, looked into his blue eyes, and whispered, "You look sexzzzyyy," kissed the blush in his cheek, and pushed his shades back down.

And we rode. We rode with the wind in our faces, the sun on our backs, rode like kids again, not a worry in the world, at least not for the next couple hours.

As we ate our picnic by the lake, the wind continued to caress us. Even Sophie seemed to drink in the warm, fresh air as if she knew fall was just around the corner.

On the way home, we stopped by the shop to grab a landscape knife so I could clean out the flower pots before they froze hard. Then Kenny walked me around the shed to show me what needed fixing. It was painful to see.

The happiness from our day dissipated as we walked past all the broken-down trucks and pieces of equipment. By the fourth out-of-order commercial mower, my heart had sunk as low as it could go.

I wondered how Kenny could face this scene day after day and manage to keep going with no working capital to buy parts or repair equipment. I wanted to cry. I was amazed that he saw each broken hunk of machinery as fixable.

Now I realized why I avoided the shop. Everywhere I looked, there were heaps of what to me looked like junk.

I didn't tell Kenny how hopeless it looked to me. I knew he was dispirited, too, and I didn't want to add to his misery.

But I felt even worse when we got home. Our garage and house were disaster areas, too, with stuff accumulated everywhere. Although all the kids had moved out, piles of their belongings remained.

Part of me wanted to rent a giant dumpster or call Goodwill and tell them to pick it all up. I'd been trying to overlook the mess, but ignoring it wouldn't make it better. I knew I'd begun to see only what I wanted to see: smiling faces, a blue sky, the hens scratching in the backyard hosta patch. The mail had started to go unopened, some bill collection phone calls unanswered.

I thought of the depth of sadness that had sent me into the hospital and on a three-year road to recovery. I refused to ever go back. Each morning, when I reached for my low-dose antidepressant, I felt grateful for where I was in my life. Being with people in the low-stress receptionist position at TDS helped me forget the dire situation of our business. Hardly two days ever passed without me swinging by the girls' homes to see the grandkids, whose innocent faces always lifted my spirits. I continued to be physically active and worked at being gentle with myself, an important survival strategy in the midst of business turmoil.

I would pray for strength. I would pray for a miracle, an angel. I would keep writing, releasing the sadness and struggle through my fingertips.

I looked at the mounds of mail building up in the office. Sitting next to the desk, I started shuffling through it, throwing the junk mail into the recycle bin.

"I learned years ago at an administrative seminar to sit next to the recycle bin when going through the mail," I told Naomi and Maron, who were sorting their own piles of paperwork at their desks.

"Great idea," Maron said.

"Thanks for helping with the mail, Mom." Naomi smiled.

"It's kind of a no-win task," I noted. "When I'm done sorting, I know what will be left — a heap of bills."

"I remember when I used to freak out when a bill collector called," said Naomi.

"I know. Now we just roll with it," Maron chimed in.

"The lack of working capital is killing us," I said with a sigh. "If we could pull out of this mess, I know exactly how I'd reorganize our business. We would focus on creative design, skilled installation and maintenance, with relationships at the heart of each project. That's where our passion lies. We would outsource lawn mowing and snow removal, which just drains our spirits. I can just see it. In fact, I dream about it."

"I think about how much easier my job would be if I weren't always worrying about how to divvy up the scarce money that does come in," Naomi said.

"And have you seen Dad lately?" Maron added. "He looks worn out. Something has to give. We can't keep this up. One of us is going to get sick from the stress."

"Believe me, I know," I said. "Friends wonder why we don't just give up the business."

"That's easy for them to say if they haven't stood in our shoes. Our jobs are everything to Naomi and me. We love what we do. We feel it's worth fighting for. And look how Corey has found himself in the business! He lives to work beside Dad." Maron's eyes met Naomi's in agreement.

"I'm so proud of all of you," I said. "And seeing you become such key parts of the family business is a dream come true for me."

Things will get better, I thought. *They just have to.*

I was dressed for work. Thank heavens it was casual attire. My afternoon shift at TDS was a chance to turn off the perpetual-worry switch in my head and lose myself in the simple tasks of greeting people and answering the phone.

The morning had been a string of chores around the house: Start the laundry, feed the pets, load the dishwasher, and submerge myself in a sketch for a client, a small landscape project. While I drew, Naomi and Maron arrived to work in the downstairs office and needed a helping hand with their little ones. With baby on hip, I tossed something together in the crockpot for supper.

I had just enough time before work to swing by Polk Farm Conservancy and eat a turkey sandwich beside the most beautiful sunflower field I'd ever seen. I jumped into the Jeep and a few minutes later was beneath a blue sky, staring at a sea of sunflowers, their uplifted faces following the track of the sun. The simple pureness of the moment seemed to quench the country yearning inside me.

I imagined how the sunflowers would look later. By day's end, as the sun sank, pulling a deep blue sky along with her, the little heads would follow, bowing toward the west, drooping their weary heads, ready for rest. Looking at their golden faces made my heart sing. *A flower that follows the path of the sun and grows plump seeds to feed the birds — how perfect is that?*

I headed back to the Jeep. Several years earlier, Kenny had spotted the sunflower-gold Jeep for sale in a car lot. He'd told me he saw something he knew I couldn't resist and he was right. It was a rugged ride, short and compact, built like a tank for off-roading with the top down. Whenever I drove the sunflower Jeep, with the SUNFLWR license plate, surrounded by the words: "Sunshine All Day Long," I would get smiles, waves, and thumbs-up, and it made my day. It made two of us smile.

There's something irresistible about the bright, happy face of a sunflower. In the language of flowers, the sunflower stands for honesty, happiness, and faith.

～ﻌﻌ◡◡◠

He emptied his pockets, just as he had every night for thirty-eight years.

Thirty-eight years, seven days a week. That was more than fourteen thousand nights, not counting the years he'd emptied his pockets before our paths ever crossed.

I glanced at the two small piles that spilled onto the ivory countertop beside our kitchen sink: a few coins, his favored pocket knife, a metal washer part from one of his mowers, a few blades of grass, a dash of grime and dirt, and in the midst of it all, the little crimson glass heart I'd given him years ago. Every day he carried my heart in his pocket.

He downed two full glasses of water, then asked about my day. I gave him a kiss.

"It was OK. How 'bout yours? Or do I dare ask?" I traced the rim of his ear with my fingertips. I loved his ears. He would joke that the teacher pulled them when he got into mischief.

"How was my day? I don't want to spoil your evening." He shook his head. His cheeks were now weathered, worn, and sunburned. The sparkle in his blue eyes was gone, replaced by a sad fog.

I knew what he faced each day, keeping the landscaping equipment running, making sure the crews got to their jobs on time, handling the clients, and what complicated it even more was dealing with the weather elements. The elements I'd grown up with, my best friends, my buddies, had now created day-to-day challenges as we tried to earn a living at landscaping.

Where was the joy? The joy in watching a gentle rain shower or a rumbling thunderstorm roll in. The joy of sharing a mug of coffee beside the fire while huge white snowflakes drifted from a white sky. Where was the joy in our day?

Sue Massey

Scraping the contents from his pockets into his drawer, he said, "Isn't that pathetic, to work this hard, and for what? I have forty-seven cents in my pocket."

"You're home now. Let's have a glass of wine, a little supper, and try to unwind. Sophie misses you."

He glanced down at his cell phone. "No wonder I feel drained. I took 126 cell phone calls today."

"Oh, my gosh. That's ridiculous." I walked over, pulled open his drawer, and set his phone inside. Running my fingers through his hair, I said, "I'm sorry, sweetheart. I want so badly for our lives to turn around." I pulled him close.

A muffled ring came from inside his closed drawer, and he instinctively reached toward it.

"Really, Kenny. Just let it go."

"I would, but it's probably Corey. He was having problems with the brakes on his truck. I have to answer it."

I turned to the oven and pulled out a tray of roasted root vegetables. All these years of someone, somewhere always needing him. Anyone else would have folded long ago, but not Kenny. I didn't know how he kept enduring.

The recession was still taking its toll. The future seemed uncertain, but one thing I knew: The little red glass heart he carried in his pocket stood for my everlasting love for him. The elements might cause things of nature to crumble, but Kenny and I always knew we were stronger together. My heart would always be safe and secure, tucked into his pocket.

"Mom, now that Maron and I are moms and working in your business, we honestly don't know how you did it," Naomi said. I was sitting on my bed with my iPad in my lap, and she was in the nearby rocker, texting and talking at the same time. "To think, you had all five of us before you were thirty."

I looked down at the threadbare cuffs of my favorite, worn black hoodie and vividly remembered the days my nerves matched the frayed edges. "I'll be honest. At times, it was no bed of roses. We all needed each other to survive, to make it work, to not let the overwhelming responsibilities break us apart as a family."

Naomi nodded. "I think that's at the heart of our family. You taught us when our plate gets too full, prioritize, tuck some demands behind a door in our heads, and deal with one task at a time."

"I learned that in therapy. Sometimes it's not till after you dig your way out of adversity that you realize what you learned, the skill that will help you conquer the next obstacle."

Naomi leaned over, kissed my forehead. "Here, let me show you quick how to change the font on your iPad, then I'm off to run payroll downstairs in the office. Call me if you need anything. Let's catch up this weekend."

She clicked a couple buttons on the iPad and disappeared, her ponytail flopping as she closed the door behind her. I was so glad that she and Maron had taken over the office. For twenty years, I had done it all. I'd managed the crews, the office, hired, fired, trained new employees, run reports, overseen the marketing, sales, design, flowers, purchasing, everything, and I'd hit a wall — couldn't take one more complaint call, one more pile of paperwork. I'd begun easing out of the business and spending more time writing.

Naomi and Maron had added a crib and playpen to the basement office and often had their little ones in tow. I loved hearing the babies' voices prattling. It rebuilt my spirit. When they were in my arms or toddling nearby, I thought of nothing but the fun of watching them grow and develop. I was thrilled that I could be there whenever a grandparent was needed, just as my parents, and Kenny's, had been for us.

The blowfish was a brilliant aqua blue, covered in tiny porcupine-like spikes that lightened in color when his sides puffed. He looked

Sue Massey

like a small squeezable stress ball. I watched as he swam effortlessly like a hot air balloon floating in midair.

My mind dropped into the five-foot aquarium in front of me at the Dean Clinic. I thought of all the times I'd sat in medical waiting rooms: If I wasn't pregnant, it was for annual physicals for the kids, the full range of childhood illnesses, a continual string of appointments relating to Corey's ADHD and cognitive development challenges. This visit was for me. I needed a physical so I could get my camp form signed. Then I would spend a week in the north woods with a hundred women, ages eighteen to ninety, all of us sharing a thread of loving support as we had every summer for over twenty years. It would be a week of heavenly bliss.

The theme of the camp — The Choice Is Yours — beckoned me every year to pull out my camp gear. We would frolic, free as the wind, during our week in the woods. We women ran the camp. I learned to cook in a commercial-sized kitchen; the pans and bowls were as large as some of the buckets we used to feed the animals on our farm when I was growing up. It took three women to hold and scoop mashed potatoes out of the stainless steel tub into ten serving dishes, one for each table in the lodge dining area. It was like farming. When you work elbow to elbow together, a bond forms. Sweat dripping from our brows, we would run to the lake and jump in for a cool dip, laughter rippling across the mirror surface.

Thoughts of swimming in the lake drew my mind to the water, the aquarium in front of me. I admired the way the artist had designed the colors and shapes inside the tank, the brilliant coral, seaweed-like grasses, burnished stone, a sunken ship with a window that a yellow fish swam through. A string of bubbles gurgled out of the sponge anchored to the pebbled bottom.

My mind circled back to the fall of 1989 when, for the first time, I took the part-time receptionist job at TDS, which turned into the communications editor position. For those eight years at TDS, I had been like the sponge in the aquarium, learning so much that I could feel my brain expanding.

I recalled the joy of starting our landscaping business, the eagerness with which I embraced the freedom of being outside all day again, basking in the elements. I had felt as weightless as the little blowfish that hovered over a piece of chartreuse coral.

In so many ways, I had come full circle. The receptionist position was still a great fit for me because I enjoyed people and liked helping employees and visitors. I had spent a good portion of my years answering phones in all capacities. On the other hand, it was hard to step back into an employee's shoes when I'd grown accustomed to managing a company. I'd swum my way to the top and couldn't help but wonder: What now? Ideas were continually bubbling up from inside me with no place to put them.

I looked at the little aqua-green fish that kept nervously bobbing his head against the glass as if he wanted out. And if you were out, you would die, I thought. He needed a diversion, a new window to swim through, something to capture his energy and drive.

The nurse called my name, and I followed her into the office for my physical. I decided not to overthink things. I would continue to entertain myself, seek ways to make life interesting, and stay close to nature. Magic was all around, even in a doctor's waiting room, and I would find ways to find it and keep it close to me. With the gift of an iPad from our son-in-law Shawn, I played with photography and writing whenever I wanted to get lost in the creative chambers of my mind.

"Sue, how's your mom doing?" a fellow employee asked as I helped him with a temporary security badge from behind the TDS reception desk. It caught me a bit off guard. I collected my thoughts while handing him a form to fill out.

"I don't know if you remember, but she did some alterations for me, way back when. Time slips away. Goodness, what's it been, fifteen years ago?"

"Oh, my, I'd almost forgotten." Mom and Dad had retired from the farm, built a small ranch house on a corner parcel of their farm where Mom could have her garden and Dad a shop to putter in. I remembered now. I'd made a business card for her when she said she wanted to take in mending and alteration jobs. Her hands were never idle. I paused, remembering the excitement I felt as I pressed the pushpin through the little business card and into the cork bulletin board in the TDS break room. "There, Mom is officially open for business," I thought.

Mom was a wizard when it came to alterations. Her Singer sewing machine would buzz, fabric would twist and turn, she'd mutter a few soft "darn this thread" comments, and within minutes, she would emerge, holding an altered garment and grinning as if she'd completed a marathon.

I was the go-between. TDSers saw her "Alterations" ad on the break room bulletin board and gave me garments to deliver. A week later, when I returned the altered clothes along with a bill, I'd hear, "Two dollars? This can't be right. She replaced a zipper for me."

"That's my mom. Sewing is her passion."

Now I searched for the right words. "How sweet of you to remember my mom. We lost her to cancer back in '99."

"Oh, dear, I'm so sorry to hear that, Sue."

"It was a bit of a shock. She was only in her late sixties, and I think I was in complete denial until the last ten days of her life. She just kept working, kept sewing, kept cleaning, gardening, and cooking."

"It's that farm work ethic, it runs deep." The depth of his understanding startled me. I wondered how he knew. He stood before me in a crisp, starched-collar dress shirt in a Fortune 500 company. But, clearly, somewhere in this man's past, he had known or been touched by the hands of those who work the land.

"Thanks for asking about my mom. That took me back. It was during my first tenure with TDS."

He smiled and nodded. "I'll never forget the alterations your mom did for me. She sure had a way with needle and thread."

"She sure did. I have Mom's thread collection on a shelf in my office at home. It's a little wooden box that opens like an accordion, opens to layers of thread spools in every color imaginable. When our grandbabies toddle and play in my office as I write, I place it on the floor and let them explore and have fun with it. Can't hurt a thing."

It warms my heart to think their little fingers are touching the thread my mother once did. And with those pieces of thread, the little spools of color, she made a difference. I hope I'm able to leave behind a thread of color, a spool of hope, of something mended and repaired, and something new, an idea, an inspiration worth following.

CHAPTER 22

Little Boy in a Crate: Finding a Voice

Little Boy went into a crate, bewildered but not timid or scared. He might be more feathers than bone, but his spirit was mighty.

I knew this day would come. It's impossible to keep a rooster in town. Our neighbors had been remarkably patient, but when he began his consistent 6:00 a.m. wake-up call, his fate was sealed.

Unfortunately, Little Boy had stolen my heart. I would miss his strutting about, protecting his harem of hens in our backyard coop.

Hoping against hope that there might be a way for me to keep him, I Googled "how to quiet a crowing rooster." The results weren't good. The experts agreed that roosters were born to crow, born to develop a voice. I read of a rooster who gathered his seven hens into a coop, then went back outside to ward off the hawk; it cost him his life. They're called cocksure for a reason.

For now, I placed Little Boy in a small metal dog crate, and I fed him everything he loved: dried meal worms, wet cat food, melon rind, and fresh water.

Today, I just want time. Time to gather my feelings and figure out who might give a new home to this special Little Boy, once named

Yang when he was merely a cotton-ball-sized bit of fluff. He was identical then to little Yin. But one day, Yang grew a deep red comb and stiff tail feathers, and I realized my hen was actually a rooster.

I'll place his crate on the table in my office while I write. I'll listen to his intermittent cackles as he scratches, flutters about, and seems to wonder why he is in a crate.

He doesn't belong there. He deserves to be free, where his voice can be heard. If only I could buy the farm over the hill, I would take Little Boy there. Together we would both be free.

"Mom!" Maron burst through the open door of our bedroom. She was the early bird; her two little boys were now her five o'clock wake-up call.

I was sitting in bed with my iPad, my fingers fluttering over the keys, still in my comfy nightshirt. Kenny had left an hour earlier to organize the day's landscaping work.

"I know you're writing, but this can't wait," Maron said. "I just took this message off the voicemail, called Dad, and he said I needed to read it to you immediately."

I took a deep breath, braced myself. I had heard these messages before: Sometimes they could make or break my day.

"Get this," Maron went on, looking down at the scribbled note she'd taken off the business voicemail. "It's a message from a neighbor who owns a lot beside Blackhawk Church. He calls Dad every year and has him mow his empty lot. This year when he called, Dad told him no; he said he's done it too cheap for too many years and it ruins his mowers. The guy was speechless. Well, I guess he tried it on his own and discovered what a 'deal' he was getting from Kenny Massey. He told Dad it took the engine out of his mower, and repair would be over $600. He called to thank Dad for all the years he mowed it — and so inexpensively!"

Maron held the note as if it were a winning lottery ticket, knowing what it meant to her dad — and to me.

Sue Massey

I set my coffee mug on the stand beside our bed and looked to the heavens. "He's found his voice, Maron, he has finally found his voice! I'm calling him right now."

"Morning, Sue," Kenny greeted me when I called him. I heard engines and skidsteers churning in the background.

"Hey, I know this is the worst time to call you, in the midst of dispatching crews to work sites, but I'll make it quick."

"You're fine. What'd ya need?"

"I need to tell you how proud I am of you. Maron just read me the note from the client. You've found your voice, sweetheart."

"Well, thank you, Sue." His usual steady tone had a hint of pride.

I thought of all the times I'd urged Kenny to stand up for himself more. I loved his giving heart and the way he would go to extremes to help others. But a person can go too far in that direction. Over the years, I'd tried to gently explain that to him, but it seemed as though I were talking to the wall. Being partners in marriage and business at the same time was no easy feat. I finally gave up, decided to accept him going out of his way to please others even if it cost our business a great deal of money. It was frustrating, but it wasn't worth an argument. Now, however, I was thrilled to hear that he'd finally told a client, "No."

After I hung up the phone, Maron and I grinned at each other. "Ma, can you believe it?" she asked me.

"No, I'm still in shock. I'm amazed the client took the time to call and tell Dad how much he appreciated him."

Maron nodded. She sat, legs crossed, work boots on, ready for the day.

"Appreciation is big, isn't it, Maron? That little note will fuel and fire our souls through the day ahead."

"That's for sure," she said.

"Since the recession knocked us off our feet, I've so wanted to give each of our dedicated employees a raise, but the money just hasn't been there. You, Naomi, Dad, and I are last in line to get paid, and sometimes we don't. I have such appreciation for everyone who continues to show up for work, and of course that includes you. Your hard work in the office makes it possible for me to take some time for writing, knowing everything will run smoothly under your hand."

"Thanks, Ma. I feel your appreciation every day, but it's always great to hear it!"

We shared a quick hug. Then Maron picked up her bag, and her soft footsteps made their way down the staircase to the lower-level business office.

I thought of Kenny, born and raised to be a farmer, to tend the crops quietly and faithfully — a simple life now filled with layers of responsibility. When two people stand face-to-face, hand-in-hand, at an altar, making lifelong vows to one another, only fate knows what the years hold for them, this couple who have joined together until death. They share their dreams, their hopes, their desires, and then life happens.

There was a note. A piece of white paper taped to the stained-glass panel of our front-door window.

I noticed it with curiosity as I made my way up the walk. I was feeling so satisfied because we'd met our goal of planting spring flowers for all the clients who'd placed orders.

The economy was picking up, and we had plenty of landscaping work again. But that hadn't put an end to the stress in our lives. We were still whittling away at the debt we'd fallen into during the worst of the recession. And it was a challenge to find time to accomplish everything we needed to do.

The growers and greenhouses had been a bustle of activity since the first of the year. There didn't ever seem to be an off-season. The whole industry was a mad beat that followed the seasons.

It was Memorial Day weekend when Maron and I pulled up in our van to install flower planters for a client's lakeshore home. We were almost giddy. We were ahead of schedule, a rarity. There were always last-minute calls coming in: "Am I on your list? I may have forgotten to call. Can you fit me in?"

Maron and I pulled fifty-pound bags of potting soil from the van and fell into our routine: filling pots with soil, carrying flat upon flat of flowers around the side of a house that felt like half the length of a football field.

An hour later, filthy, wearing a layer of potting soil, wiping sweat from our brows, we stood by the backyard pool, and I knew we shared the same thought: *I would drop my clothes in a heartbeat to jump in.*

"I'll start the blower and begin clean-up while you stack the empty flower trays," Maron said, and I nodded.

The garage door opened, and out pulled a black Escalade with two jet skis trailered behind. The owner of the house opened his car window and called out, "Looks great. Thanks! Have a nice weekend."

I gave a thumbs up and waved, wondering who was going to water the flowers we had just kicked ass to install, since the owners were clearly off for the holiday weekend. There must be a maid, a gardener, someone on staff to water, I hoped. We'd had disasters in the past when homeowners didn't understand the importance of giving new plantings a few days of generous waterings. We always left our clients a list of instructions and reinforced the message verbally, but miscommunication still occurred now and then, and I felt dreadful if anything we planted ended up dead or struggling to survive.

The blower fell silent, the van door creaked open, and Maron hopped into the driver's seat.

"We did it, Mom! Check that one off our list," she said as she held her clipboard against the steering wheel, grinning ear to ear, reviewing the list of names. "That's it! We're done! Now we get two days off."

Maron turned the key and backed out of the brick-paved driveway.

"Do you have weekend plans?" I sipped a Propel.

"I would be happy to do nothing! You?"

"Nothing sounds fabulous, doesn't it? Dad mentioned he'd like to take a drive to Galena, wander through some antique shops — and you know your dad, some of 'em are actually junkyards. Maybe eat at that Italian restaurant; you know your dad, if it's covered in tomato sauce, he's in heaven."

Maron turned the engine off. "Well, whatever you do, have fun. Try to rest up, and I'll see you bright and early Tuesday morning." A kiss, a "Love ya, Ma," and we parted ways.

The overnight trip to Galena was a sliver of heaven. Kenny and I checked out a handful of shops, walked hand in hand beside the river, and had a fabulous Italian meal at the top of the hill, followed by dessert in bed.

My thoughts were still lingering in the playfulness of our evening as I started toward our house and saw the note taped to the front door. I pulled it down.

Sue Massey, you are fired! I came from our home in Florida to our Madison lakefront home, which was an appalling MESS! Weeds everywhere. I am embarrassed, no appalled, to think what our neighbors must think. I am disgusted and disappointed in you. I will no longer need any of your services!

My shoulders went limp, and my purse and overnight bag fell to the ground, taking my spirits with them. I sat down, the brick walk cold beneath me. I felt chilled by the letter from a client who, moments earlier, I had considered a friend.

Kenny's car door banged shut as he walked up, carrying a bag.

"Sue, what's wrong? What happened?" Just an instant before, we had been laughing and singing "Red, Red Wine" to Neil Diamond's CD in the Jeep.

I handed him the letter. He scanned it. "What's up with that?" he asked. "What's she talking about?"

"Good question. Two weeks ago, I called and left a detailed message on her cell phone. I hadn't heard what services she wanted this year, if any. I didn't know if she was back from Florida or if her house was for sale or even sold for that matter. Last I heard, she was thinking of selling it. She never returned my call, so I figured she was over-the-top busy, and when she found the time she'd call."

"Looks like she found the time to drive over, find our home, and deliver a nasty note to our doorstep."

"Well, if she wanted to slice my heart in half, she succeeded."

"I'm sorry, Sue. You don't deserve this." He reached for my purse and bags. Then he crumpled the note into a ball and stepped on it, squashed it like a bug, unlocked the front door, and together we walked into the house.

As I sorted through my thoughts and feelings, I tried to envision the soul from which those ugly words came. They clearly must have emerged from a place so sad, so drenched in hurt it was beyond imagining. I'd made my share of mistakes, but I always tried so hard to learn from them, become a better person, talk things out and reach for an understanding.

My first impulse was to call the client and try to straighten out the misunderstanding. My second thought was "no." I didn't ever want to work for her again. I wanted to surround myself with people who encouraged and appreciated our work.

I looked through the sunroom skylights at the blue sky, a puff of clouds drifting overhead. I gave the ungrateful, angry words to that white cloud. Perhaps she could take on the note, filter the words, find the purity of forgiveness, and allow me the freedom to let it go.

"How you managed to have all five of us will forever be a mystery to me," Kelli said. Now in her early thirties, she was a registered nurse in labor, delivery, and newborn care. "In my daily work, I get a glimpse of what you went through — the premature labor, the IVs, high-risk complications, hospital stays, bed rest, the extra care needed to raise preemies. It leaves me speechless."

Kelli was home from California for a visit, and we were talking in the sunroom. As she spoke, my view of her as an adult child shifted, and before me stood a beautiful, articulate, caring young woman who had found her path in life. A peaceful, contented feeling filled my heart.

"I remember when you were eighteen and about to graduate from high school," I told her. "For the first time, I realized how concerned my mom must have felt when I told her I was getting married at eighteen." I smiled up at Kelli. She stood five feet, eight inches with an athletic build, thick hair the color of her dad's.

"Grandma Johnny was very special," Kelli said, using her nickname for my mother. "I think she knew you'd figure things out, and it'd be on your terms."

"Probably. I always felt as though I grew up with you kids. In fact, I still feel like a kid at heart." I carefully arranged my thoughts into words. "Are you planning to have children?"

"I don't think so, Mom. We've talked about it. Shawn is OK with it either way, but I'm so happy in my career. I get to hold newborns every day and help parents learn to care for them. So I get my baby fix and my freedom, too. I know that's probably not the answer you wanted to hear." Kelli looked at me, trying to read my reaction.

"Actually, I'm not surprised. I just hope your decision isn't because of your role as a second mom during the years before and after we lost the farm and my depression that followed."

"No. Not at all. In fact, in high school when I did a lot of babysitting, I sort of knew then I might not need to have children of my own." A butter-yellow finch caught her eye and she pointed outside toward the bird feeder that hung on a nearby birch limb. "Mom, look!" We shared a moment of pleasure, watching the finch pluck black thistle seeds from the feeder.

"I totally understand," I said. "I certainly don't believe a person has to have children to feel complete. I'm sure your sisters have told you how having kids has flipped their worlds upside down."

Kelli's smile turned wide, "Yes, they have."

I checked the time on my cell phone. "It's almost time for my shift at TDS. What are your plans for the afternoon?"

"I'm planning to take a run, then visit my sisters."

"Perfect. Corey will be here for dinner tonight. I know he's looking forward to spending time with you too. It's great to have you home."

"Great to be here. I've already been in your brownies, Ma, the ones on the counter. I sure miss your cooking."

"You make yourself at home. What's ours is yours. Love you, sweetheart."

The Americano, with two shots of espresso, tingled against my lips as the steam warmed the tip of my nose and nourished my senses. I snuggled into a comfy, pumpkin-colored café chair beside my good friend, Tee.

"How have jewelry sales been?" I asked her. "Have you noticed a dip since the economy bottomed out?" I sipped the strong coffee.

"Not bad. Gold and diamond sales have been steady, thank goodness." Tee loved her sales position at a jewelry store and was very successful at it. We often got together to talk business; we could identify with each other's ups and downs. "How about you? Has the economy had an impact on landscaping?" Tee's eyes peered out above the rims of her trendy, green-framed readers.

"It's horrible. I mean, we've been busy, sales have been strong, but we're behind in taxes, and it sucks. No matter how many hours we work, it barely puts a dent in the back taxes."

"Oh, Sue, I'm so sorry to hear that. I wish there were something I could do." Her quiet voice matched her soft brown eyes. She tucked her curly auburn hair behind her ear.

"It helps being able to vent. You know, when the kids moved out, Kenny and I finally had some privacy, our own personal space, and I thought life couldn't possibly be better, and then this happens. We're working too many hours. It feels like we're drifting apart again, and I know it's the stress. I scheduled a few marriage-counseling sessions."

"Sue, I can relate. The fact that you're both willing to work on your marriage is a testament to your love for each other."

Her face softened, and for the first time since I'd met her, she spoke of her failed marriage. As the coffee warmed me, her words filled my head, and the hustle-bustle inside the café dropped away. So foreign were the experiences she shared that I was shocked into silence. If I felt tormented by these images, I wondered what she must have felt. Unable to hold my silence any longer, I cried out, "Oh, Tee! For nineteen years?"

"Yes, for nineteen years, I just took it. My mother told me to be a good wife. I thought this was part of it."

"I'm so sorry," I said. "I feel so awful for you."

I tried to get my head around her ordeal. I envisioned the huge man groping, thrusting, and inserting himself into this little woman, my dear Tee.

She lies beneath him, counting the minutes until it is over. He moans, releases, rolls off, and falls asleep. She feels brief relief at completing her day's final task. She is sore, but knows she'll feel better by morning. If only he doesn't wake early and want it all over again. She feels the stickiness of his body trickle out of hers and onto the cotton sheet. She yearns for a shower. The suds would leave her clean, and she would have her body back with no trace of him left. But she is too tired to move. She tries to focus on happy thoughts, her children — a boy and a girl who fill her days with such an abundance of joy that she is able to survive the nightly ritual. Her mother's voice in her head: "He may stray now and then. Just ignore it, and be a good wife."

Nineteen years she endures it until one day she awakes to a new voice. A voice she doesn't recognize, a voice within herself.

The kids are nearly grown, she thinks. She looks around. Beautiful home. Framed picture of a handsome businessman husband. Comfortable lifestyle. Is it worth it? It feels like a lie, but she has never known it to feel any other way.

The phone rings. Her husband's young mistresses have begun to call the house. "No, he's not home. Who am I? I'm his wife." She walks

Sue Massey

into their bedroom, pulls out the suitcase, and begins to pack. No longer chained to the voice in her head, or being someone she isn't, raped for the last time.

I thought of Kenny and the thrill we discovered beneath the sheets, two hearts throbbing, gasping for air, every cell awake and on fire. The warm feeling of opening, touching, rubbing, thrusting, climbing, wanting, desiring, reaching, higher, higher, nearly there, coming, coming, almost, almost, more, more. . . "Oh, my God, oh my God." Eyes closed beneath lids of darkness splintered with brilliant fireworks in the arms of shared pleasure. A cool sweat bead trickles down my forehead and onto his chest. He flips me over effortlessly, and I caress his back with my fingernails — he loves this. We enjoy the gift of each other, aglow, bliss, pleasure pulsing. I love this feeling. Having this feeling makes me only want more.

I sipped the last drop of coffee from my now cold mug. I stood, embraced Tee, "I am so proud of you! You're a wonderful person and you deserve only happiness. It took a lot of courage for you to stand up for yourself, and you did. You're an inspiration to others in the web of unhappy relationships: raped no more, only shared pleasure."

I was so grateful for our marriage. It was far from perfect, but whenever Kenny and I became aware of an issue, we embraced the steps of change that would help us overcome it and make it better.

"Maron, your dad asked me where I would like to go for a trip if we had the chance."

"So what did you tell him? Where would you like to go? " Maron sipped her morning coffee as she packed work orders for the landscaping crews into her bag.

"The first thought that came into my head was, we so need a new dishwasher, and then, I would go to TJ Maxx and buy a set of silverware." I savored a scoop of my favorite breakfast fruit and yogurt.

"Mom, you're so not a normal mom. I didn't want a normal mom. I wanted a fun mom, and I got one."

"True, I'm definitely not your norm. I'm so tired of opening the silverware drawer to find it empty, and what few utensils we have, they're in the dishwasher, and I don't know why I bother to run it because only half the dishes come out clean. It needs a part, and the part costs more than a new dishwasher."

"That sounds familiar," Maron said.

"Right. That's the story of our life: rob Peter to pay Paul."

"Oh, Mom, that was so Dad yesterday. A part broke on one of the commercial mowers, and rather than buy a new part, he ran to the junkyard, wrenched a part off a piece of junk, and had his mower running in no time. I think he knows every junkyard within an hour of Madison, maybe even statewide. Well, I have a nine o'clock with a client, gotta run. Love ya, Ma."

Leaning back in my chair, I stared at the ceiling fan as the paddles went around and around and around. It made me think of when I was a kid, perched on my windmill hill, listening to the windmill paddles creaking and moaning as they pulled fresh water from deep within the earth. I could hear the water gush into the cup, then into a pipe that filled our well — the well that provided an abundance of ice-cold water for us.

Some days, I liked to think about that simpler time. We always found moments to connect; it was during chores that we chatted about the day. We worked shoulder-to-shoulder in all types of weather and helped one another find our way.

There was nothing worse than to be stuck, caught in a circle going around, again and again, over and over. Our family had tried everything to break out of this ceaseless circle of debt that kept slapping our heads like the paddles on the fan. We didn't dare stop, had to keep moving, keep doing. Perhaps our greatest fear was being unable to earn a living at what we loved to do — working with the land, breathing life into our ideas. To not follow our dreams seemed like living a partial life.

All I knew was to place one foot in front of the next. I tried not to dwell on yesterday's soured milk, for it made the most delicious sour cream coffee cake — like a bite of love, a forkful of sweet cinnamon comfort to feed the soul.

Sour Cream Coffee Cake

Cream until fluffy:

1/2 cup butter

1 cup sugar

2 eggs

Sift together and stir in:

2 cups, flour

1 tsp. baking soda

1 tsp. baking powder

1/2 tsp. salt

Add:

1 cup sour cream

Stir together filling:

1/3 cup brown sugar

1/4 cup white sugar

1 tsp. cinnamon

1 cup chopped nuts (optional)

Grease a 9 x 13 baking pan. Alternate a layer of dough, then filling, and sprinkle the top with remaining filling. Bake at 350 degrees for about 35 minutes. When cool, I like to drizzle with:

Boil:

2 T butter

2 T cream

Stir in powdered sugar until consistency of frosting.

Add:

1 tsp. vanilla extract

The door opened, and Maron popped in again. "Mmm, it smells really good in here!"

"Sit down, let's talk if you have a spare minute," I said. "The cake's almost done." I stood by the oven with a potholder in my hand.

Maron shuffled onto a kitchen stool. This would be the perfect time, I decided, to ask her something that had been nagging at me.

After we were settled at the table with small wedges of cake, I posed the question.

"Maron, when you were little, do you remember the time I packed a suitcase and went to stay with my brother?"

"The time you wanted Dad to go to marriage counseling with you and he said no?"

"You do remember."

"Oh, yeah." Her voice shifted in that way she had of encouraging me to say more.

"Be honest, were you scared? Did you think I might never come back?" I braced myself for her response, thinking if I was brave enough to bring up the subject, I had to accept the answer. I flashed back to my stay in the hospital for depression when the doctor called my family together for a group session. The questions, the answers pulled from me like pieces of my heart, and the horror in the circle of eyes was more painful than giving birth. I worried that my doctor would pull my deepest secret from me and that once I gave voice to those awful words my family would never speak to me again. Someday I knew I would need to bring my secret out into the air. But that would take more courage than I had at the moment.

"No, I wasn't scared," Maron replied. "My first thought was: Dad, you're screwed. You better say 'yes' to the counseling."

"Did you worry, or think I might not come back?"

"No. I remember calling you on the phone, just to hear your voice, and you always answered, gave me your undivided attention, and I felt reassured."

"Oh, good. I feel better." I was relieved that I hadn't scarred Maron through my actions, but I knew each family member had a unique take on every situation. When I had the chance, I would ask the other kids the same questions. I'd learned never to assume anything. One can't possibly know what another person is thinking. It's always best to ask.

"The first few times you and Dad went to counseling," Maron said, "I remember you coming home looking drained. But after a few weeks, it was like a cloud lifted. You started talking to each other more, even touching again. It was magical. There was a happiness in our home again."

"We had homework assignments from those sessions."

"Like what?"

"We learned about boundaries," I said. "We created a certain time of day to talk business, make decisions, and discuss finances. Then we would put those issues away and not let them interfere with the rest of our time together. We also started a weekly date night. One week your dad picked what we would do, and the next week it was my turn. We worked hard on respecting each other's differences. Acceptance, mutual support, and understanding can rekindle love."

"Wow, that's a lot. No wonder you looked exhausted when you came in from a session."

"Relationships are hard work, there's no doubt."

"Lately, it's been a tough go," Maron said. "I love being part of a family-owned business, but the lack of cash flow is a killer."

"True, but look at how our family has responded: We've pulled together, reorganized our efforts, turned to our God-given gifts, and kept pushing on."

"It's amazing how we've all branched out into second jobs and found ways to make extra money by following our hearts," Maron agreed. "That's one good thing about the bad economy. It's forced us all to innovate."

"That's right, and your art work is taking off. I'm so proud of you. You really have a special eye for colors."

"It's been fun," Maron said. "And Naomi loves her new side job selling those trendy women's bags and bins. Not to forget Dad's sculptures — who would have guessed he has such talent for that? Recycled metal, who'da thought?" Maron grinned.

"I know. I'm so glad he has that outlet," I said. We'd all been astounded when Kenny started creating beautiful sculptures out of recycled metal. On reflection, it made sense, because Kenny was a wizard at making something, with seeming ease, out of minimal materials. The surprise for me was that old, rusty junk could be transformed into such breathtaking, almost ethereal beauty. Not only were people paying good money for his sculptures, but many of our landscaping clients had asked Kenny to hold a welding class so that they could learn the skill. Kenny considered that the highest compliment of all. He held teachers in the greatest esteem.

"Do you ever think about what life would've been like for us if we hadn't lost the farm?" Maron asked.

"Oh yeah, it's crossed my mind a time or two."

"And?" She sipped the half coffee, half milk, two teaspoons of sugar concoction in her mug, eyes studying mine.

"I always wanted you kids to have the experience of growing up on a farm, the way I did. But life on the Massey farm was totally different than life on the Johnson farm, where I grew up. Even if we'd stayed on the Massey farm, I could never have recreated my childhood for you. It just wasn't the same. And, honestly, I might have outgrown the farm in the sense of wanting to grow, explore, meet new people, travel. I'm drawn to the unusual. In a larger city like Madison, I feel as though I blend in more, and I like the differences among people. It makes life interesting. There are also so many opportunities at our fingertips. If it weren't for the effects of the recession, I would say I'm living my dream."

I tossed a blanket onto the lawn, and my grandkids and I lay on our backs and discovered the clouds. I told my four grandchildren — Adam, Troy, Savannah, and Klay — how I would lie on top of the ridge of my childhood farm in a soft mound of meadow grass and watch the clouds.

"Weather is the result of sunlight mingling with the earth's air," I explained. "Mother Earth rules because she controls the weather. I picture her clouds as her children. Each one is so fluffy, so unique, just like each of you. What do you see when you look at the clouds?"

Troy saw cotton balls. I saw a swan, a cat, a snowman. The kids laughed as I pointed out the animals and people I saw in the sky. Adam was now six, followed by Troy, three, and Savannah and Klay, both approaching two.

A handful of hens emerged from beneath the huge blue hosta leaves. They scampered over, eager to see if we had treats for them.

Troy pointed at one of the hens. "Bingo," he said, calling her by name. I was excited to see that he could tell the hens apart by their color.

I looked again at the white airy clouds, each beautiful in its own way, like people. I thought how fortunate I was to lie on a blanket with my grandchildren around me as I discovered their unique beauty.

A crisp greenback dropped onto the hardwood floor between my bare feet. Kelli had tucked it into my birthday card.

I reached to pick up the bill and read the numbers: 1-0-0 dollars. I sat down in the corner blue chair, held Kelli's card to my heart, and thought about how wonderful our relationship was as mother-daughter friends. That alone was the best birthday gift a mom could ask for. If the day ever came when she wanted to talk about the time we'd spent apart, I would listen with an open heart. For now, I was just happy to be part of her life.

We used to give each of our kids a hundred-dollar bill for their birthdays. Those days ended with the recession. If Kelli only knew: Her hundred-dollar gift arrived when Kenny and I were down to three dollars between us.

Despite our meager finances, I'd arrived at a peace-filled, happy place in my life. Little of it was material based, though I was proud of what we'd earned by working as a family team.

I grabbed the birthday card and the hundred-dollar bill, jumped in the Jeep, and headed for the grocery store. There I picked out the essentials, adding them in my head as I placed them in the blue plastic basket. Then, at checkout, I watched the numbers total on the screen, holding back two items that were possibly wants rather than needs. It came to $57. I still had money for gas, my favorite wheat bread at the bakery, and meds at the pharmacy.

I looked toward the heavens and thanked God. We'd made it one more day. Enough food to get us through until my TDS check arrived. It wouldn't be much after the IRS garnished business taxes and health insurance was pulled, but it was something.

Many folks were far worse off. I vowed never to forget these days of trying to get by. I smiled down at Kelli's sparkling butterfly card. If there was one gift we gave our children, it was the will to survive. Our goal as parents was to work ourselves out of a job, and I knew our kids were survivors. They had each other, and they could make it in a world of unrelenting uncertainly.

I sat on the patio, looking out past our back yard to the sprawling farm field behind it, listening to the wind chimes that I'd hung from a branch in the birch tree. The corn was gone; only golden-brown, chopped-off stalks remained. The sun was lowering behind the wood's edge, leaving half the field sunlit and half in shadow. The owl in the white pine would soon call to its mate, then swoop over the jagged corn stalks for its nightly meal of field mice.

The wind played with the chimes. A few hours earlier, a turbulent north wind had tossed the chimes till they tangled in the twigs and their melody was hushed, only a ping echoing now and then. I had reached to untangle them, set their voices free, and now a gentle

Sue Massey

breeze played a soft intermittent tune, letting me know that evening was closing in. Soon the wind would quiet, and so, too, would the chimes.

Penley Wind was the pet name I gave to my friend the wind — Penley because I loved my pen the way I loved the wind. It was like a baton in the hand of a conductor, a way to express the melody that flowed through me.

Like the chimes, my thoughts and feelings could become so tangled that my voice was cut off. But as I learned the art of acceptance and surrender, I spent far less time trying to unsnarl them. My voice became clearer, gentler, freer, and my song rang more true, attuned with the world around me.

CHAPTER 23

Humble Pie

I woke early on Thanksgiving morning, looking forward to getting together with family. With our parents gone, we three siblings had each selected a holiday to host. My brother, Bruce, who lived across the field from us — as the crow flies — had Thanksgiving. My sister, Sandy, who lived an easy forty-five-minute drive south in Janesville, had Easter. Christmas dinner was at our home. Though I was in charge of the meal, my real excitement lay in watching everyone open their gifts.

I was so grateful for family, especially now that my siblings and I had settled into a place of acceptance and understanding, of not dwelling on the past but rather appreciating one another. There was a time when my sister and I had lost touch. It wasn't until after she completed a grueling chemo regimen for breast cancer that I learned why my relationship with Sandy had become so distant.

"You know, Sue, I've been thinking," she said one evening when she dropped by. "My experience with cancer made me think about a lot of things, especially family. I remember when we were little. You were always the funny one. You made me laugh. And you had such high spirits, such a sense of adventure. I don't think Mom knew where you were half the time."

Sue Massey

She rocked gently in the rocker that filled a corner of our bedroom. I sat cross-legged on the bench that rested at the foot of our bed.

"Did anyone know where I was?" I joked. "They still wonder where I'm at." Our laughter filled the room.

"Then, in high school," she continued, "about the time you started dating Kenny, I broke up with my boyfriend. From that point on, it was like your life kept moving forward, and mine stopped. On top of a broken heart, I felt like I lost my best friend, my little sister. Before I knew it, you were engaged, married, and having kids. It all happened so fast. You know, I think the world of Kenny, but the closer you became to him, the less I saw of you. I began to retreat into my bedroom."

My heart ached. All these years, and I never knew what had happened to the close bond I'd once shared with my sister. I just accepted that the demands of raising a young family had sent me in a completely different direction with little free time.

"Then, when I had cancer, I re-evaluated everything," she went on. "I was in so much pain sometimes, I have to be honest, I just wanted to fall asleep and never wake up. Sue, it was just terrible. But when I could muster enough energy to go to my computer to open emails, there was always one from you, every day. Even though you were working and faced so many demands, you always reached out to me. You'll never know how much that meant. I'm so sorry for those years I wasted not talking to you, the distance I put between us, over petty stuff that didn't even matter."

I walked across the room, scooped her into my arms, and said, "What matters now is that we're closer than ever. All these years, I never knew you felt Kenny replaced you. No one ever replaces a sister. We shared so much growing up. You know me so well. You laugh at all my funny ways. You get me, and you still love me." There was no holding back; the tears fell. "I think through counseling and group therapy, I learned how important it is to reach out, let people know how much I care about them, talk things out if there seems to be a communication glitch. Thank you for telling me how you felt. I had no idea."

As I sat back onto the soft nap of the bedroom carpet, Sophie came near to comfort me. I felt a heavy stone lift from my heart and love for my sister fill the space. I looked at Sandy, her eyes red in the flickering candlelight of our bedroom. "Isn't it odd how something as horrible as cancer can make us realize how precious each day is to us?"

I jumped up. "This calls for celebration." I ran to the kitchen and poured us each a glass of Lambrusco wine. When I returned, we clicked glasses and cheered to "sisters forever."

I thought about Sandy as I lay in bed that morning. I was glad I'd be seeing her at Bruce's later that day. I was to bring buns and my mom's favorite sweet potato dish. Even those who aren't fond of sweet potatoes love this recipe.

Sweet Potato Hot Dish
From: Ma Johnson

Peel six four-inch sweet potatoes, cut vertically into one-inch pieces, place in a saucepan, and cover with water. Toss a pinch of salt into the pan and another over your shoulder for good luck. Boil the sweet potatoes until almost tender. Drain and place in a buttered casserole dish. Set the oven at 350 degrees.

Mix and bring to a boil in the microwave:
1/2 cup orange juice
1/2 cup brown sugar
1/2 cup white corn syrup
3 T cornstarch
Dash of cinnamon if you'd like.

Pour the sauce over the sweet potatoes and bake for 30 minutes. If you're lucky enough to have leftovers, stir into a loaf of sweet potato bread.

I know that when I stir the recipe together my thoughts will be with Mom. I miss her helpful hands and caring ways. She was a pie-baking queen. We had her homemade pies almost every Sunday after church, along with a buffet of other extraordinary dishes. My dad was a meat-and-potatoes kinda guy, so she didn't dabble too much with fresh herbs and spices, but each dish was created to perfection with a sprinkle of her love folded in.

I've learned to make many of her trademark recipes, and they're cherished by everyone in the family. One of our favorites is her vanilla cream pie. Our kids love it so much that they request it as their birthday cake.

I lie back in my warm bed, thinking. The late November dawn is slow to rise, and yesterday we had our first snow. I think of Thanksgiving. I think of pie, and the many slices of humble pie I've been served in my lifetime.

Sometimes, when I pour my heart into an effort and it doesn't go the way I'd hoped or someone perceives it differently than I'd anticipated, I have to fight off the demon of disappointment, the childhood perfectionism ingrained in me. I once interviewed an executive who told me he was a recovering perfectionist. It made me chuckle.

Having children is humbling. Having five in a family with limited income pushed me to become resourceful. I found ways to entertain them on a dime. This didn't happen overnight, but rather from years of trial and error and a splash of therapy here and there.

A typical ten-inch pie is cut into six to eight portions. I would need two pies cut into twenty segments each to symbolize even a portion of the humbling experiences I've encountered in my lifetime. Some were a result of my naive, overzealous, excited nature. In my fifties now, I have a clearer understanding of who I am and am better able to settle my emotional self to match my surroundings. I remember years ago freaking out over little things that today would be nothing, a small clump of butter that didn't fully mix into the pie crust. I've learned to go with the flow, be flexible, accept what I cannot change, and move forward.

I'm saddened when I think back to the days when the children were young and I was so stressed I'd come home from the office thinking what to make for dinner and get upset because the house was a mess. The kids were being so good, playing happily, the older ones caring for the younger ones. Today, I tell my younger self: Really? Was my frustration helping anything? No.

I think what a different mom I would be today. Thankfully, I've learned from my mistakes and continue to evolve, though I'm certain some slivers of humble pie will be served in the future, amid all the drama that comes our way as our creative, multifaceted family lives, learns, and grows together.

Bruce opened the door to his house wearing a colorful paper turkey hat. He and his wife, Lisa, had set up a craft table for the kids to make their own turkey hats as they arrived for Thanksgiving dinner.

Although we all missed Kelli, who was still working as a registered nurse in California, it was wonderful to have our four other kids and their families together. Listening to the clamor as they enjoyed the dinner and each other's company, I smiled with contentment.

After we finished the grand feast and cleaned up the kitchen, I motioned for my sister Sandy to sit with me. She pulled up a chair and began to grin.

"Sue, remember that time you picked a poppy from the neighbor's yard?" Sandy loved to bait me, toss me a hook and let me run with it. It made me feel as though we were kids again.

"Do I remember? Like it was yesterday! I kept admiring that patch of orange poppies on the way to and from school. They were so beautiful! One day, I couldn't stand looking at them from a distance anymore. I picked one, walked up the hill and in the door, and held it up to Mom."

"Yes, I remember how your eyes sparkled and you had such a happy look on your face," Sandy said.

Sue Massey

"Yes, but it didn't last long. Mom said, 'That sure looks like the poppies in the neighbor's yard.' I told her, 'No way. The teacher gave it to me and told me I could give it to my mom,' She looked me in the eye and said, 'Susan, tell the truth.'"

Sandy laughed at the gruff voice I used to mimic mom's stern disapproval. "That's all it took, then you burst into tears." She leaned forward to hold her ribs in laughter.

"And that wasn't the worst of it," I recalled. "Mom sent me down the hill to give the flower back. I remember standing at the door shaking with fear when the lady looked out and said, 'Honey, you just keep it.'

"I told her, 'No, my mom said I couldn't,'" and I set the flower on her stoop and ran back up the hill, sobbing the entire way."

It was so fun to look back and laugh. I had always been the clown of the family, and Sandy was my one-person audience.

I reached into my purse and pulled out an envelope. "Hey, you guys, you have to see what I came across." All eyes turned toward me as I held up a handful of old photographs. "Here's a picture of Dad and Grandpa on top of a horse-drawn wagonload of hay. This has to be back in the forties. I think I'll scan it and give it out for Christmas."

Corey got up from the floor where he was playing with the grandkids. He loved children and was the awesome uncle who tackled and wrestled with the little kids on the carpeting. Now he looked over my shoulder, interested as always in anything that had to do with farming.

"Here's one of Corey and Maron playing pirates in a boat cut out of a cardboard box," I said. "Dee, you had to be the mastermind behind that creation. If we didn't have money for new toys, you guys made them."

Dee grinned as she reached for the photo. "Wow, that brings back memories." Tall and slender with a head of curly hair that brushed below her shoulders, Dee was now working on an interior design degree in Madison and lived near us again.

Sandy was hovering like a hummingbird, setting out plates of pie while trying to view the pictures. With Mom gone, Sandy had taken over her role.

"Naomi, look at this one of you at the cabin holding a jar of minnows."

"I look like Savannah in that photo, don't I?" Naomi said, smiling as she held one-year-old, curly-haired, blue-eyed Savannah in her lap.

"Let's take a few pictures of the grandkids before it's time to leave," I said, grabbing my camera. "Adam, Troy, Savannah, and Klay, come sit by the fireplace." The excitement in my voice usually captured their attention and they came running to see what I had in store. As I lined them up, I said, " If everybody smiles and is patient, I'll have a treat for you afterwards." They gathered around, and I began snapping pictures. When I had enough photos, I ran to my purse to get a small treat from Halloween to divide amongst them. Dee's six-year-old, Adam, stood quietly beside me like a little mouse waiting for a morsel of cheese.

Having raised five, I was a near master at conjuring up diversions and bribes, and they always worked. I had taken so many pictures of our gang of five that when they caught a glimpse of the camera, they automatically fell into line. My camera fit my hand like a favorite glove. The curve of it felt like a comfortable pen, a paintbrush, a wooden cooking spoon that warmed in my grasp. I would look at an everyday scene and see pictures waiting to be captured and tucked into scrapbooks for generations to come.

Only two placemats rest on our kitchen table. The days of daily rollicking, noisy family dinners are past — though when I feel the urge to cook, the kids are close by to join us.

Now, there's a new mat in my life: a yoga mat that I've fallen in love with. Many times through the years, my kids had urged me to do yoga. I always told them I had too much energy to slow down, meditate, and relax.

Sue Massey

That, they told me, is the very reason you should do it. That, they explained, is the whole point.

I finally tried yoga at Women's Week camp up north. I was surprised how much yoga reminded me of growing up on the land. I felt that same connection to the earth while lying on my yoga mat, gently moving through the poses and matching my movements to my breath.

After camp was over, I discovered Inner Fire Yoga Studio in Madison and began to attend. It feels sacred to me, a place I can be alone, mindful of my thoughts while letting the outside world drop away. It's a special place, a community, where I feel at peace.

Shortly after I discovered yoga, a friend loaned me a memoir she'd just read and thought I would like.

I hesitated, but I didn't want to offend her, so I smiled and thanked her. I didn't let her know that I probably wouldn't read it.

I could count on my two hands the number of books I'd read in the past thirty years, and most of those were cookbooks or guidebooks on child-raising. I did love listening to books on tape while in the car. I even started a book club with a friend and enjoyed discussing books with the group. But if someone suggested a book that I couldn't get on tape, I wouldn't read it. I would resort to my long-time alternative — skimming.

It began when I was in fourth grade. I remember the scowl on my teacher's face as she said she was moving me to the slow reading group. I devised a technique to speed up my reading time. Whenever given something to read, I would go to the ending first, jump back to the beginning, then skim everything in between.

It wasn't easy to take tests when I'd only glanced through the material. And if the test was timed, worry consumed me. I grew to dislike school intensely.

After I left school, I was happy to put aside the anxiety that reading provoked in me. Reading for pleasure wasn't part of my life.

Now, holding the paperback my friend had loaned me, I decided to give reading another chance. Yoga had opened something in me, a flexibility, a receptiveness that was new to me.

I sat down in my favorite chair and slowed my mind and my breathing as I'd learned to do in yoga. I opened the book to the first page.

And, then, for what seemed like the first time, the world of reading opened to me, and I dove into the adventure between the pages.

The chaos inside my mind quieted, and I was able to focus. I became lost in the story.

For the rest of the week, I took the book with me wherever I went. If I was stressed, waiting in line, or unwinding before bed, I looked to my book, the ongoing story in my mind.

I stopped skimming. The narrative drew me in like the luring aroma of fresh bread. I wanted to savor each word as if a bite of my mom's warm cinnamon raisin loaf.

Soon I always had at least one book nearby to read. And while Kenny liked to speed-read his way through books, I discovered that I wanted the opposite. I wanted to pause between paragraphs, linger at delicious sentences, contemplate the characters and reflect on what made them tick. I grew to love biographies and memoirs because I wanted to know someone on a deep level.

With yoga and with books, I was beginning to feel a tranquility flow over me, an acceptance of who I was, along with an understanding of my voice. Slowly, my life was making sense, and I was learning to love the person I'd always been.

One piece remained: the deep, dark secret I'd carried with me most of my life. Was I ready to speak of her, and if I did, would the words release the control she held over me? What if sharing the truth left me vulnerable, open to harsh criticism? Would my friends think less of me, shun our friendship? The thoughts haunted me, but I was learning to let life happen, not to push such sensitive, personal decisions. *If or when the time is right*, I thought, *it will happen.*

Sue Massey

CHAPTER 24

Stardust

It was late afternoon on Friday, payday. The phones at the TDS reception desk were quiet. I reached for the desk phone, a separate line for non-customer-related calls.

My fingers knew the Masseys Landscaping number by heart. I was anxious to know whether Maron had been able to pay our landscaping employees. With money so tight, it was always touch and go. Luckily, we'd never had to ask our employees to wait for their paychecks, but I lived in fear that it would happen.

As the numbers on the keypad bleeped beneath my fingertips, I thought of Wednesday, two nights earlier. We'd gathered as family and shared pizza as we sat on the floor of Maron's new home just down the street from us.

Eight months ago, Maron, Naomi, and their families had sold their first homes and moved, all seven of them together, into Gram Betty's house, which was two doors away from ours. Betty had recently been moved into assisted living, leaving her house vacant.

The four adults — Naomi, Dannon, Maron, and Seth — and three kids — Troy, Klay, and Savannah — had managed to make the cramped two-family living arrangement work for nearly a year while

Maron and Seth went through the process of buying a house across the street. Wednesday had been the first night in the new house for Maron, Seth, and their two little boys — a double reason to celebrate.

Having two of our daughters, their husbands, and their kids living so close to us was a wish come true. It was a moment of triumph we felt as a family, a goal we'd all worked hard to achieve.

"Masseys Landscaping, how may I help you?" Maron answered the phone.

"Hey, Mar! How was night two in your new home?"

"I love this house!" Maron exclaimed. "I keep pinching myself to be sure I'm not dreaming. I actually have a studio in which to paint."

"I'm so happy for you," I said. "And I'm so proud of the way you kept working toward your dream till you made it a reality."

"Thanks, Mom. On the other hand, we barely made payroll. I emailed our banker, told him a couple large deposits would be coming in over the weekend, and asked if he would cover the payroll checks. He said OK."

"Good thinking, Maron. It sickens me that we have to live so close to the edge when our sales are booming and we're having one of our most successful years ever. If only the IRS would let us set up a payment plan to pay back taxes instead of insisting on taking $38K of our working capital in one large chunk. That's what has us in this pickle."

"Why do you suppose the IRS won't listen to reason?"

"I'm not sure. You'd think they'd want to help hardworking, honest folks trying to make it in the world of small business. Did I tell you the latest? The IRS is forcing Kenny to take 'early retirement' — air quotes — even though he's only sixty-two, and do you know why? So they can garnish most of his social-security check on top of everything else."

"Social Security! That's a shock."

"I know, it feels odd even to say the words." When I looked at Kenny, I still saw the twenty-one-year-old guy of my dreams.

"It's hard to believe the IRS has so much power over the fate of small businesses," Maron said.

"I know, and it doesn't make sense. What good is it to the economy if struggling businesses can't make it? These small-business casualties cause a rippling effect. Look at our business. If it fails, twenty-five people will be without work, with no way to pay mortgages or bills. Everyone's better off if we keep trying to make it."

"Oh, I totally agree, Mom, we have to keep going. Sometimes it's so hard, though. Naomi and I are sitting here with the Friday blues. It's been six weeks since either of us have had a paycheck, and for you and Dad, it's been twice that long."

"I'm so sorry, honey. When we hired you and Naomi, we meant to make your lives better, not worse! I never thought you'd get caught up in such a financial mess."

"Well, we're in it. Up to our ears." I'd never heard Maron sound so low.

"I know, and it breaks my heart. I think most parents hope the next generation will have a few less struggles than they did. Well, I have to lock up here, Maron. I'll be home in ten, and we'll talk more then. I love you. Without paychecks, we'll have to make our own fun this weekend. How about if I pack sandwiches and take the little ones to the zoo while you finish moving into your new home?"

"There's no bread in the house."

"There will be. I just picked up my TDS paycheck, and Dad and I are cutting down a tree tomorrow morning. A cash job on the side for a neighbor friend for $500. We'll split up the money and feel rich."

That was our family, I thought as I hung up the phone. If someone hit a wall of darkness, someone else stepped up to find the window of sunshine.

"I knew there would be perks to living in my parents' neighborhood, but I never imagined this!" Maron laughed into the phone. "One night I walk out of your house with a tray of amazing plates-to-go for our supper, the next morning there's a warm quiche on the counter for breakfast, and today when I'm tired from a rough night with the boys, Dad drops off a cup of coffee on his way to the shop. Is this for real? If it is, I don't want it to end."

"We love doing it, Maron," I said. "We'd love it if all five of you kids lived in our neighborhood. With you almost next door and Naomi's family across the street, it feels like when my mom and her sister, my Aunt Elsie, lived on farms near each other in Blanchardville, and the two of them were on the phone every couple days to catch up on the news. Your dad can't figure out how you two girls can find anything to talk about in the evening after working together in the Massey office all day."

Maron chuckled. "After supper, I walk across the street to Naomi's, and we sit at a little table in her garage. Our hubbies have the little ones. Sometimes we strategize and sometimes we just vent like best friends. Think how lucky our guys are: They don't have to listen to us."

We laughed together. "I love having the grandbabies close by so I can be part of their life every day," I told her.

"Little by little things seem to be coming together," said Maron.

"Yes, it's all good on the family front. Thank goodness we just keep shooting for the stars."

"Well, count me in. I'm on this ride with ya, Ma. Now, gotta go, I'm off to take the boys to day care. I'll see you at the home office after your yoga class."

"Love ya, Maron. " I grabbed my yoga mat, towel, coffee, Sophie, and was out the door. I beeped the horn as I drove by Naomi's and again as I passed Maron strapping her boys into their car seats.

"Mom, did we ever tell you the story about stardust?"

Maron looked at Naomi, and they shared a smile.

"No, tell me." I was mixing up a batch of chocolate cookies while they sat on stools at the kitchen counter.

Sue Massey

"Well," Maron began, "one reason we want our children to grow up here in the neighborhood near you and Dad is because we loved going to our grandparents' homes when we were little. We want our kids to explore and enjoy your backyard garden, your hens, and the farm field with you. It's almost like living together on the farm."

A warm glow of sunlight shimmered in Maron's blue eyes as she glanced toward Naomi. I stopped stirring the cookie dough and leaned forward on the counter to hear their story.

"When we stayed overnight on the farm with Grandpa and Grandma Johnny, we would play board games or put puzzles together." Naomi took up the story, sipping from her water bottle. The two of them were about to begin their workday in the downstairs Massey Landscaping office, the business the accountant had changed from an LLP in our names to an LLC in their names.

"Grandma Johnny would help us into our pajamas, tuck us in bed, read us a book, and then pretend-sprinkle stardust over us. We would close our eyes and feel her breath on our foreheads when she leaned over to kiss us good night," Maron said.

God bless our parents, I thought. We would never have made it through if it weren't for that magical stardust they sprinkled on our family.

"Sue, I'll be honest. I'm sure not excited about my birthday."

"Honey, it's just family," I assured Kenny. "We're keeping it simple. The kids are ordering pizza, and I made your favorite Death by Chocolate birthday cake."

I hurried around the room lighting candles for an evening glow as the front door opened and the kids and grandkids burst in. I could hardly wait to scoop the little ones into my arms.

Everyone pitched in, pizza boxes flipped open, and the aroma of garlic bread filled the kitchen. Setting pizza slices on a plate, Maron winked at me, then whispered in my ear, "Dad said no gifts, right? Well, wait till you see what walks through that door."

I was puzzled, but before I had a chance to ask a question, the front door opened, eyes looked up, and Mario and his Mariachi band walked in. Mario, one of our employees, was like family. He, his wife, and a friend were dressed in Mexican style, carrying guitars.

As they played and sang for us, I couldn't stop watching Mario, thinking of this hard-working man who excelled at everything he touched: brick, carpentry, landscaping, and now those same hands played beautiful music with deep meaning. The little ones were wide-eyed, clapping and nodding to the beat.

For an hour, Kenny never stopped smiling. I'd almost forgotten how handsome he was when he smiled. Then he stood and asked if they would play a song for us. It was soon to be our thirty-ninth wedding anniversary.

He held out his hand and asked me to dance. And we did, as everyone clapped and sang along. The mood within the house was aglow, soft and warm and filled with love.

Later, as we crawled into bed, I said, "And you weren't excited about your birthday?"

"That was the best time ever." Kenny was still smiling.

I leaned over and kissed his cheek. "I don't know what it is about family birthdays, I just love being together to celebrate."

"Well, thank you, Sue, you always throw a nice party."

I still remember how happy I was when I closed my eyes that night. It was a good thing we had that evening as a family, I thought later, considering the shock that would totter our world just a few days later.

Sue Massey

CHAPTER 25
A Patch of Sun

"Girls tell you?"

"What?" I asked, turning toward Kenny as he came into the bedroom.

"Bob, our landlord, died last night. Heart attack."

"Oh, no," I said. Bob owned the lot and shed where we stored our landscaping and snow-removal equipment and vehicles. We'd been so lucky to find the spot, just a couple minutes from our home.

I felt sad for Bob's family and then wondered how it would change our lives. "What do you think that means?"

"It means our leased space is history," Kenny said. "Bob's family will sell it, some big developer will buy it, and our landscape shop will be bulldozed over."

My heart sank, for I knew we would never find another place like it, and the idea of moving all our paraphernalia made me feel as heavy as granite.

Kenny sighed. He sprawled next to me on the bed, where I was writing on my iPad. "And to think fifteen years ago Bob wanted to sell it to us for $350,000, and we couldn't afford to buy it," he said. "How great would it be if we owned the space and didn't have to worry about losing it."

Letter from the *Heart*

"There's no way we could have worked any harder than we did," I reminded him. "We had no way to raise that kind of money."

"It's a five-acre parcel of prime real estate," Kenny said. "The land is zoned commercial, worth well over a million. They'll likely build some huge development project. Now what'll we do?"

"Well. . . " I wished I knew what to say, what to do. Always the one scrambling for the optimistic view of a situation, I could think of nothing.

"I just wish we weren't behind on rent for the space," Kenny went on. "Bob's daughter wants to meet with me tomorrow. I'm sure they want to close the estate as soon as possible and they'll probably demand back rent. There's no way we can pay it. God, this is my worst nightmare."

Again I searched for some heartening words and came up short. Was this the final debt, like the money owed for chicken feed that had tipped our farm into bankruptcy and foreclosure?

No, no, no, I can't do this again.

Sophie sat on the floor, her large brown eyes moving back and forth between us, feeling the sad, worried energy between us.

"Is there anything I can do to help? Go to the meeting with you?" I offered.

"Not really. I just wish I had a check for back rent to hand them, and I don't."

Earlier in the week, he'd been smiling so widely at his birthday party that I'd caught a glimpse of the carefree Kenny of our youth. That seemed a lifetime ago. "Well, I better keep moving," he said. "I have trucks to fuel up before the work crews arrive, and I've gotta figure out how I'm gonna get through that meeting tomorrow." He closed the bedroom door behind him.

I lay back against my pillow, burrowed deep into the familiar warm spot that felt like my mom's embrace, hoping an answer would come to me. Sophie jumped up and circled close to my face, her warmth and presence a comfort.

I put on "Send Me the Sun," a favorite CD by Kimmie Rhodes, and turned the volume so high the notes and lyrics vibrated through me.

Please, please, please send us the sun, I thought. Just a little sunlight.

I hit "repeat" so many times, I lost count.

"You gave me the best advice, Ma," said Dee.

"What's that? What advice did I give you?"

"You told me that if I ever woke up so sad that I didn't want to get out of bed, I needed to drag myself into the shower and keep placing one foot in front of the other. You were right. To this day, I hear your voice, Mom, and it has helped me many times. The steam in the shower clears my head, and I'm able to plan my day. Before I know it, I'm dressed and out the door."

"Well, believe me, that tip came from personal experience," I said. Her words seemed like a gift from heaven. For the first time in years, I'd had a hard time getting up that morning. After kissing Kenny good-bye and wishing him luck at his meeting with Bob's daughter, I wanted to crawl back under the covers and sleep until the meeting was over and we knew what our future was going to be.

I hoped there would be a resolution today. The last thing we needed was another black cloud over our heads. The worry over losing our leased land and shed brought back all the feelings that had hung over me when I feared losing our farmstead.

But at least this time Kenny and I were able to talk about it, share our feelings of anxiety and dread. Knowing that I wasn't alone with my emotions gave me the fortitude to face the day. As I hugged Dee good-bye, I resolved to follow my own counsel and find something constructive to do with the day.

I was busy at the stove when Kenny came in later that morning. I had turned on the Food Network, which always inspired me to cook something special.

I turned the burner down and spun to face him. From the look on his face, I knew.

"Tell me," I said. "What happened at the meeting?"

The relaxed, contented look on Kenny's face melted into a smile. "It went fine. Bob's daughter says she wants to work with us. Even though we're behind on the rent, she likes having us in the spot. She extended our lease."

"Phew. Thank goodness!" I wrapped my arms around Kenny's neck and squeezed him tight.

"It's just a short reprieve," warned Kenny. "We still have to make payroll, and I don't know where that money's gonna come from. But, wow, it's good to have one less thing to worry about."

"I couldn't bear to think about moving everything you have in that shed," I said. "It's such a relief when someone is willing to work with us rather than against us."

"It's lucky we have such a good relationship with Bob's family."

"That's mostly your doing," I reminded him. "You've always been so helpful to them. You're the definition of a good neighbor. Kindness and generosity like that always return themselves."

"Well, I'd better get back to work."

"When you get home, we'll celebrate. I'm making chocolate and vanilla cupcakes. Chocolate for you, vanilla for me."

"Can't wait," he said and gave me such a big kiss that I murmured, "Are you *sure* you have to go?"

He laughed in a way I hadn't heard for a long time, teasing, joyous. I was so happy I felt like dancing.

I gave him some fairy kisses on his ears. His ears are beyond precious. They lie tight against his head. They are just adorable.

"I'm sure," he said. "We'll celebrate later."

He gave me one of his famous bear hugs that I never wanted to end. I kissed him one more time and turned back to the stove to finish making the frosting.

Whenever I baked for Kenny, he said it didn't count unless it was chocolate. His standing request for his birthday cake was Death by Chocolate. It's so chocolatey, a half-inch piece goes a long way.

I'm vanilla through and through. When I was a senior in high school, I remember filling out a form for the school newspaper. My favorite foods? Vanilla ice cream cones in the summer sunshine and hot buttered popcorn in the winter. They're still on my list of favorites. I like vanilla cake, vanilla Oreo cookies, vanilla steamers, and vanilla/white chocolate. If it's vanilla, I'm in.

When the two of us swirl our chocolate and vanilla together, we make a great pair. After nearly four decades of marriage, we have our swirling down to a science, a perfectly choreographed dance. When life beats us down and we fall out of sync, we aren't afraid to seek professional guidance. A few marriage counseling sessions, and we're back in step again, instinctively knowing when to dip, when to twirl, as we sweep across the smooth, dusted dance floor.

I've never been drawn to a suit and tie; I love a more rugged, outdoorsy, hard-working type of guy. I am five six and Kenny five eight, so we pair nicely on the dance floor and in bed.

Death by Chocolate

Mix until well blended:
One chocolate cake mix
3 eggs (from our free-range chickens out back)
1 cup water (or milk if you prefer)
1/2 cup oil
1/2 cup sour cream
3/4 cup dark chocolate chunks

Pour into a greased bundt cake pan. Bake at 350 degrees for about an hour, or until a toothpick inserted into the center comes out clean. Remove from oven and cool ten minutes. Gently tip the cake out onto a platter.

Break two chocolate candy bars into pieces. Shove them into the sides of the cake while it's still hot. Cool completely, then frost.

Chocolate Frosting

Microwave until melted:
1 small bag dark chocolate chips
1/2 stick butter
4 T. water

Stir in until smooth:
1 bag powered sugar
1 tsp. vanilla

Drizzle and swirl the frosting over the cooled top. Garnish with ground almonds and shaved chocolate. If this isn't chocolatey enough, serve with a scoop of chocolate ice cream.

Sue Massey

CHAPTER 26

Shooting Star

Happiness is neither virtue nor pleasure nor this thing nor that, but simply growth. We are happy when we are growing.

~William Butler Yeats

I set a clear, triangular vase beside my office computer screen. The tiny vase held five stems of shooting stars I'd picked along the woodland trail while taking Sophie on her morning walk. I couldn't resist bringing home a piece of the field of wildflowers that covered a grassy knoll beside the trail.

I sat down in my office chair and gazed at the pure white beauty created by nature. I lifted a single bloom from the vase to study it. I tipped the flower right side up, then tipped it down. Depending on how I held it, its five petals could be a rising star or a falling one. The five petals seemed to represent our children, with Kenny and me as the center from which they grew. I reflected on all we'd been through together. I knew a family crisis could tear a family apart or tighten the bond. I was so glad our family chose "shooting" rather than falling star.

My eyes drifted to the wall to the right of my computer screen, where I'd hung one of my favorite paintings by my daughter: "Self

Portrait by Maron Massey." It was a semi-abstract depiction of a na-ked, knee-crossed young woman with large eyes that had the power to pull you in.

I remembered asking Maron to tell me about the painting. She said it had been an assignment given to the students in her MIAD (Milwaukee Institute of Art and Design) class. The painting reflected where she was at that time in her life: first-year art student in a new city, new apartment, and one of the teachers (soon to be terminated) had been rude and acted inappropriately toward her.

As Maron explained the painting, I could see all the struggle, all the pain painted into the large sad eyes on the canvas looking back at me.

That's what artists do: They paint, or sing, or write, or sketch, or create whatever is in their hearts to release their feelings. When freed, the emotions are given shape, direction, and meaning. Slowly but surely, we were weaving the frayed edges of our family into the most colorful, harmonious pattern I had ever seen.

⁓∽∽⌐

"Mom, you do know you aren't normal, right? What person wakes up at five, works on writing her memoir, then presents and sells a fifty-thousand-dollar landscape plan in an hour, has apples baking in the crockpot for supper, and is heading off to a second job? You real-ize that's unusual, don't you? But, hey, you go, girl, and we'll stop by for some of those baked apples tonight."

Although Maron had said it before, this time there was something about the "not normal" that hovered in my mind. I always knew I was different, with my emotional see-sawing, sensitivity, and restlessness. I'd always accepted this as the way I was. But something had hap-pened yesterday that shocked me into a new awareness.

I had a short med-check appointment at the clinic and walked out holding a printout of my medical history. I sat inside the Jeep and read the top line: Diagnosis: Cyclothymia. *My God, what is that?* After seeing professionals on and off for so many years, I couldn't

Sue Massey

believe that I was finally reading a diagnosis — and that I had no idea of its meaning.

I Googled the term on my iPad, and was astonished. Cyclothymia was a mild form of bipolar disorder. Now it all made sense: my bursts of energy, my almost euphoric view on life, my flights of fancy. While the endless swirls of thoughts inside my head were fun at times, they were also exhausting. I recalled how I'd reach for Xanax or Diazepam to calm the craziness inside my head.

I thought about our entire family. There were anxiety, obsessive-compulsive, attention-deficit-hyperactivity, and mood disorders. These were conditions within our brains, not of our choosing, conditions we were born with and had little control over, that lived within our genetic make-up. We simply had learned to adapt until we discovered there was treatment: cognitive therapy, medicine, personal wellness initiatives, and guidelines to help each of us manage our symptoms.

I sat in a daze reading WebMD. There was something about a clear-cut diagnosis that made me feel better. For one thing, it meant I wasn't alone; I could connect with others who suffered the same symptoms. For another thing, I could now do research into the disorder and learn more about myself. I could become a truer version of myself. I would still have to cope with the same challenges, but putting a name to it made it seem more manageable.

This information shed a whole new light on my past, present, and future.

That November, Kenny and I celebrated our thirty-ninth wedding anniversary. He looked as handsome and sexy to me as the day I first caught a glimpse of him across the flickering dance floor. I continued to cherish the same things that first drew me to him: his wavy sun-bleached hair, his slightly downcast blue eyes, his striking high cheekbones and perfectly shaped ears, his rugged build, his smile and friendly wave to everyone he met. With every day that passed, my love for him deepened. Things that long ago might have ruffled us were nothing, just a quiet breeze that swept on by. We had settled into the loving comfort of knowing who we were as our respect and appreciation for each other grew. We had learned to accept and embrace our differences.

He had stood by me through my depression, my new diagnosis, and the secret I'd kept buried for such a long time. He loved me no matter what.

I discovered an intimate women's writing circle, and my daily writing began to take shape as a memoir. There were so many feelings yet to express. I plunged further and further into my past, sorted through my strangled emotions, and released more and more of the anguish that had haunted me. My voice grew loud and clear.

"I have no choice," Kenny said. "I need to buy new parts for the plows. I can't put off the repairs or we won't be able to meet our snow-removal contracts. It's great that business is picking up and we have so many clients, but that makes it even more important to be sure all our equipment runs smoothly. If a plow breaks down in the middle of a snowstorm — well, you know what a nightmare that is."

"I agree," I said. "We've put off maintenance on all the vehicles for way too long. You've been a genius keeping them running, but you can't do it forever without new parts. How much is it going to cost?"

"A lot. Thousands. And we're going to be short on money for payroll, too, if something doesn't give."

"We've cut expenses to the bone," I said. "I can't remember the last time I had a grocery run. Then, we have a tax payment due, and you know if we don't pay the IRS, they'll force us to close the doors of Masseys Landscaping for good." I sighed. "Kenny, what are we going to do?"

"I've been thinking, and there's only one thing we can do. We have to ask for another loan from the bank."

"But we're still paying off the last loan."

Sue Massey

"I know, but where else can we turn?"

"OK," I said. "I'll make an appointment for us at the bank."

"I'll get the papers together to show them what a good year we've had," Kenny said. "The money will be coming in if the bank will just be patient with us. Remember the year we cleared three hundred thousand during snow-removal season? We can do it, Sue. I know we can."

Ah, Kenny, I thought. *You're the master of clawing out of deep holes. But this chasm's so deep that sunlight can't reach the bottom.*

"You mentioned snow," I said. "Sometimes I feel a whisper of relief at the thought of having you home during a snowstorm. The two of us sipping hot chocolate in front of a fire, watching and enjoying the snow rather than having to clear it. No more sleepless nights of worry, wondering when to dispatch the trucks, call the crews in. I think of all the holidays and family events postponed or missed because of the snow. Oh, how I would love to watch it snow together, you here beside me. I know you say it pays the bills, but you're on call for the entire winter, and it's a thankless job."

"I know, but if the business doesn't make it, I won't be home at all. I'll probably have to spend the winter out West, helping with the wheat harvest or hauling water in the oil fields and sending my check home. That's the only way I'd be able to make enough money to keep our family going."

The recession was officially over, but a recession is like a drought: Its effects linger for many years. It takes time to rebuild and recover.

Every day I searched for the silver lining. We could no longer afford cable TV, so we were doing more reading. Our dishwasher took a dive, so we washed by hand. Our dental insurance was canceled, so we brushed and flossed more often. Thrift stores had become the place to shop. We learned to relish the gift in having basic needs met. We were warm, we had food, we had work, and we had each other. But deep inside, there was a lurking fear that our lives might crash the way they did in 1986. If we threw in the towel, we would lose everything: our home, our hard-earned reputation as a company, everything.

Sadness clenched my heart. For over two decades, Kenny and I had poured all of ourselves into the business so we could leave it for those of our children who shared our passion, and now this. I knew we weren't alone, given the economic downturn, but that didn't make it any easier.

It was the cusp of spring, and I wished I could embrace its beauty rather than feeling burdened by the uncertainty in the air around me. I longed for the darkness to lift so that I could see the path intended for me. As the magnolia blossoms began to open beneath a warming sun, I waited to learn our fate.

Sue Massey

CHAPTER 27

Taking Root

A week later, we sat in the bank waiting to talk to Josh, a banker who had arranged loans for us before. I clutched my portfolio of papers, hoping against hope that he would help us again.

I was frightened. And I was so weary of being afraid. Did everything always have to be so difficult?

Josh greeted us with his usual warm, friendly smile and ushered us into his office.

I laid out my papers and started explaining the situation. Almost at once, he was nodding in understanding. "You're right," he said. "The economy is tough on small businesses like yours. You have the benefit of being nimble and able to take advantage of trends, but when a recession hits, you don't have much leeway. I understand why you're struggling."

"Oh, thank God." Relief rushed through me. Finally, someone who understood.

"There's some small-business funding I can earmark for you. Take a look." He handed some papers across his desk.

"It's rare to find people who understand the challenges of running a business like ours," I said. "I think of people like you as angels."

"I believe in you guys," Josh said. "Ever since Masseys Landscaping installed my back patio, all I can say is: Wow. I would recommend your landscaping services to anyone. Everything you do is top-notch. It would be a shame if you couldn't continue doing what you do so well."

"Thank you, Josh," I said, feeling the tension in my hands soften.

We discussed the terms of the loan, and it sounded almost too good to be true. With this low-interest money, we would be able to catch up on our overdue rent, do most of the necessary equipment repairs, and have a cushion to assure that we would meet payroll.

"We can't thank you enough," Kenny said as he shook Josh's hand. I gave Josh a hug.

"I plan to stand with you," Josh said.

"It sure will be good to have some breathing room," Kenny said. "We really appreciate it, Josh."

I nodded in agreement, thinking that maybe tonight we could actually get a good night's sleep. The whole world seemed brighter having Josh on our team.

"I think his belief in us means more than the money," I said on our way back to the truck.

"It means the world," Kenny said.

"I hope someday we'll be in a position to give someone a helping hand as life-changing as the one Josh just held out to us," I said.

Kenny nodded. "Success would be nothing if it meant fighting against people rather than with them."

"That's what life's all about," I said. "Helping one another."

Finally, after decades of struggle, I was able to connect the pieces. At last, everything fell into place and made sense to me.

My doctor had told me that one day my eating disorder would burn out and disappear. I'd seen different therapists over the years, but this psychiatrist was the person I trusted most. He was the one

I saw when I arrived at the hospital in a pit of depression so deep I thought I'd never climb out.

He had helped me then and many times since. He'd always said he wasn't overly concerned about my eating disorder, partly because my weight didn't fluctuate and I never suffered the health problems that some do. Whenever anguish about my dark demon filled me, I held on to my doctor's words. I pictured releasing my eating disorder like a captured bird, letting it soar into the sky. I wasn't sure when or how it would happen, but I trusted that it would.

My doctor was right. One day I realized that the moment of complete freedom had arrived. The wind had taken my deadly, suffocating secret and swirled it away.

Talking with Kelli on the phone, I told her, "Ever since I began writing my memoir, I've had a chance to understand myself better. And you won't believe what happened."

"What, Mom?" I could feel her compassion through the phone.

"My eating disorder has gone away, just like the doctor told me it would. Food is no longer my enemy. I've learned to accept who I am."

"Mom, that's fabulous. I'm so happy for you. Even if your book never gets published, it was worth every minute for you to write it and release the feelings bottled up inside."

"Thanks, Kelli. I can't believe how free I feel, like the soldiers at war within me have set down their arms and decided to march to the beat of my heart rather than against it."

I looked out the patio doors at a hen picking up sunflower seeds on the deck beneath the bird feeder. From this vantage point in my life, the view was crystal clear. I grew up in a household with two perfectionist parents. The only time I saw clutter or messes was when I went to someone else's home. Though my parents showered me with love and freedom to roam, I never felt I could measure up to what was expected. As I grew into my teen years, I felt more and more a misfit, and when I didn't know what to do with my feelings, I would stuff them down with food and then release all the feelings and the food into the toilet bowl. It was a constant war within me.

As my life unfolded and uncertainty spanned from horizon to horizon, the stuffing and purging continued. Each evening, I released all the stored hurt and confusion of that day into the toilet. Almost immediately I felt euphoric, as if I'd crossed the finish line and another day of racing to survive was over. I didn't have to figure out the toxic brew of emotions churning inside, just spew them into the bowl and forget them.

How many times I'd vowed to myself that I would stop, but when I tried, it grew worse. It was only when I poured everything locked inside me into writing about my life that the day my doctor predicted arrived and I felt a giant burden lift.

The issue wasn't food but feelings. As I wrote my memoir, I discovered that I couldn't tell the story without digging deep and articulating my struggles. Putting those buried emotions into black-and-white print made them into something I could confront instead of the amorphous shadows I'd been unable to pin down.

One reason it had been so hard to face my eating disorder, beyond the fact that it was an embedded addiction, was that it was so humiliating to me. Like a prostitute, my eating disorder appeared at night for the release of my daily burdens, and then she would turn and disappear into the darkness. Part of me wished she would never return, while another part lusted to lose myself again in her ravishing embrace.

Though I'd worked to overcome my clinical depression, my Diazepam addiction, and my cyclothymia, the stigma that hovered around an eating disorder seemed far worse to me. I knew how unhealthy, even life-threatening, the disorder was, yet the addiction's power was too great for me to resist. I wondered why an eating disorder seemed worse than other addictions: drugs, alcohol, sex, overwork. It started so innocently. I just wanted to drop some weight, fit in with the high school kids: I would do it just this once, or just one more time, until the day I discovered it had become my daily fix. It seemed to be the only thing I could control, until I realized it had begun to control me.

When the day arrived that I didn't feel the need to visit the bath-

Sue Massey

room after dinner at the end of a long day, I thought at first I must be sick. Then, two, three, four days passed, and soon I realized my eating disorder had "burned out" as my doctor had believed it would.

I began to write about my feelings surrounding the eating disorder in my memoir. The day I hit "send" on the eating-disorder piece to my editor friend, I held my breath, envisioning her as she read my words. She called me at once, and her caring response and unconditional acceptance made me realize that the secrecy was what had made it seem so shameful, so unspeakable. The next step was to move out to my next circle of close friends, to be open and honest and share the secret with them. Finally, I was brave enough to do so.

My palms were sweating, even though it was twenty below outside. I was meeting one of my dearest friends to chat. I'd never imagined this day would arrive, and now that it had, it felt bittersweet.

I'd woken that morning knowing I wanted to tell Sherill about the terrible secret I'd kept hidden most of my life. I had shared my recent recovery with Kenny and the kids, my sister and brother, and, just recently, my friend and editor, Jill. When I worried aloud what people would think when I told them, Jill assured me they would understand. If they didn't, she said, they weren't the kind of people whose opinion I needed to care about.

I felt strength grow as I formed the words in my mind and began to role-play, trying to prepare myself for whatever reaction Sherill might have. No matter how this turned out, I thought, it would be the release of a load I was tired of shouldering.

Now, at a corner table at our favorite coffee shop, I smiled at Sherill, braced myself, and began.

"Sherill, thanks for meeting me on such short notice. This morning I suddenly knew I wanted to tell you something that I've never dared speak about."

She looked at me intently, questioningly. I gathered all the strength I could find within me.

"Something has happened to me while writing my memoir." I cupped the warm mug of coffee between my palms.

"Sue, what is it? Good, I hope." There was a hint of concern in her voice.

"Even better than good. It's amazing." I leaned toward Sherill, grasping her hands. "My nearly lifelong eating disorder has lifted, gone away."

I held my breath, waiting for her reaction.

She looked stunned. "Huh, Sue, I had no idea you had an eating disorder. I always thought you were a healthy eater. Oh, my God, I am so proud of you. To think that after all you've been through in your lifetime, you also had the burden of an eating disorder on your shoulders." Sherill clicked her tongue and shook her head side to side. "I've always admired you, but now I admire you even more. You're the strongest woman I know, Sue. Seriously, I have never seen the equal."

She stood and hugged me, and I cried tears of relief.

After telling Jill and then Sherill, it was easier to tell my other best friend, Tee. When I broke the news to her, she too expressed surprise, then held my hand, looked deep into my eyes, and said, "Sue, you are not your eating disorder. Don't you ever forget that. An eating disorder is just that, something that happens to someone. I'm honored to be your friend."

I knew why these three women were my best friends. Long ago, my doctor told me to surround myself with positive people who honored and loved the person I was. And I had. I was blessed with the three best, closest friends ever. All my life, I'd sought this type of friendship, one with open communication, love, encouragement, and acceptance.

As my courage grew, so did my voice. At a routine appointment, I decided to tell my dentist what I'd been hiding for so long. He didn't seem surprised. "Sue, I have a number of patients with eating disorders," he said. "Often I can tell who has bulimia just by looking at their teeth, because it tends to erode the enamel. It's very rare for a bulimic to have teeth as good as yours. It's pretty incredible how you were able to channel your feelings into your book to recover. I think you'll be astonished how much you can help others by sharing your struggle. In fact, I want several copies of your book for my patients."

After thinking about it, I saw that the eating disorder had been one of my coping skills. But now I had discovered much better ways to cope — writing, yoga, losing myself inside the pages of a good book, talking to people I trusted.

Now free of my disorder's choking arms, I was able to explore one of the greatest joys in life, food. As I stopped depriving myself of food, my body reacted beautifully. As I ate what I was hungry for, I felt satisfied even if I'd eaten only half of what was on my plate. It was a miracle — one of the happiest miracles in my life. I'd dreamed of this moment for more than thirty years, and now there would be no looking back, for the sky before me was a vibrant, crystal-clear blue, and my thoughts soared with the clouds.

"Corey, let's talk." I sat behind the kitchen counter, sipping a cup of strong coffee.

"'Bout what?" Corey clomped in from the garage with his dog, General, behind him. "Say, Mom, did Dad go out plowing snow last night?"

"I woke up once, and he wasn't in bed, so I guess so." I stirred my coffee, watching the fluff of whipped cream disappear into the dark brown coffee swirls.

"Mom, that makes me so mad. Why didn't he wake me? He told me he wanted me to stay here last night in case he needed me to help plow. Then he doesn't call me. Dang."

"Corey, sit down a sec." After he perched himself on the edge of a kitchen stool, I told him, "Sometimes things aren't the way we perceive them."

"Like what do you mean?"

"Well, Dad said you had a hard day yesterday at the funeral of your friend's dad, and then you saw an old friend you hadn't seen in a while, and it was upsetting for you. Yes, he wanted you to sleep here, but I think he wanted you here so we could support you through this tough time, not just to plow snow."

"Oh."

"So how did it feel seeing that old friend?" Looking into his solemn blue eyes, I saw the boy who struggled every day of his life, learning to deal with a myriad of never-ending mental challenges. I couldn't fix his troubles, but I could lend an ear.

"Really upsetting, Mom. It's all because of him that I got in trouble. Now he and I have to pay back nineteen grand for the copper he took. I'm in such a hole, I don't think I'll ever get out. Mom, *he* asked to borrow our truck; I didn't know he planned to steal copper from a building site. It just sucks, Mom. I just can't seem to get ahead."

"Corey, I think it might help you if you write a letter. You don't have to send it, just write down your feelings. You've always been good at expressing yourself. Tell your friend you miss his friendship, but you're hurt that he doesn't accept more of the responsibility surrounding what happened that night. You don't have to send it. You're very articulate and in touch with your feelings, Corey. I know you can do this."

"Yeah, maybe." He leaned down to pat his dog.

"Did I tell you what happened to me as I wrote my memoir?"

"No. What?"

"You won't believe it. My eating disorder went away."

"Wow. That's awesome, Mom!"

"I can hardly believe it myself. It's such a joy to view food as one of life's pleasures and not as my nemesis."

"That's great, Mom. Really."

"Writing has been a way for me to cope with stress. Unlocking my feelings through words has been the best therapy ever. I'd really like to help others through my example. That's why I thought if you wrote down your feelings it might help you, too."

"I'll try it, Mom. I do get so frustrated sometimes. I don't want to say anything against Dad, but I hate the way he waits until the last

Sue Massey

minute to hire extra guys to plow, and then he can't find anybody, and we all end up working too many hours."

"I know. I think your dad likes to run lean, save money. He always thinks we can handle it, and we rarely can. Snowfalls always take longer to clear than expected. It's too hard on the sidewalk crews to shovel more than eight hours."

"Exactly."

"I hear ya, buddy. I like to plan ahead too. When the holidays are coming up, I like to call around and hire extra people a couple weeks in advance so we're prepared."

"Exactly, but not Dad."

"But you know what? I've found that anger is a huge drain of positive, creative energy. It only hurts the person who's angry. I'm working on forgiveness, acceptance. That doesn't mean you shouldn't express your feelings. I discovered the hard way that it's not a good idea to swallow your emotions. But it helps to look for the learning experience within each challenge. The bad economy has caused us grief, but look how each of us has grown both personally and professionally."

"Yeah, you're right."

"Just think of all the skills you've acquired. You've built a little home for yourself, and look what you learned by building it. You taught yourself all types of skills: working with vendors on supplies, learning how to wire, hang windows, insulate, and lay drywall. It's all about the journey, Corey, don't ever forget that."

"Yeah, I know."

"You've been blessed with many gifts, Cor. Clients call and tell me, 'Corey is such a polite young man, so thorough and meticulous, wonderful to work with.' And how do you think that makes me feel?"

"Like you trained me well."

"I'm so proud of you, Cor. I know we'll get this figured out. Hang in there, buddy. Your little niece and nephews are counting on you to play and wrestle with them. They love their Uncle Corey." I tucked my yoga mat and towel under my arm. "Well, I'm off to yoga."

"And I'm off to split wood. That's how I release my stress, Ma."

"And that's great, Corey; please don't overdo it." Corey was such a hard worker. I was always encouraging him to balance his life between work and free time. "Hey, Dad's been asking me to make homemade pizza. Want to join us for supper tonight?"

"That sounds great. That'll be something to look forward to." He pulled on his coveralls. Ever since he was little, he always loved being warm. He knew how to dress for working outdoors in all types of elements.

"Feel free to bring a date; crash downstairs and watch a movie if you want — if there are any movies you haven't already seen, that is."

Corey grinned. "So I love movies. Anyway, I'm not dating anyone at the moment. It's just my dog, General, and me, and that's just fine for now."

Corey had brought home some lovely young women through the years, but I knew he enjoyed being single. Still, I had a feeling that if the right person came along, he'd settle down and make a great partner in life. He had a really good heart.

"Well, I'm off." He zipped up his hood. "By the way, last night's scalloped potatoes and ham were awesome."

"Saved by the crockpot again. Love ya, buddy."

"Love ya, Ma. See ya tonight."

Christmas was coming. I'd been thinking about the menu. Kelli had texted me that she'd been dreaming of my hot apple cider for a month. Naomi requested my stuffed mushrooms. A show on TV had sparked my interest in trying a crown roast. I decided to stuff it with wild rice. I immediately thought of a favorite wild rice recipe that was in my card file.

The handwriting on the worn card lit warmth within me. It whispered of my earlier days at TDS when I found myself in the communications editor's position. Maggie, the administrative assistant to the president, took me under her wing. Maggie now lives in Ken-

Sue Massey

tucky, and when we occasionally connect on the phone, the gratitude and love I feel for her is immense. During therapy, I was taught to surround myself with good people. I have, and it's why I stand where I stand today.

As I added the wild rice ingredients to my grocery list, I could envision each of these people who encouraged, supported, and accepted me along my path. Each was a priceless part of the circle of strength that surrounded me.

Maggie's Wild Rice Casserole

Sauté:

1 cup wild rice

1 stick of butter

8 oz. can of mushrooms (I like to use fresh)

1/2 cup slivered almonds

3 T chopped green onions

Place in 2-quart greased hot dish pan. Pour over: 3 cups of chicken broth. Cover and bake at 350 degrees for 1-1/2 hours. Stir occasionally.

I also like to add: dried cranberries, apples, and sautéed celery. Sometimes I use pine nuts instead of almonds. At other times, I'll add browned sausage and bread cubes and turn it into a stuffing. That's what I planned to do for the crown roast for Christmas dinner.

I thought about the stuffing of my feelings in years past and how now I was free from the worry of ever having to stuff them again. Free.

I was reading part of my memoir to Maron and Naomi to get their feedback.

"I like it," Naomi said. "I have a feeling when I read your book, I'll know so much more about you." She was sitting in one of the corner rockers in Kenny's and my bedroom. Our whole family often gathered here. Because our bedroom windows looked out onto our gardens, there was a feeling of being in a cottage in the north woods away from all worries and concerns. It had the soothing feeling of a nest, a cocoon.

Maron sat beside Naomi in the adjacent rocker. "I like how you refer to your eating disorder as your little, dark, secret friend," she said. "What's important isn't how it sabotaged you in the past but how you cope with it in the future."

"I'm not going back," I said. "I'm certain of that. Every day I feel so good, so healthy. I no longer need those past crutches in my life. I have new coping skills to carry me through, and my family and friends are everything to me."

"Do you remember when your eating disorder began?" Maron asked.

"I remember the very moment," I said. "I was a freshman in high school and felt unattractive and overweight. I stepped on the scale and was shocked to read the numbers. I was desperate to trim down. I wanted so badly to be pretty and popular. Then later that same evening, just by chance, I saw a TV interview with a girl who confessed to throwing up her food so she could maintain her slender figure. And I thought: Wow, what a great idea. I could eat anything I wanted and still be thin. Like a typical teen, I completely ignored the point of the TV segment — that this was a horribly unhealthy strategy.

"Suddenly I had a way to feel in control of something, if only my weight and appearance. At dinner, my parents would hand me bowl after bowl of food and tell me to fill up. I didn't want to disappoint them, so I found myself eating to please them, then going to the bathroom to get rid of all the food. My life was a series of cover-ups, trying to hide my secret. It made me feel like a terrible person, a fake, an imposter. Pretty soon, I didn't know who I really was anymore."

"It sounds awful," said Naomi. "I can only imagine the turmoil you felt."

"I remember a couple times, growing up, when I saw you eating a huge amount of food and it confused me a little, though I brushed it aside at the time," Maron said. "It seems like you eat very differently nowadays than you used to."

"That's right," I said. "I eat when I'm hungry, stop eating when I'm full, and eat what I like. It sounds so simple, doesn't it? And it is. But it took me a long time to realize that this is the way to live."

"I understand the cycle of binging and purging, but what about the anorexia? How did you handle that?" Naomi asked.

"The worst of my anorexia occurred when I was in high school," I said. "Some days all I would let myself eat was an apple. I would run laps in the gym till I dropped. I was starving all the time. I made excuses to my parents about how I'd eaten earlier or I wasn't feeling well, but it was hard to sustain that routine for long. I became starved for food. Then, when I would eat, I would feel so guilty, like I couldn't wait to get the food out of me. It was a horrible vicious circle."

"Did things change after high school?"

"I thought they would. I was sure that when I left home and was on my own, I would leave my secret friend behind. But she followed me. Whenever I tried to shake loose from her, she would grip tighter. I would tell myself, over and over: This is the last time. But then the daily frustrations and demands would threaten to crush me, and I would turn back to her, my understanding friend who could release the avalanche of emotions and fears. It became my only way to cope with life's demands. For five minutes, after I expelled all my stress into the toilet, I felt light as a feather. But just as quickly, life closed in again, and the cycle resumed."

"Oh, Mom, how sad."

"I feel so much better being able to talk about it and knowing you kids support me. You and your dad have been so accepting. You are part of my recovery. And now that it's out in the open, it doesn't seem so dark and scary and shameful any more."

"Just think," Maron added, "what wonderful things you can accomplish with the energy that was once wasted on a secret friend who did you only harm. And I know you'll be able to help others dealing with additions."

The magic of the season is upon us. It's the voices of children in the snow, laughing in the joy of simple play. It's Sophie coming in from outside covered in clusters of tiny snow pillows. It's my mom's sugar cookie recipe, the sweet smell of butter and sugar mingling in the air.

Snowflakes flurry from a white sky against a pine-covered backdrop. As I sprinkle birdseed in the feeders outside our bedroom windows, the birds chirp a light song, waiting for me to step inside so they can swoop in for their seed-fest. I hold my mitten out, and I catch five snowflakes on the palm of my periwinkle mitten.

I think of our five children. It has been a year of challenges for each of us, and we cluster together to support one another, forming a lattice as intricate as a flake of snow.

Kelli and Shawn flew in from California. "Mom, please give us your holiday grocery list," Kelli said. "Shawn and I want to buy everything on it as part of our gift to you." Kelli's wide smile and sparkling blue eyes reminded me of when she was little and pleading to go to some ball game.

"Oh, no, Kelli, that's too much," I said.

"Sus, we're serious. Give it up," Shawn chimed in.

My inclination was to refuse, but then I thought of what I'd learned about accepting help when I needed it. I could see Kelli and Shawn really wanted to do it, and it would take one huge task off my to-do list. Still, I hesitated.

"Kelli, it could be two to three hundred dollars. Our cupboards are almost bare, and the list includes the special meat for Christmas dinner."

"Please, Mom. Let us do this one thing for you. For our family. We don't have a dish to pass, so let us buy the groceries. We always stay up late, so we can go tonight and have everything ready for you to start cooking in the morning."

"Wow, I don't know what to say."

"Give it up, Sus." Shawn's eyes were direct and penetrating.

"Well, OK." I ran to my bag and pulled out my long grocery list. I scribbled a few explanatory notes on the side, hoping they'd be able to make sense of it.

"I'm speechless," I said. "This is beyond kind. I can't thank you guys enough. If you have any questions about the list, just wing it. Whatever you bring me, I'll make it work. The door's unlocked, so if we're asleep, just toss the groceries in the fridge."

"Sounds good." Kelli tucked the list in her pocket.

In the morning, I found our cupboards filled with an abundance of fresh fruits and vegetables and the most magnificent crown pork roast I'd ever seen. I pulled out the fresh mushrooms to make stuffed mushroom appetizers and saw they'd bought four boxes of them. It felt like Christmas in our kitchen.

Of course it snowed on Christmas day, which meant most of our family was out shoveling and plowing for Masseys Landscaping clients while I was scampering around the kitchen. I was glad we'd set mealtime at 4:00 p.m. By that time, the little kids would have finished their naps, and the snow work would be done.

The dinner table was a rainbow of colors and aromas: mashed potatoes, cauliflower with mustard sauce, brussels sprouts with bacon and pecans, crown roast of pork with wild rice stuffing, cornbread and honey butter, Jello salad from my sister. Soaking up the moment, I thought how wonderful it was that we were all together. I said a quiet prayer for all who were less fortunate.

I received another extraordinary gift two days later while telling Kelli and Shawn good-bye at the airport, just before their flight back to California. "Thanks for everything, Mom," Kelli said. "It was the best Christmas ever, and that was because of you — the way you let Shawn and me buy the groceries, the way you went with the flow, whichever way that took us. You were so calm, accepting, flexible, at ease with everything. There's a serenity about you that I've never seen before. I felt I could relax, too, and be with you in a whole new way. It was tremendous."

Shawn nodded in agreement. "I hope you give yourself credit for that, Sue," he said. "You've made some dramatic changes in yourself, and that's not easy to do."

"Aw, you guys are too sweet," I said. "I can feel inside that I'm a different person than I used to be. Writing down everything that's happened in my life and letting out all those trapped feelings has been a metamorphosis; I feel reborn. I can sit back and enjoy whatever happens without trying to control events or become anxious if things don't turn out the way I planned. I can lower my expectations. I can let go of irrational beliefs about how things 'should' be." I made little air quotation marks around the "should."

Both Shawn and Kelli nodded and smiled.

"I hadn't realized how much I used to strive for perfection, way beyond what was reasonable, until I let go of the need to do so," I told them. "I hadn't even comprehended what perfectionists my parents were — and how much pressure I felt to do everything exactly right — until after talking with my therapist, who became like a trusted friend. I have to give her — and a handful of others over the years — much of the credit. Therapy, yoga, and writing — those are the teachers that helped me find myself."

"That's another thing, the way you can talk now about being in therapy, about your eating disorder, all the things you used to feel ashamed of and hide about yourself. Hearing you speak so honestly and openly makes me feel I can be totally myself with you," Kelli said.

"It's great to hear that you can see the difference in me. The other day, my sister thought I looked slimmer. I told her it was 'body by yoga.' Ever since I started my three-times-a-week yoga classes and healthy, normal eating habits, my body seems firmer, and I feel so good. I'm learning to look in the mirror and see myself — not the flaws, not the shortcomings, but me. The transformation has been phenomenal."

"There's no doubt about it, you really have changed," Kelli said. "This was a Christmas we'll never forget. It's not about perfection, it's all about family, love, being together, and embracing whatever comes our way."

Sue Massey

It was Valentine's Day. A dear-neighbor friend gave Kenny a hundred dollar bill for plowing his driveway and told him to take his bride out. I was so excited to go out to dinner: a real dinner I could enjoy, relishing every bite of food and sharing tender conversation with the love of my life, Kenny.

I handed him a stack of white pages, the manuscript of my memoir, tied with a huge, red, velvet bow and anchored with a card that held a key, a key to my heart.

"You know, Kenny, it's a miracle that we're together," I said, sitting across from him at the restaurant. "I was on a medical website last night. It described eating disorders as closely related to obsessive thoughts of perfectionism. Hmm, imagine that. Then, add the cyclothymia disorder. Do you know less than 1 percent of the population is diagnosed with cyclothymia? Lucky me. Maron's right on the money when she says I'm not normal. My doctor once held his hand up and showed me a gentle linear curve and said, 'Sue, this is where most people live.' Then he placed his hand high above his first line and drew a line with deeper peaks and valleys and said, 'This is where you live.' "

"I can see that." Kenny smiled as he took a sip of Merlot. I felt a deep closeness to him. Our recent evening class on couple's communication had enhanced our feelings for each other.

"And you know what, Kenny? That's exactly what it feels like — like my head is in the clouds — and I wouldn't change it for the world. Can you imagine viewing the world from a parachute or hot air balloon every day? I get to. I sail with the wind, skip from cloud to cloud, and look down on earth's beauty. Kenny, it's amazing up here." I paused to order the sea bass and place my crisp white napkin on my lap.

"I was reading about the highs and lows of the diagnosis, and I thought how fortunate I am to have found the right medication to bring them closer together while I can continue to enjoy the floating highs. I love channeling that energy into the grandkids or my designs. When I'm in a creative zone, there's nowhere else I'd rather be.

"When I think back to being a kid, it all makes sense now. During my lows, I lost all confidence and self-esteem, hated myself. In my highs, I sometimes acted before thinking through the consequences, which made me feel even worse about myself. I was tormented whenever I let myself down, which was daily. I was a wreck inside. I had become desperate, and I turned to trying to control my weight to cope with all that didn't feel right in my life: a form of self-medication."

Our waitress placed the plate of steaming beef in front of Kenny and white sea bass in front of me.

"This looks wonderful, Kenny. I can't believe how excited I am to be eating out with you tonight." I lifted a flake of perfectly cooked fish to my mouth and closed my eyes. It tasted heavenly.

"I never thought I would live to see this day, when I could savor delicious food like this. Seriously, it's a miracle. All the years of torment, when I thought of food as my worst enemy, are over. When I knew I was planning to 'get rid of it,' the food never tasted as wonderful as it does when I'm eating to nourish my body. I honestly don't know how I survived all those years. What a revelation this has been."

I reached over and grasped Kenny's hand. "Thank you for being so patient and understanding with me. You've never pressured me to do anything I wasn't ready to do. You know me so well, sweetheart. Mom was right. You're the perfect guy for me: for richer or poorer, for better or for worse, in sickness and in health. Though our lives may teeter on the edge of drama and uncertainty, it's our love that helps us endure."

I picked up my wine glass. "Here's to almost forty years of Valentine Days together, and many, many more. I love you, Kenny."

"I love you too, Sue."

We clicked wine glasses, and our eyes met at the tip of the flickering candle flame between us.

Then Kenny shot me a mysterious smile.

"What? What is it?" I asked.

He reached inside his coat pocket, pulled out an envelope, and handed it to me.

"A Valentine card? How sweet is that!" I slid my finger under the flap and lifted out a large pink card. Something fell on the floor.

I reached down and picked up a yellowing envelope. I recognized the handwriting. It was mine from a long time ago.

I looked up at Kenny. "Is this what I think it is?"

He smiled and nodded gently.

"Wow, Kenny, it's my letter — the letter I wrote you when I was eighteen! You kept it! After all these years, where did you find it?"

"I was downstairs looking for my old high school annual, and there it was, tucked inside. I'd forgotten I'd slipped it in there. Too many moves, too many years."

I glanced down, and the years turned back in my mind to the September 1972 canceled postmark on the envelope, addressed to Kenny Massey, Hollandale, Wisconsin. I remembered writing it that way because all I knew was that his family farmed near Hollandale. How right I'd been when I said it was a miracle we were together. What good fortune that the postman had even delivered it.

I pulled out the letter and read through it. I was struck by the simplicity of the handwriting and the words I'd written. Today my handwriting was more mature, and I was perhaps more wise in life experience. But I had no regrets. I felt a surge of empathy for the girl who'd written the letter, following a strange yearning in her heart.

Kenny placed his hand on mine. "Sue, I'm so glad that you had the courage to write the letter and that I decided to go to the dance. I almost stayed home that night, but I thought maybe you'd be there, and I couldn't get your letter out of my mind. If I hadn't seen you that night and offered you a ride, I'd have missed all the fun."

"It has been fun, hasn't it?" I agreed. "Thank heavens I wrote that letter. If I hadn't, I can't imagine what different roads I might have traveled, but I'm sure they wouldn't have been nearly as exciting." I thought for a minute, then asked, "Kenny, if I hadn't sent that letter, do you think we would be together today?"

"It's hard to say," he said. "Although I'd noticed you before, it didn't occur to me to ask you out. I never dreamed you'd be interested in me. But when I got your letter, it started me thinking. The more I thought about you, the more certain I felt that I'd better make a move, or some other guy would."

"I'm glad you made the move. I'm so happy that we took the plunge together. The waters may be turbulent at times, but the ride and the views have been spectacular.

"Cheers to the journey." I clicked Kenny's wine glass, leaned in for a brief kiss to seal our deal.

My eyes open to an early morning dawn. It looks very cold outside. The fireplace is aglow, and Kenny has left for the day. I view the idle seeds in the bird feeder outside. My feathered friends are missing, hiding from the biting cold.

I remember the first time I had a seminar that flew us to Florida in the dead of winter. As the plane landed and I saw a landscape of lush emerald green instead of a blanket of snow, I felt my spirits lift and realized why people travel to warm climates in the winter months. I would love to travel and discover new places and cultures. I imagine where I would go as I lie back in my warm nest to dream: the gardens across Europe, my homeland Norway, and a zillion places across the United States which I have yet to see.

The hardest part would be leaving my grandbabies, family, and pets behind. As much as I would love to travel, I love my nest. I love coming home, slipping my comfy clothes off the hook in my closet, getting lost in cooking, or playing with the little ones before crawling into one of the most soothing places in my life — the arms of my bed, beside the love of my life.

I glance at my mat rolled tight as a Tootsie Roll on the chair in the corner and think of the way I've learned to focus on my breath, to be aware of my body. Nowadays, whenever my mind swirls too fast, I think of the warm studio, the community of yogis, the mindfulness

I've learned from my practice.

I pick up my iPad and open an email from a nursery vendor. Only twelve weeks until dig season. I've had time to renew my spirit, submerged myself in my writing, and I feel ready to return to the field: to push up my sleeves and reclaim my place in the land of flowers, to work outdoors beneath warm brilliant sunshine.

It may be below zero outside, but inside my nest, it is warm. I cuddle with Sophie and glance with fond memories at the oil painting of my childhood farm on the wall, and beside it, the picture of my mom as she stands in her flower garden. I imagine the white, frigid landscape outside to be a lush, green carpet of hope. It is a new year, and I plan to embrace it.

This is, I realize, as close to life on the farm of my dreams as I'm likely to get in my lifetime. With the cornfield in back and a handful of pet hens in our garden, two daughters and their families living on our street and a son who crashes downstairs during snow-plowing events, I have the togetherness I always wanted.

I'm surrounded by family, working side by side with them, able to cuddle my grandbabies whenever I want, to dig in the earth when I feel the urge. Money will probably always be a problem, but that's one of those things I've learned to accept rather than fret over, as unfixable as the weather. I'll do what I do in the cold Wisconsin winter — bundle up, put my tongue out to catch the snowflakes, and turn my eyes to the sun — let the frigid days deepen my appreciation for the warmth of a fire, a touch, a friend. I will do what I've learned in yoga class — relax into the moment and stay here, now, in this one breath, keeping silent enough to hear the wind.

After I realized that my secret, my eating disorder, was truly gone, I also realized it was OK to talk about it — that I'd caused myself the most pain through my shame, secrecy, and self-hatred. As I've revealed myself and my deepest secret to people I trust, I've felt a lightness and bliss I never dreamed possible. My disorder has dissipated through myriad pathways — through yoga, nature's healing power, and the cognitive exercises that helped me uncover damaging, outmoded beliefs and replace them with more positive ones. One of the most healing pathways has been my love for writing stories that have settled in my heart and want to be freed.

So much of my life was unclear to me until I made the effort to put all of it down on paper. I went back over the stack of scrapbooks I kept during the days of losing the farm. I reread every letter people wrote to us in those frantic days. I burned the ones that were cruel and hurtful, lit a match to them and watched them go up in smoke, and I absorbed the warmth and kindness of the vast majority of those letters in a way I was unable to do when I received them. I went through every bit of it, step by step, and saw that I couldn't disavow any of it or wish it hadn't happened, because it led me here, to this moment of pure peace.

The one constant that has helped me through it all is my faith, which rests in the miracle of life, in my every breath. My faith has never wavered. She sings to me as I watch life emerge from a brown egg in the palm of my hand: first a faint tapping, then a beak, a head, a torso, then wings, and a tiny, feathered new life. She's there as I towel off a damp newborn puppy and watch as her new lungs inflate, her head begins to wobble, her limbs stir, and then, with a faint dove-like purr, her voice begins. My faith was with me as I felt that same miracle of life flutter and grow inside me, then held a new child in my arms, a gift beyond words.

Following the farm foreclosure, in the darkest of days, all the gestures of love, kindness, and empathy carried me when I could not walk. And I know, as my life continues to unfold, my faith will be there if ever I need to be carried again, too sad, too weak to find my way.

I don't necessarily need a church to feel my faith, and I don't need a gravestone to draw my departed close. They're with me in the air that gives me life. They're the handwriting on a recipe card, the pictures in my office, their scent in a coat they wore, a family ring I've been given, a look of understanding, a color, a texture, a feeling, a thought, a smile. They are with me always.

Whenever I see a clothesline with sheets flopping in the wind, I am with my mother. Just holding a clothespin between my fingertips

Sue Massey

brings her vividly to life. The taut lines strung between two T posts send me back to myself as a kid, playing and dangling on the posts, watching my mom's handkerchief-covered head bob up and down between clothes basket and lines, hanging our clothes in the fresh air to dry.

Each time I see a watermelon, split open and laden with tiny black seeds, I'm with my Grandmother Gunhild. She and I are sitting on the wooden picnic table under the giant canopy of our maple, seeing who can spit a seed the farthest, while waiting for Grandpa George to bring the next wagonload of hay bales for us to unload into the barn.

We pass an A & W stand, and I'm on our wrap-around porch, perched on our hilltop farm overlooking Blanchardville. I've just ridden with Dad in his pickup to retrieve a gallon jug of A & W root beer from the little stand we can see from our porch. It's the end of a sultry summer day of hard physical work putting up hay, making meals, and milking the cows, and we gather to treat ourselves to root beer and popcorn in the breeze of the open-air porch. The crickets are in full song as the lotus bug arches a familiar buzz in the nearby oak, and moths swarm the yellow night light beside the porch door.

An empty glass Kerr canning jar catches my eye on a store shelf, and I am elbow-high to my mom watching her ladle peaches, apples, and tomatoes into the mouths of sparkling jars, preserving her orchard and garden produce for the months ahead. And when a deep down-like blanket of snow covers the land outside, I can hear the suction release as she opens the sealed jar and a bit of summer seeps into our kitchen.

These are everyday moments that live within me as if I were a kid yet today. These memories are the epitaphs engraved in my heart like the etchings on the gravestones that honor those we love.

It is the faith in me that looks for goodness in all people. Though it's hidden at times, if I search I will find it, or an understanding of the endless string of "whys" that haunt us when bad things happen to innocent, good people.

My faith is the whisper of the wind. She is with me always.

1. Glimpses of dawn: taking root, our backyard gardens evolve. 2. Friendship garden: Jack-in-the-Pulpit. 3. Finding beauty in the twisted and tangled.
4. Pots and patios — blooming where planted. 5. Kenny's vision, our backyard treehouse. 6. Finding our niche with the land.

Sue Massey

7. Growing Places by Sue. 8. Winter color. 9. Working draft of children's book with illustrations by Maron Massey. 10. A new generation, Dee, Corey, Maron, Naomi, and Kelli. 11. Jack the Cat wondering why the hen came into the house. 12. Sophie dressed in her pet therapy vest: ready to volunteer. 13. Turning to the earth.

14. Yin & Yang (Little Boy).

15. Hidden Talent — Kenny's recycled metal art sculptures.

16. Welding madness: Hearts Aglow.

17. Dee and Maron welding with Dad.

18. Like father, like daughter.

19. Falling Tiers sculpture.

20. Cranes and Beyond by Kenny Massey.

21. Dad's funeral — crystal cross.

Sue Massey

22. Our Norwegian Dinner Prayer. **23.** West Madison 19′ Massey snowman icon.
24. Survior Sandy — inspired Sue. **25.** Joy. **26.** Stems of coneflower in a sea breeze
by Maron Massey. **27.** Our grandchildren, Adam, Klay, Troy, and Savannah.
28. A stroke of luck: Sue wins a Harley, and the kids name her Pearl.
29. Massey-Johnson — Best Christmas Ever.

The End

Acknowledgements

As we express our gratitude, we must never forget that the highest appreciation is not to utter words, but to live by them.

~ *John F. Kennedy*

Gratitude unlocks the fullness of life. It turns what we have into enough, and more. It turns denial into acceptance, chaos to order, confusion to clarity. It can turn a meal into a feast, a house into a home, a stranger into a friend. ~ *Melody Beattie*

My heart is bursting with gratitude beyond words.

I recently overheard someone say, "Why, anyone can write a book."

Only a writer can possibly know the painstaking, lonely hours of living inside the mind and bringing feelings into fruition, giving them voice. After laboring and giving birth to *Letter from the Heart*, my understanding of what goes into each and every book has deepened immensely. A book is a work of art, with words the medium, like the brush strokes of a painting, the notes of a lyric, the smoothing of clay between water-dripped fingertips. I am left with a profound respect for the process of writing, editing, publishing, and marketing a book.

A year and a half after I began this book, my heart is filled with gratitude for what feels like a lifetime of blessings. My life has been touched by so many, each of whom lives within me. They are the beautiful woven threads in my life, each thread a unique color. Each has been sewn into the very fabric of my being.

I have asked myself: Why does one choose to write a memoir, a story so personal, so open to public viewing? It takes an enormous amount of courage, and I went to great lengths to handle sensitive areas with the utmost care. My hope in sharing my story is that a spark may flicker and ignite a flame within someone searching for answers in their life, grasping for hope, yearning for change, desperate for ways to cope with life's adversities.

My deepest thanks go to:

My family: Kenny, my one and only, and my children: Kelli, Danelle, Corey, Maron, and Naomi. It has been each of you, with your unconditional love, your supporting and encouraging strength, who has carried me when my footprints left the sand. I am so profoundly grateful we are family and share the nest we call home.

Jill Muehrcke: my editor, my saving grace, who sometimes serves as a trusted therapist and mentor as well as editor. A book begins as a seed, an idea that gets pounded out onto paper or keyboard. Then it passes to someone who loves the art of arranging words: cutting, tightening, rewriting, and whirling her red wand in the name of proper grammar, punctuation, spelling, and the perfect combination of words to create beautiful, compelling stories and pictures in the mind. Early on, we knew we made a perfect team. I love to write, and she loves to edit. To my editing queen, my muse of inspiration who teaches me her art and craft with words and sentences: I am deeply, deeply grateful. Thank you.

Relatives and friends near and far: Just knowing you were there was a comfort beyond words. I have felt your loving support carry me at times, like the wind, my closest friend.

Farm Aid: (Willie Nelson and family) and country-band Alabama (and all), even the media who tucked us beneath their wings, and all who reached out with gestures of kindness, prayers, letters, cards, offers, a healing hand, gifts, a touch or a hug. I shall never forget.

To each and every one of you who have touched our lives: My life feels full and beyond abundant. Thank you.

As you read, please remember, this is my story, my voice, my views. As the years unfold, time and space make it feel less personal. At times, I can speak of it as if from a third person, from an outsider looking in at my life. A friend imagined I would feel a gentle wave of lightness when the book went to print, a letting go of all the unfinished, unconnected, confusing thoughts and feelings in my mind. I think she is right. A goal complete, a legacy to leave behind for generations to come, it has been a challenge, a thrill, and a flight higher and farther than my wildest dreams.

Sue Massey

About the Author

When I was little, my mom told me to stick up for myself. She said if I didn't, no one else would.

It seems as though I've been searching for my voice most of my life: trying to connect my deep feelings to the outside universe. Whenever I struggle to make sense of a situation, I reach for a pen, or my iPad, and words are released like a creek rushing with the spring's melting snow. My soul settles, and I am home, at home with my thoughts and feelings.

I believe in voice, a voice in positive change.

In writing my memoir, I released a voice that I didn't know existed. I let go of a secret I'd never verbalized. Once I articulated it, the secret lost its power, and I was free of its pain and burden. Free to take flight into the wind.

Come fly with me. Together, we shall find voice: the essence of peace within.

Sue Massey
Author, *Letter from the Heart*